THE BRANDYWINE TRADITION

THE
BRANDYWINE
TRADITION

HENRY C. PITZ

ILLUSTRATED WITH 16 COLOR
AND 32 BLACK-AND-WHITE PLATES

WEATHERVANE BOOKS • NEW YORK

To Molly

PREFACE

ANY AUTHOR who pauses upon the completion of his book to take a long look back over his sources and who enumerates all the helping hands that have put him in possession of his material, is likely to be astonished at the spreading network of his obligations. I realize mine go back to the picture-book years of my childhood, then to the teachers of the art-school years and finally to the many friends and acquaintances who played some part in shaping the Brandywine tradition. Almost all of these are gone and I have only my memory of their conversation and stories. A large part of the book stems from them; I can only list their names: George Harding, N. C. Wyeth, Harvey Dunn, Violet Oakley, Jessie Wilcox Smith, Wuanita Smith, Clifford Ashley, Walter Everett, Margaretta Hinchman, Thornton Oakley, Herbert Moore, Thomas Wells, Stanley M. Arthurs, Joseph Chapin, Katherine Wireman, Elizabeth Shippen Green, William Aylward, Clyde DeLand, Gayle Hoskins, W. H. Koerner, Arthur Becher, Anna Whelan Betts, Ethel Franklin Betts Bains, Sarah Stillwell Weber, Emlen McConnell, Olive Rush, Henry J. Soulen, Harry E. Townsend.

Of the greatest help have been the hours spent with Gertrude Brincklé and Frank Schoonover. Miss Brincklé, a family friend of the Pyles' from childhood and later a secretary to Howard Pyle, and Mr. Schoonover, one of Pyle's earliest students and a close friend for the rest of his life, have opened their memories to me. Mr. Schoonover's pictures have been an important contribution to the story of the Brandywine.

Howard Brokaw, a grandson of Howard Pyle, has been most generous in giving me access to his important Pyle collection and has loaned me his files of clippings, letters and memoranda. Miss Constance Moore, former Director of the Delaware Art Center, has also been helpful. Mario Cooper and Grant Reynard have both furnished me with material on their former teacher, Harvey Dunn. Mrs. Mary B. Knowles of the William Jeanes Memorial Library, Plymouth Meeting, Miss Ellen Shaffer in charge of the Rare Book Department of the Central Branch of the Philadelphia Free Library and Mrs. Miriam Leslie of the Art Room of the same library have assisted me in many ways.

Sylvester K. Stevens, Executive Director of the Pennsylvania Historical and Museum Commission, Norman Kent, Editor of *American Artist*, and Oliver Jenson, Editor of *American Heritage*, have given me permission to use some of the material in my writings for their publications. Cass Canfield of Harper and Row has kindly given permission to quote some letters and other material about Howard Pyle, and Paul Horgan has permitted me to quote from his book, *Peter Hurd, a Portrait Sketch from Life*.

Leonard Dennis of the Historical Society of Pennsylvania has put much valuable material at my disposal and Miss Edith Emerson, Director of the Violet Oakley Foundation, has given me much information about Howard Pyle and Violet Oakley and permitted me to examine the Violet Oakley collection. Edward Wilson has recalled for me his early days as a Pyle student.

Mr. Charles Scribner has kindly given permission to reproduce "Blind Pew" by N. C. Wyeth from the Scribner Illustrated Classics Edition of *Treasure Island* by Robert Louis Stevenson and also to quote from the letters of Howard Pyle and Edwin A. Abbey published in the Scribner edition of *Edwin A. Abbey* by E. V. Lucas.

Of the greatest help has been the generous cooperation of Bruce St. John, Director of the Delaware Art Center, and of Rowland P. Elzea, Curator of the Collections, and the Art Center staff. This collection of the work of Howard Pyle and other Brandywine artists is the most complete and invaluable source material for the book.

Mr. and Mrs. Andrew Wyeth have helped me in countless ways, beyond my ability to itemize. From the beginning I have had the support and help of Mrs. Newell Convers Wyeth, Carolyn Wyeth, the John McCoys and the Peter Hurds.

I am very grateful for the patient editorial help of Mrs. David Ehrlich, for the careful production supervision of Mr. Arnold Paine and the printing expertness of Mr. Robert Hart. The color and black-and-white plates owe much to the photographic skill of Mr. Arthur d'Arazien. Mr. Lovell Thompson made the book possible.

HENRY C. PITZ

Plymouth Meeting, Pennsylvania

CONTENTS

CONTENTS

COLOR ILLUSTRATIONS

THE COMING OF LANCASTER, Howard Pyle

THE BATTLE OF BUNKER HILL, Howard Pyle

PILGRIMAGE OF TRUTH, Howard Pyle

FATE OF A TREASURE TOWN, Howard Pyle

BLIND PEW, N. C. Wyeth

THE ORE WAGON, N. C. Wyeth

CANADIAN TRAPPER AND WOLF, Frank E. Schoonover

GENERAL HARRISON AND TECUMSEH AT VINCENNES, Stanley Arthurs

PLOUGHING UNDER THE BUFFALO BONES, Harvey Dunn

LA FÉE AND BERTRAND, Elizabeth Shippen Green

MAY DAY, Andrew Wyeth

SMOKEHOUSE, Andrew Wyeth

CHICKEN HOUSE, Carolyn Wyeth

N. C. WYETH IN HIS STUDIO, Henriette Wyeth Hurd

LANDSCAPE WITH POLO PLAYERS, Peter Hurd

SPRUCE HEAD, John McCoy

following page 126

BLACK-AND-WHITE ILLUSTRATIONS

following page 222

THE BRANDYWINE TRADITION

I

THE VALLEY AND ITS PEOPLE

ART HISTORY is largely the story of happy conjunctions. The mystery of talent thriving in a given place and under a given set of circumstances is the riddle which art historians either merely report or attempt to unravel. A great city, a crossroads of trade and cultures, a thriving place of accumulated wealth — these are the places where we may expect to find a flourishing of the arts. But talent can take root and flourish in the unexpected, the quiet and the unnoticed. It has its own willful way and its own instinct for the essential sources of nourishment. So a small valley, threaded by a modest stream winding down through the southeastern corner of Pennsylvania and into the northern miles of Delaware, can be and has been a nursery of picture making for at least a century, giving rise to a tradition that seemingly has reached its peak yet shows no sign of abatement. The Brandywine Valley has been a snug enclave of talent.

Strung along the slender thread of the Brandywine River or Creek (for it is called both), the valley with its flat meadows and rounded hills stretches back from the marshlands of the broad Delaware into Pennsylvania and the high ridges of the Welsh Hills. The country is not spectacular, but beautiful through every season of the year. After more than three centuries of the white man's cultivation, it is still very little scarred by the reckless claws of industrialism, although some of our earliest industries were born on the banks of its stream. The valley has kept its unmarred, wholesome look and remains a haven for the untormented eye. History has decorated it with an important battle, it has been a meeting place of many races and finally it has been touched by talent. In a sense, it is largely undiscovered still; it has not advertised itself, it is content to be; yet, its gifted sons and daughters have touched many threads of the national life. Its artists have profoundly influenced the development of American illustration. Brandywine pictures would fill many a gallery, and the valley has produced not only its local literature but also has made a contribution to the national culture.

Commerce has never moved down the Brandywine — it is a canoe and rowboat stream except for a two-mile-long estuary which flows out to the broadening Delaware. It is not a boundary river of geographical or political import, but a tidy size proper for damming — its waters being diverted into mill races. From earliest colonial days it has been a mill-stream that saw the various stages of development of flour, gunpowder, paper and textiles along its banks. The farms that dotted the valley were fertile and abundant. Its roads were busy with traffic to and from the backcountry. Solid and secure, there was bustle and achievement beneath the region's benign aspect. In fact, the valley may be a quieter place today than it was a hundred and two hundred years ago.

In its modest length of perhaps sixty miles, the Brandywine changes its character a number of times. The river rises from a two-pronged source, each fork bubbling from springs high on the hump of the Welsh Hills which separate the Susquehanna and Delaware watersheds. The two brooks tumble down through woodlands and hill farms, circle away from each other and then touching lower levels move toward each other and unite a few miles above Chadds Ford. The hill brooks become a sizable stream, deceivingly docile, for it has its sudden spring rages. Mostly placid and often sluggish its quiet waters nudge through meadows, under sycamores and circle around hills, slipping by former millsites and tumbling over several dams. Few houses line its banks. The Wilmington road borders the water in places, but the stream is more apt to flow through private estates, farms and the territory of the Brandywine Conservation Area.

At the edge of Wilmington the river abruptly changes character again and, having reached the edge of its upland plateau, plunges down to the coastal plain through a beautiful rocky gorge. The water drops through a series of falls and rapids, a descent of a hundred and twenty feet over a distance of four miles. Once it arrives at the low level of the Delaware marshes it flows broader and deeper for just a few miles, joins its twin stream, the Christiana, and so through the widened channel to the Delaware. The gorge with its considerable drop of water naturally attracted some of the early, sharp-eyed settlers who shrewdly recognized its possibilities as a great power source. This location saw the founding of one of the earliest industrial concentrations in the colonies.

But the Indians knew the area first. At the coming of the white man the reigning tribe was the Leni-Lenape — they were river Indians, semi-agricultural and not particularly warlike. The length of the Brandywine was their territory. To the south were their kindred, the Nanticokes; to the west, over the watershed, were the Susquehannas, an Iroquoian tribe. The Susquehannas controlled the broad basin of the Susquehanna River, reaching far north into the Iroquois country. Their wide river was a trade route into the fur country and down it came packs of skins — deer, beaver, mink, bear, otter, lynx and fox — together with arrowheads and bundles of dried tobacco. Much of this activity went to the east, over the watershed, down the trails of the Brandywine Valley or the waters of the Christiana. So the valley was crisscrossed with trails from early days and many intersected where the Brandywine and Christiana met. Here at the first platform of rock rising above the marsh level, the Lenape exchanged some of their harvest of the shad and sturgeon run, wild peas and rice, squash and maize with the northern traders. This system of barter was already established when the white traders appeared with their beads, knives, pots, bolts of cloth and rum. The newcomers from overseas did their trading at the same point of rocks where the Indians had met and exchanged for centuries.

The Dutch explored the Delaware and some of its tributaries first but made no enduring settlement; however, they built a fort near what is now New Castle, Delaware. Wandering Dutch and English traders may have camped at the Brandywine mouth or probed up its ravine. But the white man came to stay in 1638 when the *Kolmar Nychel* and the small yacht, *Vogel Grip,* sailed past the entrance to the Brandywine and unloaded their cargoes of Swedish and Finnish pioneers on the banks of the Christiana. They built a fort and a little town grew up around it. These Swedes and Finns had come to make homes and they possessed the requisite skills and determination. They brought from their native land the knowledge of how to build log houses, a crucial asset. They were soon snug in their warm weathertight homes, while to the north and south their English, Dutch and French neighbors shivered in makeshift wood and bark wigwam-cones and stake-walled houses. Thus, the log cabin, later to be such a potent symbol of America's expansion, had its beginnings as a regional achievement among the Swedish settlements scattered along the lower Delaware. The technique of log-house building spread slowly through the colonies until it became an accustomed skill of the westward trekking American.

The Swedish and Finnish peasants knew how to work with the wilderness. They were able to grow crops almost immediately, for they planted them in the rich, open acres of the river flats. Cutting openings into the forest walls could wait. Their hands were accustomed to tools, their minds were neither diverted by gold hunting nor very much by trade. They seem to have had an instinctive knack for understanding and getting along with their new Indian neighbors. With the exception of a few of their leaders they were illiterate and left few records.

The Dutch from New Amsterdam captured their fort and settlement, but the conquerors did not disturb their way of life. A new flag was flying over them but they were still secure in their homes on their own acres. The Dutch occupation lasted for only a brief interval, for they, in turn, were swept aside by the proliferating English. The little settlement that was to become Wilmington was then under its third flag and in its future was a fourth. In the meantime, the town was gathering momentum as a trading center. The small cluster of log houses on the edge of the great wilderness was already a bustling meeting place of races. Indians of various tribes, Swedes, Finns, Dutch, English and a sprinkling of other nationalities mingled on its streets and wharves.

But the settlement was a tiny atom on a continent of frightening size. At the time of its capture by the Dutch in September of 1655, there were less than four hundred white inhabitants in the New Sweden territory. They lived almost entirely north of the Christiana and Brandywine, a thin ribbon of pioneer holdings along the Delaware which seldom penetrated the forest of trees that hemmed in the scattered settlements. The Dutch moved the government of the province to their former center at Fort Casimir, near New Amstel. They made no particular effort to bring in settlers — they were satisfied to trade and administer. They may have had a premonition that their days as North American colonizers were numbered, for they were content to allow the Swedes to continue to farm their fertile acres and raise their large families of healthy children. The Dutch chapter in the history of the valley came to a close when New Amsterdam fell to the English, and in 1664 an English force sailed up the Delaware, reduced Fort Casimir and looted New Amstel, now New Castle. The English were brushing aside the smaller nations and readying themselves to grapple with France and Spain for the provinces of North America which fronted the ocean.

William Penn touched briefly at the site of New Castle and then moved up the river to Philadelphia. His grant from Charles II was annoyingly indefinite, but it certainly covered the area of what is now northern Delaware. Penn initiated a high tide of immigration which brought in English, Welsh and Irish Quakers and some Germans largely from the Rhine country. Philadelphia grew up rapidly, a Quaker town except for the German mystics on the Wissahickon and the solid German settlement of Germantown. The Quakers spread out into the circle of farmland around the town and they soon discovered the fertile meadows and hills of the Brandywine. There were the usual treaties with the Indians, destined to be misunderstood and disputed by races whose ideas of equity and principle had little in common. Although the incoming Quaker farmers were peaceful people of principle, they had their share of concealed rapacity and they had the advantage of numbers and power. The first mills and dams on the lower reaches of the stream had stopped the spawning of the sturgeon and shad upstream — the fishing grounds of the Indians had vanished. Outmatched, the red men deserted their village above the forks, slunk into the hills, over the hump into the Susquehanna basin, and eventually were driven westward toward their point of disintegration as a tribe in Oklahoma almost two centuries later. A few remained behind, some intermarried with the whites. The last descendant died in 1803. Some graves remain. The only other Indian monuments are the fine, distinguished heads of their sachems painted by the visiting Swedish painter Gustavus Hesselius, probably the first artist in the valley.

The white invasion spread quickly. To the north, in what was to become Pennsylvania's Delaware County, and in the Chester Valley to the northwest, the migration was mostly Quaker; to the west, beyond the Welsh Hills, the early comers were Germans and beyond them settled the Scotch-Irish.

To the south, the flat coastal plain stretched down into Maryland and Virginia and became plantation country. This area was all fertile land, and industrious estate owners with slave labor began to produce enormous crops — wheat, corn and other grains, vegetables and fruits. There were many mouths to feed — the growing population needed food and shelter, but there began to be large surpluses for export. Power to multiply the productivity of the individual hand was necessary and the available resource was falling water. The flour mill began to take the place of the hand mortar, the sawmill replaced the laborious ax and adz trimming. The Brandywine was an ideal millstream of manageable size. Some tributaries were usable as well.

Not all of the stream's sixty-mile length was serviceable. Although it fell almost a thousand feet from source to tidewater, the first miles of tumbling brooks were too narrow to produce power. But from the forks on, the volume was sufficient and the drop was relatively even. The stretch between the forks and the gorge was ideal for small mills. The gorge was a different story. The sharp fall of one hundred and twenty feet constituted a great concentration of power which was difficult to harness without elaborate construction. However, the fall represented an enticing potential and later it was to become a power nucleus of impressive proportions. At the foot of the drop, ideally again, was a navigable channel open to barge and shallop from the bay and ocean.

The first mills were tentative and vulnerable to floods. They were all of wood, except possibly their foundations and their wheels were almost certainly undershot. Secure dams, solid stone foundations and millraces with proper gates were difficult to construct — time, experience and capital had first to be accumulated. Spring floods often swept the frail structures into matchwood. These floods were not an unexpected risk — the jerry-built frames were, in many cases, considered expendable. The Brandywine was not an exception as a millstream; to the north were many millstreams — the Chester, Ridley, Cobbs, Crum and Wissahickon Creeks among others — and they all experienced the same hazards and benefits. Today one may come across some stout foundation stones embedded with iron bars to which the wooden superstructures were fastened. Until time elapsed and the settlers learned to build the thick-walled, three-storied stone structures that could breast the flood (some of which are still standing), milling was considered a risky enterprise.

There is a record of a Swedish grain mill above the falls built earlier than 1687, but at a time when records were few, there could have been predecessors. The first mill of any size was built in 1727, with a stout dam that apparently was enlarged over the years. Its construction signaled the beginning of the great years of the Brandywine flour industry. These were the years when the most was made of the area's geographical advantages. Thus, the richest wheat-producing areas in the colonies could be reached by barge or wagon and at the foot of the river's falls there was anchorage to load sloop and schooner which would bring the mill's exports within reach of the coastal cities, the West Indies and Europe.

Barge and shallop could carry the harvest from the creeks and inlets of the eastern shore or inland down the Christiana, but most crucial to the industry and the Pennsylvania farmers was the development of the Conestoga wagon by the Germans of the Susquehanna basin. Their wagon builders had brought their skills with them; they had been apprenticed to the making of the curved-bodied farmer's wains of southern Germany. Now they enlarged the body, made hoop-shaped supports for the canvas cover and heightened the wheels. The new wagons were an impressive sight, lumbering after their six-horse teams with clanking harness and jingling bells, carrying their great loads down the primitive dirt trails to the waiting mills. Gradually the fame of the Lancaster County Conestoga wagon spread, its form and appurtenances changed only slightly and it became the prairie schooner that followed the retreating Indian into the West.

The valley's meager roads which followed the meadow lands for the most part were easily flooded; fords were difficult and bridges few and frequently washed out. Farmers and millers complained loudly and often. Gradually the roads were built up in the boggy stretches, bridges were added and the link between the lower mills and the junction with the great western turnpike at Downington became a much used artery.

Statistics of any sort are hard to come by for these early years. Several sources estimate the number of mills on the stream at more than a hundred. Not all were flour mills. Gilpin's paper mill was started in 1787. A census taken shortly after the Revolution listed 50 wheat-flour mills, 1 furnace, 4 gristmills, 8 forges, 2 slitting mills, 4 paper mills, 3 oil mills, 7 fulling mills, 1 snuff mill, 1 tilt hammer — all run by Brandywine water. At about the same time the output was estimated at about 400,000 bushels of grain received, from which were milled 50,000 barrels of the finest flour and about 2,000 barrels of cornmeal. Corn which earlier had been a preponderant crop had shrunk to a small fraction of the wheat output.

This expanding activity spread prosperity up through the valley and well beyond its borders. The valley's appearance changed. The meadow flats were full of cattle, many of them descendants of the red cattle brought by the Swedes. The more gradual slopes of the surrounding hills were mostly cleared and in crop. Substantial stone houses gradually replaced the log homes although often the original log house was left as a wing. A few of these wooden structures still stand in the valley. The workable soft gneiss which underlay much of the valley was used to raise the orange-brown and plum-colored walls of houses and barns. A strip of green serpentine provided stone for what were possibly the only green stone houses in early America. Quite a number of these still stand. By the eve of the Revolution the valley had been transformed from wilderness relieved only by a few Indian clearings into a comfortable pastoral landscape dotted with structures of indigenous stone. Much of the look of that period survives today. However, all but a few of the mills are gone. As the Revolution approached, a new economic factor appeared. Iron, copper and lead were discovered in the Welsh Hills and in the country beyond. Lime was also available for smelting and there were thick forests of tall growth for making charcoal and providing wood for furnace fires. The date of the earliest forge was about 1760, and the number increased through the Revolutionary years and during the early nineteenth century. Although relatively short-lived, this was an era of great activity and prosperity that produced a unique society of its own in the folding hills and fertile valleys just beyond the watershed.

These years established a breed of ironmasters — industry barons who were supported by a nearly feudal society. The ironmasters needed huge holdings, not only for the mineral deposits but also for their timber which would supply the greedy furnaces. They built great houses surrounded by workshops, stables and the houses of their servants who labored as forgemen, miners and charcoal burners. This self-sufficient community, existing directly under the ironmaster's eye, flourished and faded but left its legends behind. Several of the furnaces have been preserved and restored and from these inert monuments the bustling past can be reconstructed.

The iron foundries were built just beyond the boundaries of the Brandywine proper, but the backcountry was now linked with the Atlantic slope and iron ingots, stove plates and firebacks were transported down the valley in a steady stream to the mills and the shipping in the estuary.

The various populations were mingling more and more. The bulk of the valley population was still Quaker but the two neighboring races, the Pennsylvania Germans and Scotch-Irish, were beginning to make themselves felt. The Scotch-Irish were attracted to the East Branch, and one of the valley towns, Downington, was settled by Germans. The eve of the Revolution found the valley prosperous, comfortable and bustling with enterprise — a place of abundant crops, teeming industrial production and active trade. Unwittingly, merely by exercising native gifts, the settlers of the wedge of land that encompassed the Brandywine and the Lancaster and York areas beyond had contributed three of the most potent factors in the development of the new nation. These factors were to become mystical symbols of early America in the popular mind: the log cabin, the Conestoga wagon or prairie schooner and the frontier rifle. The log cabin was first seen in the Swedish river settlements; the Conestoga wagon had been developed by the Lancaster County Germans, and the skill of the Black Forest German riflemakers fashioned the frontier rifle, miscalled the Kentucky rifle.

The unrest that finally exploded into rebellion did not stir the valley deeply. The preponderantly Quaker population went about its business, aware but not committed to participation. A few of the young men enlisted but they were not applauded by their elders. Delaware mustered one of the hard-fighting, backbone regiments of the Continental Army. Over the watershed, Daniel Morgan raised several companies of Pennsylvania German riflemen for his famous corps. News of the fighting filtered into the Brandywine but war seemed quite remote, until the logic of military strategy dictated a battle on its very banks.

II

THE BATTLE OF THE BRANDYWINE

THE QUIET VALLEY's dramatic entrance into history came as a surprise to its inhabitants. The settlers were conscious of the war cloud that hung over all the colonies and were somewhat affected by the scarcity of overseas imports as the blockade of the British ships off the Delaware Capes tightened, but the region was self-sufficient and crops were good so there was little real hardship. Warfare itself seemed remote, although from time to time militia and troops of the Continental Line moved through Wilmington or north and south along the Philadelphia-Baltimore pike. Few young men of the valley were involved. There were some Tory sympathizers and a leaven of patriot hotheads and local militiamen, but the Quaker farmers, who were neutral, plodded about their business and tried to ignore the war.

Suddenly, with little warning, the war was being fought on their acres. Indifferent to military strategy, the farmers were barely conscious that large armies were on the move and that Lord Howe's decision to capture "the rebel capital," Philadelphia, might mean the trampling down of their countryside. Even General Washington and his strategists were surprised, for they expected Howe to make the obvious advance from New York across a hundred miles of New Jersey countryside, and it was across this countryside that it was planned to interpose the Continental Army.

When word reached Washington that Howe was not marching overland but had embarked his army and was at sea with the British fleet, the American leader felt virtually certain that the advance would be up the broad Delaware. He put his army in motion southward to the Delaware and waited for news of the fleet. Howe's transports had put to sea on July 24, and on July 30 reports came from Cape Henlopen of a host of sail on the horizon. This seemed to betoken an attack on the Delaware forts, but shortly thereafter the fleet was sighted off to the south where it disappeared into the wide ocean. For weeks there was no word of it, and uneasiness set in. There was some conjecture that it might be beating down the coast to capture some of the southern ports; but at last the fleet was sighted in the Chesapeake and sailed up to the head of the bay at the estuary of Elk River. Howe was now fifty miles south of Philadelphia but he had been more than a month at sea. His men were sick, stiff and bored, and many of the horses had died or were in poor condition.

Washington's doubts were finally resolved. He marched his army with fife and drum and green sprigs in their hats through the streets of Philadelphia, as smartly as possible, and out on the Chester-Wilmington road. At the Brandywine he took position on the steep hills which overlooked the stream and mills below and served as a defense for the ferry and ford passage. While Howe delayed at Elkton, Washington moved nearer to the line of Red Clay Creek and the Christiana with his left flank at the Delaware marshes. He expected Howe's advance to be up the shore road through New Castle; and indeed some skirmishing did take place in that direction with a small engagement at Cooche's Bridge. Finding that the British seemed to be moving northwest toward the middle Brandywine, Washington, by a night march, shifted to intercept. He deployed on the hill slopes of the stream's eastern bank, above and below Chadds Ford. It was a strong position. The stream valley was narrow, scarcely more than a ribbon of meadow land and hills commanded the fords on either side.

The story of the battle was the story of the fords. There were fords both below and above Chadds Ford, but the fate of the battle centered about the frequent fords upstream. The ground was unfamiliar to Washington, as it was to all the officers except some of the Pennsylvania militia and perhaps a few of Anthony Wayne's Continental Line. Washington

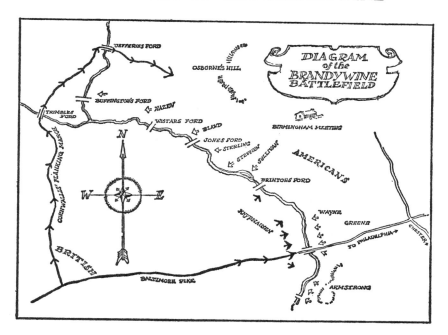

had been apprised of four fords above Chadds — Brintons, a mile and a half upstream, then Jones ford farther upstream and Wistars ford, approximately a mile beyond Jones ford. Above Wistars was the junction of the two branches of the Brandywine with Buffingtons ford over the East Branch near the junction and Jefferies ford a mile above it. Trimbles ford was on the West Branch above the junction. Washington's statements, which were confirmed by General Sullivan, indicate that he knew of the first four fords, but had been assured that there was no feasible ford for many miles above Buffingtons ford. It is quite certain that he was not informed of the existence of Trimbles and Jefferies fords. But they were to play the crucial role in the battle.

By September 10 Howe had reached the village of Kennett Square about six miles from the Brandywine. The troops had been fired upon by outposts and skirmishers but the march had been routine, except that it had attracted crowds of timid gawkers. Word had begun to spread that the British were not ferocious toward civilians. Howe had given orders for good behavior, as his inclination was toward pacification rather than force. Further, he had been told that he would be marching through Tory territory and that recruits would flock to him. He found the Tories scarce and little inclined to enlist — the countryside flocked to gape at the British, but only in apprehensive curiosity.

British scouting had indicated that the battle would develop at the Brandywine crossings. Washington had disposed his troops in readiness. His left flank, extending downstream from Chadds Ford, was held by Armstrong's Pennsylvania militia. The militiamen occupied a strong defensive position on the steep wooded hills rising from the stream. Washington doubted that a serious attack would develop here, and none did. The main body, largely tried veteran troops consisting of the brigades of Anthony Wayne, Mühlenburg and Weedon, together with the light infantry under Maxwell and Proctor's artillery, was concentrated at or near the Chadds Ford crossings. General Greene's troops were in reserve. Upstream, the troops of Sullivan, Sterling and Stephens were strung mainly between Brintons ford and Jones ford. Still farther upstream, on the extreme right, were smaller bodies of troops under Colonels Hazen and Bland and Major Spear.

The British seem to have had much more detailed knowledge of the countryside (usually attributed to Tory help) than the Americans. Washington seems to have received little information from the indifferent Quaker farmers. Howe, moreover, had a definite battle plan and put it into motion. The morning of the 11th began with skirmish action south of the stream near Kennett meetinghouse and Welch's tavern. General Maxwell had crossed the creek with his riflemen and after some sharp fighting was driven back as were two other detachments from the American center. Knyphausen with German mercenaries was leading the British advance and he took up position on the western heights facing the American center. Placing his batteries on the hilltops, he began a cannonade against Procter's guns on the parallel hilltops across the stream.

Meanwhile, General Cornwallis with more than a third of the British strength was marching north on a road parallel to the stream. This brought him to Trimbles ford which crossed the West Branch and another road which bypassed Buffingtons ford and crossed the East Branch at Jefferies ford. Passing over that, he turned southward, now securely on the right flank of the Americans. While this long maneuver dangerously splitting the British forces was carried out, Washington was preparing to attack from his center although he was aware of the possibility of a flanking movement upstream. But the intricacies and blunderings of that upstream attack and defense have defied historians who have attempted to sort them out accurately.

Colonel Bland, scouting for such a movement, crossed the stream and sighted the British column marching north. The early morning had been heavy with fog but by about eleven o'clock it was clear, and a small force of Americans were following the British column northward. A message was sent to Washington and was confirmed by another message from Colonel Hazen that red uniforms had been seen near the forks of the Brandywine. There was a possibility that Howe might be circling to the west and north to reach Philadelphia without an action. Washington determined to strike the divided enemy from his center.

But now came a message from the indecisive Sullivan that Major Spear of the militia who had scouted from the forks to Welch's tavern had heard nothing of the enemy. Sullivan had sent a sergeant on horseback past the forks and he had seen no British. Since by this time the Cornwallis advance had cleared both fords it seems incredible that neither Spear nor the sergeant had seen them or, that if the inhabitants had been questioned, they had not told. We know from eyewitness accounts that the British column attracted many onlookers, principally the young, yet the news was not transmitted to the Americans.

But at least one observer spoke up. A man named Cheyney reported to Sullivan that the British were past the forks, and Sullivan sent him on to Washington. Washington, torn by indecision, called off his attack, and a little later Cheyney's story was confirmed by a report from Colonel

Bland. Sullivan's lack of alertness and thorough scouting had allowed Cornwallis to get position on his right rear. Too late, Stephens and Sterling rushed up from their positions by the stream and deployed on the high ground near Birmingham Meeting. Sullivan, on their left, fumbled in the tricky country of hill and dell, cleared fields and dense woodland, yet never established secure contact. His force fell into confusion and broke. Late, Washington spurred on the Virginia troops and Greene's reserve. They did well and fought back from the brink of catastrophe.

Knyphausen forced the fords in the face of strong resistance from Wayne, but all anyone could do was to delay. The only available escape route was down the Chester road, and so Washington withdrew in the September dusk. Although badly beaten, the troops were not panicky — rather they were strangely philosophical. Strategy and fortune had all gone against them but they did not feel they had been outfought. They had faced the superior numbers of a professional army and man to man had proved themselves at least equal. Washington's army was staggered but not crushed. It was still a fighting unit and would outlive other bitter days just ahead at Germantown and Valley Forge. Philadelphia was open and that seemed an alarming blow, but only time would prove what an empty prize it was. Howe had no heart for pursuit. He lingered near Chadds Ford and carried his wounded into Wilmington. There was some pillaging by soldiers and rabble. When the British finally moved out to occupy Philadelphia on the 27th, the valley had seen the last trampling of warfare.

But the legend of the war lingered, to be embroidered and pass into old men's tales. Despite the Quaker reticence and reluctance to be involved, the young and many of the old could not resist the greatest drama that the valley had ever seen. They gathered from all sides to catch glimpses of the event, and there are eyewitness accounts to attest to this. It had been a widely scattered battle, with considerable interpenetration of front lines and small skirmishes and minor engagements here and there, isolated by the broken-up, wooded countryside. The fighting had been sharp and bitter but of relatively short duration. Between the intervals of combat there had been long marches, broken by rests, which permitted the non-combattants to come close and even mingle with the troops. Finally, when the fighting died and the advance swept past, there were the discarded knapsacks, ammunition pouches and muskets littering the fields, the wounded to be carried to shelter, and the stiffening bodies in woodlot and pasture.

The facts of the battle tales and anecdotes, transformed by repetition over the years, cannot always be proved, but one eyewitness account, in particular, carries the ring of truth. A Quaker youth of twenty-one, Joseph Townsend, who lived near Jefferies ford, wrote down his memories of the battle in later years. He, with his family and neighbors, was attending Fifth-day morning meeting when the appearance of the British advance column tramping down to Jefferies ford brought the congregation out of their temporary meetinghouse. The column halted, did some pillaging and broke open some casks of liquor. Joseph and his brother ran home to see to the safety of their horses and then, overcome with curiosity, walked to the nearby village of Sconneltown where the troops had again halted. The boys were allowed to move through the ranks, and then, emboldened, they entered a farmhouse filled with officers who matched curiosity with curiosity and asked questions.

Townsend wrote:

> . . . divers of the principal officers . . . manifested an uncommon sociable disposition. They were full of inquiries respecting the *rebels*, where they were to be met with and where Mr. Washington was to be found . . . They inquired what sort of man Mr. Washington was.
>
> My brother . . . replied that he was a stately, well-proportioned, fine looking man of great abilities, active, firm and resolute, of a social disposition and considered to be a good man.
>
> [One of them answered], "He might be a good man but he was most damnably misled to take up arms against his sovereign."
>
> [Another said], "You have a hell of a fine country here." [He goes on to describe the officers as] . . . rather stout, portly gentlemen, well-dressed and of genteel appearance, and did not look as if they had ever been exposed to any hardship.

They saw General Cornwallis ride by and they remarked his fine scarlet uniform. They pushed on into the ranks of the German troops and were astonished at their moustaches, a strange sight to them. Soon the troops fell back into marching order and, as they spread across the fields, bullets began to fly and Joseph made for safety, but the Germans caught him and set him to dismantling fences. At this the Quaker in him rose. "On the removal of the second rail I was forcibly struck with the impropriety of being active in assisting to take the lives of my fellow beings and therefore desisted."

Climbing up Osborne's hill, he found some of his neighbors gaping at a cluster of mounted officers. It was Howe and his staff. Unmolested, Joseph got close enough to describe the general as "a large portly man of coarse features. He appeared to have lost his teeth as his mouth had somewhat fallen in."

Then, from the direction of Chadds Ford, came the thudding of heavy cannonading; Knyphausen's batteries had opened fire. The British lines pushed on to complete their pincer movement. Behind the advance the fields were littered with discarded equipment and plunderers were at work — even in the valley there were scavengers close behind the moving battle line.

Joseph must have been dizzy with excitement. He and a few companions walked over the battlefield around the Birmingham meetinghouse. They passed among the quiet corpses and the bleeding wounded and, using wrenched-off doors for litters, carried the injured men into the meetinghouse. Finally the group set out for home as dark was setting in. To show the confusion of the battle lines, presumably in British-held territory, they ran into an American scouting party and, not responding to its challenge, were fired upon. They scattered pell-mell and Joseph, blundering in the dark into a flock of sheep, struck terror into them and himself. His account, written in later years from memory, is a remarkably convincing picture of how the fringe of battle appeared to his young, startled, unsophisticated eyes.

The tenor of the Quaker farmer mind is disclosed in accounts such as Benjamin Hawley's matter-of-fact diary: "11th Fifth Day very hot, finished harrowing the Rye — son Wm took the horse. The English engaged the Americans — the Latter defeated with much loss." And there is the story of the Quaker miller who left his logbook blank for the day, since there had been no business, and he had no interest in warfare.

That there was considerable pillaging after the battle by the British is attested to by the *Registers of Damages Sustained by the Inhabitants of Chester County by the Troops and Adherents of the King of Great Britain During the American Revolution.* The houses occupied by Washington and Lafayette as headquarters were ransacked, probably because of their temporary military use. Gideon Gilpin, the owner of the so-called "Lafayette Headquarters," filed an itemized claim. It is a long list, comprising such items as "10 Milch Cows, 1 Yoke of Oxen, 48 Sheep and 3 Colts, 1 Clock, 2 New Baggs and a history book." The claim totaled five hundred and two pounds, sixpence. There were many similar claims.

The physical marks of the battle were soon erased, but the minds of the valley folk had something to work on for generations. In a short time, the historians appeared, not only sorting out such documents as were relevant but also tramping the fields and hills in an attempt to pin down just where each unit had moved, where each contact had been made. Of course, their patient researches have been only partially succssful. It is the nature of history that there are never enough certainties — there are always times when deduction and conjecture must attempt to fill in the blank places.

Apart from the scholars and historians with their passion for certainties was the gossip and storytelling of the natives. These enthusiasts paid some lip service to the certainties but could indulge in the luxury of embellishment. For a valley filled with presumably truthful and matter-of-fact Quakers, they did very well with the arts of embellishment. Perhaps the tall tales generated by the battle heralded the unabashed romanticism of the verse and novels of later decades.

III

TALENT IN THE VALLEY

WHILE WARFARE left no long-lasting scars on the valley, it did result in some economic disabilities, but the Brandywine suffered less than most regions. It put its back and wits to work and prospered.

By chance, disaster that struck a few miles to the north brought with it some unexpected advantages. Yellow fever had broken out in Philadelphia in 1793 and struck again in 1795, 1796 and 1798. Many people fled the city and some of them moved to the Brandywine, which had gained the reputation of having a bracing and pestilent-free air. The valley was free of the fever until 1798 and then was touched only lightly. During the plague the port of Philadelphia was almost deserted, for few ships cared to venture up the river. New Castle and the Christiana and Brandywine estuary became the unloading points. Wilmington grew to be a bustling place and its population doubled in a space of about fifteen years.

When Alexander Wilson, the young Scottish immigrant who was to transmute his astonished enchantment with the birdlife of the forested continent into his great *American Ornithology*, was forced to land at New Castle on his way to Philadelphia, it was his walk northward through the Brandywine valley that gave him his first vivid impressions of the new land. Penniless and carrying his few possessions on his back, he ambled along the Strand at New Castle, admiring its line of fine brick residences with their comfortable gardens. With a companion, he walked up the old causeway built across the marshland by the first Swedish settlers. The flat country covered with thickets draped with wild grape was a part of the long coastal plain that spread northward to the bank of the Christiana where the hills began to climb.

Wilson found Wilmington a fair town. He passed the thirteen great flour mills clustered on its northwest edge that made the Brandywine the largest flour-producing center of the New World. Jacob Broom, a signer of the Declaration of Independence, was making preparations for a new cotton mill and French émigrés were running two new silk looms. He passed the old barley mill, the snuff mill and the Gilpin and Fisher paper mill. A few miles above, a new paper mill was under construction. The atmosphere was one of vigorous growth and prosperity.

He then trudged up the Kennett Pike to Kennett Square and north on the Baltimore–Philadelphia road to Chadds Ford. The rolling forested country appeared uncleared to a European's eye. "The only houses we saw were made of large logs of wood, laid one over another," he said. "What crops we could see consisted of Indian corn, potatoes and some excellent oats." He plodded northward out of the valley. Like Hesselius before him, the very young Benjamin West and some itinerant artists, his talent only touched the valley as he passed through. The valley had not yet produced its own.

The yellow fever not only diverted commerce to the Brandywine but also a body of foreign newcomers, both temporary dwellers and permanent inhabitants. The French Revolution had driven out thousands of the nobility, merchants, middle-class shopkeepers, artisans and intellectuals. They scattered into new homes throughout Europe and hundreds undertook the long voyage to the new continent. Philadelphia was a popular objective. It was still the first city of the new republic with a European reputation for its culture, its society and its opportunities. Frightened by the plague, many of the French stopped in Wilmington, for that small town had a reputation in France as well, generated by Lafayette and many of the French officers who had enjoyed its hospitality during the war years. In addition, the bloody Negro insurrection in Santo Domingo had driven out the planters and the remnants of the French colony. Some of these fugitives, too, came to Wilmington. Still later, the dislocation of the Napoleonic wars resulted in another refugee migration.

The new émigré population worked a change on the look and flavor of Wilmington. Most of the new arrivals were French and they clustered in a long street of brick and stone houses running from the Christiana to the Brandywine. This roadway was soon named French Street and still is. They furnished a still soberly Quaker town with a sprinkle of color and a sense of style — their gay natures were responsive to trivialities and spontaneous entertainments. And they brought with them their bibelots, their furniture, their dress, their manners and their talents. Some arrived penniless, but others had managed to rescue their wealth. They helped each other and most put to bread-and-butter use what talents they had taken for granted.

Many stayed for only a few years and then returned to their former homes, but they left a leaven in the social structure. One French family put down permanent roots. From a modest beginning in the Brandywine gorge, it built, step by step, an industrial empire that spread throughout the world. The amazing Du Pont dynasty began with Pierre Samuel du Pont (1739–1817), the son of a French watchmaker, who had been trained in the family craft. He was soon out of watchmaking into theoretical and practical economics, pamphleteering and editing, and in the disturbed financial and political climate of prerevolutionary France, he climbed rapidly. When the Revolution came he found himself in a precarious position. He had been ennobled and changed his name to Du Pont de Nemours, but his future seemed uncertain. His oldest son, Victor, who had been in America under the French minister, convinced him that his fortunes lay in the New World. With Victor and another son, Éleuthère Irénée, Pierre formed Du Pont de Nemours, Père, Fils & Cie., of New York and began to speculate its capital in American ventures. All but one venture turned out badly. It was Irénée who saw the possibilities in Brandywine power, bought acreage in the gorge and began powder making on a modest scale in 1802. The great Du Pont empire grew from this beginning.

The first small powder mill expanded and soon a French-speaking community grew up around it, for Irénée imported French workmen. A village of small stone houses spread itself above and below Hagley Falls. It was a self-contained, patriarchal community. The mills themselves were shaped like mortars — three stout walls of solid stone and one made of planks faced the stream. When explosions occurred, and they did in spite of the greatest care, the plank-side blew out into the stream or onto the slope beyond.

Today the powder mills are gone, or rather, they have been reconstructed on museum grounds. But in their day they brought a new prosperity to the valley, and as the young corporation progressed from the manufacture of gunpowder into the complex ramifications of chemical and synthetic products, Wilmington remained the headquarters of one of the greatest creations of industrialism. The gorge of the Hagley Falls, just on the edge of the city, has gone back to nature, but it has a tended, parklike look. The Hagley Museum, the library and the replicas of the old mills are there for the interested visitor.

The Brandywine maintained its preeminence as the country's most important grain-milling center until the completion of the Erie Canal, which opened up the yield of the great midwestern wheatlands. It held its place for so long, not merely because of geographical and climatic advantages but because of the population's native skills, farsighted cooperation and readiness to work out new methods. The local millers learned the advantages of cooperation early. They participated in a joint inspection system of their products that standardized the weight and quality of their flour. By stamping all their products with the brand name of the Brandywine Mills, they built up a reputation for flour of the highest quality.

Fortunately too, a native-born mechanical and inventive genius grew up almost in the shadow of the mills and his farseeing ideas worked a revolution in the techniques of milling. Oliver Evans, born on the banks of the Christiana of Welsh Quaker forbears, built an early steamboat and predicted the railroad, but his boyhood interest in the mills around him spurred him to grapple with the mechanics of the industry he knew first-hand. He wrote a book, *Young Millwright's & Miller's Guide*, illustrated with diagrams, that went through many editions and became a bible of the milling industry. It was on the Brandywine that Evans' revolutionary ideas were tested and perfected. His powers of invention culminated in a system of mechanical innovations that greatly increased the efficiency of waterpower and brought into being one of the first examples of industrial streamlined production, in which the machine took charge from raw material to finished product.

From the mill side, the grain could be drawn up mechanically from the loaded Conestogas on the road or shallow-draft barges in the stream below. The processes of cleaning, grinding, cooling and bolting and pouring into barrels were entirely mechanical, and only the last stage of fastening the barrel top required human hands. It was claimed that six men could handle the production of 100,000 bushels a year.

By the end of the first quarter of the nineteenth century, the valley had enjoyed almost two centuries of growth and increasing prosperity. Although the mills on its lower reaches and the forges in and beyond its more distant hills had contributed importantly to this, the chief credit must go to the hundreds of productive farms. Their crop-heavy fields, their simple but handsome stone houses, barns and springhouses dominated the pattern of the landscape. And on those fertile acres worked, for the greater part, the descendants of the Quaker settler stock.

They had inherited much from their ancestors, but some of their rugged qualities of character were being quietly eroded by the increasing comfort of the times. They were less likely to turn their faces from the visual arts, although the theater was still a suspicious activity. They had always been fervent in education — in fact, they had many new and progressive ideas about imparting knowledge and experience. They were readers. Books of a meditative and moralistic nature remained a staple, but histories, biographies, scientific works, poetry and the novel were gradually added to their bookshelves. Many of the inhabitants were beginning to be receptive to the rapid influx of printed matter that was one of the phenomena of the times. Newspapers, pamphlets, weekly and monthly magazines and books were now appearing in an accelerated flow in response to the demands created by more widespread education and increased leisure. The printed word was now easy to come by, and it is not surprising that the first stirrings in the arts should find release in the literary field.

The Brandywine was about to establish a small literature of its own generated by three native sons who went on to become nationally conspicuous in their day, but who now are no more than names in a detailed history of American literature. George Lippard (1822–1854), Bayard Taylor (1825–1878) and Thomas Buchanan Read (1822–1872), born within a few years of each other, all achieved national success, but they never lost touch with the valley and they celebrated it in novel, verse and essay. Their works were inherently sentimental, full-blown and often melodramatic, for those were some of the literary compulsions of their day. The obvious beauty of the land was not their only theme, nor even its history; their main lode was an untapped and hitherto concealed fund of half-formed folktales and legends. Self-conscious about the newness of their own country, they were delighted to find layers of history and romantic legend that might rival those of Europe. They were haunted by the unresolved dichotomy between their instinctive love of their land and the almost irresistible attraction of centuries of European culture. Their efforts to hold European influences at bay while they struggled to create an American literature had meager success, and in their hearts they knew it. The least they hoped for was to do for the Brandywine what Washington Irving had done for the Catskills. Like Irving they collected the fragmentary legends, embroidered them and invented others. Through their romantically bemused eyes they saw a valley scarcely dreamed of by their hardheaded ancestors.

George Lippard wrote many novels, but it was with his *Blanche of the*

Brandywine; or September the Eleventh, 1777, published in 1846, that he made an epic attempt to immortalize the Brandywine. In the Preface he wrote, "The legends of the Brandywine are as immortal as the hills which overshadow her beautiful valleys." His theme was the Revolutionary battle, but even that drama seemed insufficient — he poured into his tale all the fantasy, the breathless melodrama and hair-raising sensationalism he had absorbed from his reading of the British Gothic novelists, from Charles Brockden Brown and probably from his acquaintance with the pictures of John Quidor. So the Brandywine became the unlikely background for a mid-nineteenth-century Gothic thriller.

Bayard Taylor, born at Kennett Square in 1825, was a more substantial and lasting talent. He learned his writing trade on the West Chester *Village Record* and although he journeyed into many strange corners of the wide world and achieved a certain fame for his travel articles, his heart was always in his homeland. The Brandywine pervaded his verse and essays and provided the setting for his best novel, *The Story of Kennett* (1866). Like Lippard, Taylor indulged in moments of melodrama but they did not annihilate his ability to see his characters in the round. He caught the feel of the time and the countryside, and his novel can be read as post-Revolutionary social history if nothing else.

Thomas Buchanan Read, born in 1822 in the hamlet of Corner's Ketch, was the third early celebrator of the valley in verse and prose, and he seems to have been the first native-born artist of competence. He achieved national popularity and prominence by virtue of sheer indomitable ambition. Read made the most of his natural gifts and died with a reputation that has since dwindled greatly. His family, which was poor, broke up when he was still a young boy. He ran away and walked the length of the state to Pittsburgh, then worked his way by flatboat to Cincinnati. There he apprenticed himself to a portrait artist and painter-of-all-work. He learned to paint signs, decorate canal boats and chisel figures and inscriptions on tombstones.

A few years later, he struck out for himself and opened a sign shop.

The first Nicholas Longworth became interested in him, fitted out a portrait studio for him and helped him get commissions, including one to paint General William Henry Harrison. With some money saved, he moved to Boston, which was regarded as the Athens of America. He soon became the friend of Longfellow, Washington Allston and other important men. Read was now writing indefatigably, pouring out verse, articles and novels, and Allston inspired him to paint grandiose set pieces. Their titles are indicative of the sorts of pictures they were: "The Embarcation of Cleopatra," "Diana and Endymion," "Milton," "Abou ben Adhem and the Angel." Appleton's *Encyclopedia of Biography* described his work in this way: "His paintings, most of which deal with allegorical and mythological subjects, are full of poetic and graceful fancies but the technical treatment is careless and unskillful, betraying his lack of early training."

Read's regional fervor expressed itself in a novel, *Paul Redding, A Tale of the Brandywine*, published in 1845, a year before Lippard's *Blanche of the Brandywine*. They are both equally sentimental books, although Read salted his effort with humor and seemed less addicted to runaway fantasy. In *The Wagoner of the Alleghenies* he tried verse in an effort to reach an epic level, but the theme of the Brandywine battle is clotted with theatricality and rhetoric.

Like Taylor, Read fled to Europe to taste the wonders of an older culture, but a belligerent patriotism brought him back again and again to the themes of his childhood and native hills. The Civil War themes spread his fame through his lectures and propaganda writings, but he is now remembered only for his best-known painting, a large canvas of "Sheridan's Ride" and his poem of the same title. The poem was printed in almost every grammar school reader and for a generation or more tens of thousands of the young were prodded into learning its lines by heart.

Read, Taylor and Lippard were the more conspicuous forerunners of what would soon become more abundant Brandywine talent. They initiated its parochial literature, an interesting page in cultural and social history. They made the country aware that the valley was more than the site of a day's battleground or a milling center. Read is the first artist of note, except perhaps for his contemporary, William Marshall Swayne, an intermittent sculptor whose supreme effort was a head of Lincoln for which the busy President gave two sittings. None of these men formed a school or left more than a passing mark on any of the arts in America. They only served notice that talent was stirring in the hills.

*

The role of the valley as an important center of illustrative talent began when Felix Octavius Carr Darley moved into his roomy Victorian house at Claymont near Wilmington in 1859. Darley, then thirty-seven and in his vintage years, enjoyed a great reputation as America's first illustrator of importance. He was a product of America's rapidly growing demand for more and more of the printed word and the printed picture. The publishers had discovered in him the advantage of advertising a "name" artist. "Illustrated by Darley," had become a frequent phrase in the print of the day. His illustrated books were on the parlor tables of middle-class homes all over the country — to possess them was considered a badge of culture.

He came to the Brandywine region at the peak of his powers and success to work and to radiate influence. He is rumored to have sketched on the river's banks in his youthful days, for he was born in nearby Philadelphia. He seems to have preferred its pleasant countryside to the distractions of New York and when he moved to the valley with his new bride, a member of one of the older families, his presence constituted an important addition to the cultured life of Wilmington.

Darley could scarcely have known that a few miles away, a seven-year-old boy, who was to become the most renowned illustrator of *his* day, was already poring over books "Illustrated by Darley." Little Howard Pyle was greedy for books with pictures and there were some books illustrated by Darley on the family shelves.

Darley's renown has dwindled greatly since his own day. Unjustifiably, he is now a neglected artist, but his talent deserves reexamination for its own sake, for the clues that it offers to the atmosphere of his time and because he played an important part in launching our impressive art of illustration.

Both of his parents were English-born, although they were young when they came to America. Their son was born in Philadelphia on June 23, 1822. Both parents had had stage experience and, inherited or not, there was a strong flavor of the theater in much of Felix's work. He was a natural pictorial dramatist with a growing command over the easy manipulation of figures into meaningful and arresting groups. In his quick pencil sketches that searched for compositional certainties, his rapid and advantageous use of the figure can be seen at a glance.

He never had a formal art lesson. He had shown talent early, but art was not considered a worthy career for a boy who had to make his way, so he was apprenticed at the age of fourteen to a mercantile future in a countinghouse. But he had a concealed determination to be an artist, and, working in his spare time, he accumulated a portfolio of drawings and began taking it to the printing, publishing and engraving houses. In the earlier years of the nineteenth century Philadelphia was probably the most important publishing center in the country, although it was soon to lose that position to New York. Young Darley managed to sell enough drawings for publication to enable him to leave the mercantile life and to launch out as a professional artist by the age of twenty.

In 1842, the first year of his professional career, he sold several drawings of street scenes for publication in the *Saturday Museum*, a magazine edited by Edgar Allan Poe. Apparently Poe thought so well of Darley's work that very shortly thereafter, when he began to plan a new magazine to be called *The Stylus*, he retained him to make pictures for it, and an authority states, "There is a signed contract to that effect." *The Stylus* never reached publication but out of the association came two vignette drawings, reproduced by wood engraving for *The Gold Bug* when that story first appeared in *The Dollar Newspaper* for June 21, 1843. There is conjecture that these pictures were originally intended for one of the early numbers of *The Stylus*.

In the same year a series of Darley's designs were printed from lithographic stones for a collection called *Scenes in Indian Life*. They were issued in five parts, one a month, for twenty-five cents a part or one dollar for the set. The bound set was apparently Darley's first book. The drawings were in outline, obviously influenced by the style of the German artist, Moritz Retzsch, whose work at that time was popular on the Continent. These sketches no more than hinted at the skill that Darley would acquire in a few more years, but American illustration was so barren of accomplishment in those early days that the compositions drew considerable praise. Poe's friendly *Saturday Museum* said, "They abound in spirit and are in all respects meritorious," and the *Literary Age* praised the drawings as, "Superior to any specimens of linear outline as yet offered to the American public."

Had Darley remained on this level he would not have dominated the illustrative scene in succeeding years as competition sharpened. But he had great adaptability and an enormous capacity for hard work and his unusual work matured rapidly. After completing another set of outline drawings for *In Town and About*, he was enticed into a project, the four-volume *Pictorial History of the United States* which a Philadelphia publisher printed in 1843 and 1844. The history contained 350 wood engravings and many artists worked on them, although Darley contributed only a few. But it is an indication of the low state of illustrative art in the country at the time that many of the designs were copied from or retouched from the German Adolf Menzel's superb drawings for Kugler's *Frederick the Great*. The four volumes were an ambitious and pretentious publishing project that collapsed from a dearth of talent and skill. But the bungled use of Menzel's art showed an awakening appreciation of superior illustrative art and indicated the power that Menzel was beginning to exert as one of the most important seminal influences on pen technique.

In just a few years Darley had made great strides in scope, expressiveness and technique. He stood head and shoulders above his rivals, and when Carey & Hart launched their *Library of Humorous American Works* in 1846, the series overbore the statement, *"Illustrated by Darley."*

He came into prominence at a time when publishers were struggling with the problem of adjusting the accustomed methods of reproduction to satisfy the increasing demands of a larger and larger market for books of moderate price. The fine old methods of the mezzotint, aquatint, etching and copper engraving were, except in a few cases, too slow and expensive. The choice lay largely in the wood-engraving, lithography and steel-engraving techniques. The last was expensive and little used; lithography was a new process and, although many German lithographers were migrating to America, the method was less familiar and less trusted by the conservative printers than wood engraving. Darley became familiar with all three methods — the printing and engraving houses were small and intimate and he could watch the translation of his drawings into printing blocks. He worked for all three methods, but only a few times for steel engraving. Wood engraving was by all odds the most popular method, and the greater part of his best work was cut on boxwood by the engraver's burin.

By the time he moved to New York in 1848, even his amazing industry could not cope with all the work that was thrust upon him. It was a chauvinistic period, the young republic was eager to celebrate its past in text and picture and Darley became famous for his American themes. He became a friend of Washington Irving and illustrated his *Rip Van Winkle, Sketch Book, The Legend of Sleepy Hollow* and *Knickerbocker History of New York*. Other lauded authors of the time such as N. P. Willis, Henry Wadsworth Longfellow, Harriet Beecher Stowe, Donald Grant Mitchell, Francis Parkman, James Fenimore Cooper, Mary Mapes Dodge and George Lippard were proud to have their works illustrated by him.

Darley did illustrations for Dickens, Scott, Tennyson and Laurence Sterne, designs for banknotes and many pictures for the current magazines — *Harper's Magazine, Harper's Weekly, Our Young Folks, River-*

side Magazine, Health and Home and *Every Saturday*. He drew pictures for several scores of other books, books forgotten by everyone except those collectors who track them down for the Darley illustrations. It would probably take some degree of temerity to read them today but, at a distance, some of the titles can pique our curiosity — *Peter Ploddy, Some Adventures of Captain Simon Suggs Late of the Tallapossa Volunteers, The Blossoms of Morality, Aunt Patty's Scrap-Bag, Streaks of Squatter Life, Polly Peablossom's Wedding, Picking from the Picayune and Yemassee.*

When Darley moved from the bustle of New York to the quiet of Claymont he was nationally famous and without a peer in his own field. A young artist, Winslow Homer, just serving his apprenticeship in the field would shortly build an important reputation in illustration through the Civil War years and then become a painter whose fame would far exceed Darley's. Later, in the last decade of Darley's life, the pace of publication would accelerate and a company of first-rate talents would be perfecting their illustrative skills. But Darley never lost his public or the favor of the publishers. He was busy to the end. And the younger generation of illustrators, avidly studying the work of the British and Continental greats, could find an American model of first caliber only in him.

Darley, by moving from New York to Claymont, became the first illustrator to move out of arm's reach of the publishing world. Lesser artists would have feared to risk neglect and lack of work. Darley's move may have influenced Howard Pyle to follow the same pattern a few years later, a pattern that is now quite accepted. Darley gave the valley, as yet unaccustomed to talent, its first illustrator of note, but it would be years before artists were accepted as part of the local scene.

IV

HOWARD PYLE — THE FORMATIVE YEARS

THE WILMINGTON in which Howard Pyle was born on March 5, 1853, was still a small town just beginning its stretch toward city size. It was inching up the hills that rose to the north and west of the junction of the Christiana and Brandywine which resulted in a channel that flowed out to the broad Delaware. Architecturally, the town was largely red brick, still generously dotted with the Colonial and Federal and beginning on the higher levels of its hills to break out into variegated Victorian fantasies. Down by the water were the docks, the factories, work sheds and the shanties and close-packed houses of the poor. Higher up the streets, laid out in a gridiron pattern, were tree-lined with brick sidewalks which rippled over bulging tree roots. Standing cheek by cheek, the ample brick houses presented identical faces to the street with their iron hitching posts and stone mounting blocks at the curb, white marble steps and arched passageways which ran back at street level to the narrow but deep rear yards.

The white marble steps were scrubbed, an early morning chore for the housemaid. The doors and window frames and shutters were kept freshly painted, often a discreet dark green. Door bellpulls were replacing brass knockers, and lace window curtains were no longer considered ostentatious. The solid oak doors were pierced with brass letter slots and footscrapers were embedded beside the first step.

Quakers lived in many of these houses; they were the prosperous descendants of the Pennsylvanians who had moved into the valley a century and a half before. Turning their backs on the street, they lived in their pleasant high-ceilinged rooms. During the warm months, they enjoyed the trees and grape arbors of their "backyards." Inside, polished mahogany from the early Philadelphia cabinetmakers graced their rooms, sometimes replaced with black walnut by those with an urge to keep up with the times. These quiet people lived on quiet streets that only reverberated when iron-rimmed wheels bumped over the rounded cobblestones.

The youngster, Howard, grew up in just such a Quaker home and could count a long ancestry stretching back to the first Robert Pyle who had settled on his acres in the valley near Chadds Ford. By the time the boy reached maturity he would be able to claim over seventy first cousins. The clan would play its part in shaping him. His parents, William Pyle and Margaret Churchman Painter, sprang from a family tree that was many-branched, and Howard had in him the sap that had already quickened generations of useful lives.

The Pyle house was in the country just beyond the growing town. It was built in three parts — the oldest section was a modest fieldstone home put up about 1740, a larger addition was built at the time of the Revolution and then a recent wing was added before the Civil War by Howard's father. It stood back from the Kennett Pike and looked out on a wide lawn and grassy bank ideal for rolling and climbing. To one side there was a small grove of trees beyond which the moving wagons and carriages on the turnpike were easily visible. The garden toward the back was crowded with flowers and fruit trees, with cinder paths, arbors, a greenhouse, a wooden summerhouse and an outcropping of rocks overhung with trees and vines. This was the scene that nurtured his imagination. He would come back to it again and again in the pictures and writings of his creative years.

The visual details of the snug interior, the plastered rooms, the paneled doors, the recessed windows, the hand-carved moldings, the steps that led up and down from one section of the house to another would work their way into many of his pictures. Most important, the atmosphere of the house was one of warmth, comfort, concern and affection.

The house was filled with books and, in spite of the Quaker background, of pictures too. On the walls were steel engravings of Landseer, Holman Hunt and a Murillo Madonna. The bookshelves boasted a wide variety of reading matter from *Slovenly Peter* to Thackeray, from *The Arabian Nights* to Swedenborg's *Heaven and Hell*. Long before he could read or write, Howard knew scores of old tales by heart, for his mother often read aloud to him. *Slovenly Peter* was one of his favorite stories, but he was saturated with the magic of *Grimm's German Faery Tales*, *Tanglewood Tales*, *The Wonder Book* and *A Midsummer Night's Dream* before he reached reading age.

Howard was the oldest of a family of four children, and although he was often followed about by two younger brothers and a small sister, he was inclined to be solitary. His mother was one of the most important influences on his life. Much of what he was or could hope to accomplish was due to her inspiration and concern. Reading between the lines, it can be surmised that he was her favorite child and her hopes were centered on him. In every way, Margaret Pyle appears to have been a remarkable woman, warm, loving and understanding, endowed with an eager, receptive mind, an ear for the cadence of words and a sharp, independent way of working through to her own personal and intellectual solutions. So she read and talked, admonished and caressed. She encouraged his scribbles, watched and hoped.

Later Howard was to recall his first frustrated childhood effort at creation. While contemplating one of his favorite secret garden places, a large rock bedded in ivy and ferns and shaded by the garden wall, something impelled him to write his first poem. He rushed into the house and explained his wish to his mother. Having been given several sheets of gold-edged paper and a pencil, he ran back to the spot of his inspiration. With the blank paper before him he was suddenly seized with a desperate wave of frustration — he could neither read nor write.

A little later, when he had mastered reading, he could remember the good hours on the rug before the hickory woodfire in the little library with a well-thumbed volume, perhaps Dickens, open at the picture of Master Humphrey with the dream people flying about his head.

From the earliest days picture and printed word were associated in his mind, and so they remained all his life. Endowed with a dual talent that even then was struggling to express itself, it could not have been otherwise. His dawning twin gifts only intensified his imagination. He could see things in image-terms or in the continuity of words. At times the two media seemed separate and distinct and then again they merged and became one. He had inherited the Quaker penchant for meditation and looking inward, but his dreams insisted upon bursting the bonds of Quaker reticence to conjure up a world of heroic action, sumptuous color and strange happenings.

Howard's imagination was nourished by his surroundings. He could follow the large Conestoga wagons lumbering down from the upper Brandywine and the Pennsylvania German country beyond, loaded with grain or lime. They were drawn by eight trotting mules, their crimson harness studded with brass stampings and jingling silver bells. He could walk to the banks of the Brandywine and watch the grain being ground in the mills and then loaded on the coastal schooners at the docks. Small steamers were moored at the docks also, and paddle wheelers, which plied the Delaware up to Philadelphia and down to Baltimore through the canal. There were even a few large steamers bound for the New England ports, the South or occasionally the West Indies. But canvas had not yet been driven out by steam, and small boys could still send their hearts out after a receding sail.

The town was still dotted with old walls and other monuments of earlier times such as the old market sheds. Saturday-morning market continued to bring in the farm wagons at break of day and some sharp-eyed peddlers. Loads of watermelons, peaches and tomatoes from the Eastern Shore and pushcarts of fresh shad when the run was on were hauled through the streets. Wagon and carriage shops smelling of fresh wood shavings and coach varnish lined the lower streets where a small group of

young and old often gathered to watch one of the town artists paint like-
nesses of prize steers on the sides of a butcher's wagon, or a blue and buff
soldier on the Continental Moving Company van. Howard always remembered the carriage decorator with his long-haired striping brushes
bending over the involved scrolls of his seemingly effortless calligraphy.
The water-powered powder mills and gristmills which dotted the length
of the Brandywine fed his young curiosity, and the open country, mile
upon mile of field, meadow and rounded hill was within easy walking
distance.

Howard's boyhood years were also war years. Although Wilmington
was not in the battle zone of the Civil War, the conflict seemed near at
hand, for the town was poised on the very brink of the South. Its hills
were the last of a range tapering down from Pennsylvania. To the south
beyond the Christiana stretched the flat country. This delta peninsula,
bounded by the Atlantic and the Chesapeake Eastern Shore, extends down
through Maryland and a tip of Virginia to confront Norfolk and Hamp-
ton across the wide water of the Chesapeake. That peninsula country was
Southern in habit and feeling, a country of large acreages of plantation
dimensions, of easy living, of a diminishing heritage of elaborate manners,
of an entrenched agricultural society resentful of business and industrial
vulgarities. Yet these communities were too much behind the northern
lines to do more than mutter and sneak off their young men to join the
Confederate battalions.

The troop and supply trains poured through Wilmington on their way
to Washington and the southern battlefields, and back from the war came
the hospital cars and the boxcars jammed with ragged Confederate prison-
ers. Up through the Delaware and Chesapeake Canal came the scows
loaded with wounded and sick. Howard could join the crowds that clustered at the docks as the litters of injured soldiers were carried up the
streets to the hospitals. There was competition among the young boys for
the privilege of fanning the feverish faces or shielding them from the hot
sun as the stretchers swayed up the summer streets.

War was in the air, in the conversations and in the printed sheets of the newspapers and magazines. The demand for war news had brought a spate of printed matter into being and a large part of it was pictorial. *Frank Leslie's Illustrated Newspaper* and *Harper's Weekly*, both founded only a few years before, were filled with pictures, and soon the *Illustrated London News* was following suit and presenting the work of its artist in the field. The very first guns of the war had been pictured by artists on the spot. Frank Leslie had his English artist, William Waud, in Charleston drawing the Confederate batteries as they arched their shells at Fort Sumter. Several of the officers within the fort were sending sketches to *Harper's Weekly*. The immediacy of these drawings, however tamed they might be by the wood engravers who translated them into printing surfaces, was breathtaking to an audience as yet unsatiated by pictorial journalism. To the young these drawings often represented a stolen excitement which led them to outwit their parents' precautions to protect their childish minds from the horror of conflict. But in the early months of the war the horror was usually masked effectively by theatricality and sentimentality. Most of the early war artists got no closer to the front than their cubbyholes in lower Manhattan. They saw the war through a haze of Victorian habit and taboo. The waving silver sword, the heroic dying gestures, the parade-ground precision even in the face of deadly fire, the uniformly dastardly countenances of the foe — all the clichés were overworked in their pictures.

Young and old alike devoured these spectacles without critical reservations, but as the war continued, bitter truth began to purge pictorial journalism of its artificiality. More artists were at the front facing the grimness of everyday war. They rebelled against the popular and editorial dreams of war. They sketched what they saw and protested when the magazine editors encouraged their studio artists to glamorize the originals. Before the end of the war, pictorial reporting had begun to convey the real bitterness and suffering of war.

During this period, young Howard could scarcely have been aware of

the mediocrity of most of his pictorial fare. For a youngster with an innate avidity for pictures, the battle scenes were thrilling regardless of
merit. He may have detected the name of Winslow Homer under some
of the *Harper's Weekly* reproductions and had some faint intimation that
these were superior to the average, yet his omnivorous mind did not begin with quality. It needed quantity. But through those years he was
seeing American periodical illustration grope its way toward competence
and gradually abandon routine sentimentality for a more varied and robust
utterance.

One strong personality impressed itself on Howard's consciousness
through the pictures in several of the books on the family shelves, and this
was Felix Octavius Darley. This name appeared on the title pages of an
increasing number of gift books that were to be found on so many Wilmington parlor tables. They may have been put out for display, but there
were always times when the young of the family could carefully turn the
pictured pages. Howard may have learned at an early age that Darley
was almost a neighbor, living in nearby Claymont, for the town liked to
gossip about the only well-known artist in its midst. But the young Howard could scarcely have dreamed that the day would come when *his* pictures would appear with Darley's in the same book.

Darley's work made a lasting impression on Howard's mind but he saw
more of the work of the British illustrators, and they played an important
part in forming his taste. British illustration was in one of its richest periods and the British publishers, both of books and periodicals, could call
on greater pictorial and literary resources than their American counter-
parts. British publications were flooding into America and our native
productions were usually unremarkable imitations of their overseas rivals.
So Howard was able to immerse himself in some of the best illustrative
picture making of his time.

In spite of the diversity of their pictorial solutions, these artists have
been considered a "school" and are usually grouped under the label "Illustrators of the Sixties." It has proved a limiting label, for many of the

group were active in the early fifties and some persisted well into the last quarter of the century. Almost all their drawings were reproduced on wood, and the highly skilled engravers of the time with their routine and formulated technique contrived to impart an air of family resemblance to the most varied compositions. Many of these artists had their eyes on a future of painting and regarded illustration as a temporary, bread-and-butter interlude. Among these were James McNeil Whistler, Luke Fildes, Edward Burne-Jones, John Millais, Dante Gabriel Rossetti and Frederick Leighton. Others, such as Charles Keene, Arthur Boyd Houghton, John Tenniel, John Leech, Richard Doyle and Birket Foster made a lifelong commitment to illustration.

Howard pored over the work of many of these artists as he turned the pages of *Punch*, the *Illustrated London News* and occasional copies of some of the increasing number of British illustrated magazines for children. These were some of the artists who gave him some of his earliest notions of picture making. He had few opportunities in his early years to see paintings — mostly old portraits or an occasional landscape. The reproduced picture surrounded by its printed text was his daily pleasure and lesson, and this set the pattern for what was to become his lifework.

These British publications introduced him to Holman Hunt, G. E. Watts, Millais, Burne-Jones, Rossetti and Maddox Brown, who even then were abandoning illustration and beginning to form their Pre-Raphaelite Brotherhood. Their work was to influence Howard's late adolescence. Thus, the concept of the picture springing from literary ideas was ingrained in him from the start.

V

GROWING UP IN WILMINGTON

THE WAR YEARS brought the Pyle family their share of upsets. The family leather business suffered one shock after another due to the unstable financial conditions of the time. The large comfortable house on the Kennett Pike had to be given up in favor of a more modest one in the center of town. The new garden was much smaller, the house had fewer rooms and the Pyles could no longer glimpse the open country beyond the garden wall.

But there were compensations for their restricted circumstances. While the war was on, soldiers were in the streets, supplies were constantly coming through, unexpected and exciting things were happening within reach of Howard's small legs. There were more playmates, more strange households with which to become acquainted, more of everything except green space and farm animals. Although Mrs. Pyle regretted leaving her country home, she welcomed proximity to the town's social and intellectual activities that appealed to her active and inquiring nature. Mr. Pyle was closer to his business which needed more attention than before.

Howard could walk to the Friends' School across from the old Meeting House on West Street. There, for the first time, he was thrown in with a large company of children his own age and had to make his way in the inevitable group games and cope with the splitting into clans, the shifting friendships and rivalries, all the thousand and one attachments and adjustments so typical of vigorous youngsters responding to the stimulus of an exciting world. He seems to have entered into the new experiences naturally enough but he was not entirely absorbed by them. His imagination had already shaped his young mind — he could walk alone, self-sufficient, content with his dreams and images. For the first time he was encountering a school curriculum, a regimen that was plain and to the point, but kindly and wisely administered. He accepted that too, but with only casual involvement and no sharp hunger. According to his own later accounts, he spent his time largely in scrawling drawings on his slate and in his books.

Without question, he possessed intelligence but he lacked the will to apply it to the routine tasks of the classroom. He had read far more widely than the other children in his class, and mathematics bored him, but he could close his eyes and watch an endless parade of images and backgrounds. The discouraging report cards could not disclose this imaginative daydreaming — only poor marks. But his parents, although aware of his artistic talent, were still concerned about his grades and debated possible remedies for his lack of accomplishment. They finally decided to send him to a small private school, Clark and Taylor's, thinking perhaps a change of environment and different teachers might induce more interest in the usual lesson program. But Howard continued to daydream.

The subsequent school years followed the same pattern. The fact was that young Howard was learning vastly more in his solitary hours with his books and pencils or when he just stared, unfocused and daydreaming. Instinctively he was building up a repertory for his lifework, sensing what nourishments were needful, indifferent to the rest.

He fed on the things that were at hand. The arrival of each monthly batch of subscriptions was cause for excitement. But his mind was not fed solely on books and pictures. Unconsciously his eyes were noting countless things in the life around him that would appear later in picture and writing: the way hands grasped a tool, the curl of a newly plowed furrow, the tracery of a tree, the leg-spread of a body in the saddle, the moist glint of an eyeball. These impressions were part of the endless catalog of an artist's vocabulary that happily had begun to develop early and instinctively.

The school years wore on with no marked change in his unwillingness to study. Finally, his parents rallied themselves for another effort. When Howard was about fifteen, they discussed plans for his college education. Even though his parents recognized his gifts for writing and drawing and were aware that his future lay in their fulfillment, they thought several years of college would provide a foundation necessary for any lifework. But his scholastic record was not sufficient to insure his admission to college. So a program of home study was mapped out and textbooks were bought. Howard acquiesced amiably and made some efforts to cram Latin and algebra. His good intentions were short-lived however, and eventually Howard went back to sketching and daydreaming. His parents gave up their idea that he should go to college and considered the obvious alternative — art school. The family funds were too low to consider Paris or Munich. There was no art school in Wilmington, but Philadelphia was only a forty-minute train ride away and there was the old and famous Pennsylvania Academy of the Fine Arts. However, a small school run by Mr. Van der Weilen, an artist trained in Antwerp, was chosen instead. Perhaps the family had heard that the Academy instructors usually gave only one criticism a week, while Mr. Van der Weilen was in almost constant attendance.

At any rate, young Pyle's indifference to instruction came to an end. At about the age of sixteen he became a daily commuter to Philadelphia. For the first time in his life he was receiving training in a discipline of great moment to him and he applied himself with ardor. He now felt committed.

Pyle's years of study under Van der Weilen were fruitful and formed the technical basis upon which his later pictorial skills were built, but it would be difficult to measure his capacity at the completion of his training. For one thing, there are no records of Van der Weilen's classes. There are some comments attributed to a woman who was a student at the same time as Pyle, who is reported to have said that the instruction was rigidly academic — an unremitting drill at drawing and painting from still life and the model. These remarks tell us little — they could apply to most art classes of this period of 1869 to 1872. There is no indication that Mr. Van der Weilen was a particularly inspired teacher or that he placed any emphasis on more than routine observation and recording. Nor, apparently, was there any special attempt made to release and nourish the student's latent creative impulses.

*

No drawings seem to have survived from these early student days, nor from the period just following. The first concrete evidence of Pyle's artistic ability are his magazine reproductions, and they display little indication of three years of academic training. Rather than a demonstration of an academic or *correct* technique, they suggest a relatively uncontrolled and groping hand. There is really no reason to question the demonstrable evidence or to doubt Pyle's own estimate of his student skills. The awkwardness of his early efforts merely points to the gulf that so often separates the skill of imitative delineation from imaginative expression. Some never bridge the chasm, others span it only with difficulty.

That this was young Pyle's problem is certain from many things he said in later years such as,

> The hardest thing for a student to do after leaving an art school is to adapt the knowledge there gained to practical use — to do creative work, for the work in an art school is imitative. That is why so many go into portrait painting. When I left art school I discovered, like many others, that I could not easily train myself to creative work, which was the only practical way of earning a livelihood in art.

For the artist the whole process of bridging the gap from imitative recording to creative freedom requires a revolution both in thought and execution. The process has often been described as "unlearning what one has learned."

Pyle made the transition from imitative to original art gradually and with difficulty. He suffered through a period of trial and error, making hopeful experiments and experiencing disheartening failures; there were many times when the whole thing seemed of little worth. This period affected him deeply. When he finally achieved the artistic solutions that accorded with his inmost nature, he had arrived at bedrock convictions that governed his creative lifetime as a picture maker and permeated every moment of his subsequent teaching. He began to have trust in his imagination and let his artist's appraising eye be its servant.

Turning his back upon art school threw him upon his own resources. He still hoped to make pictures for the magazines but he realized his student drawings and paintings were not suitable for this purpose. They seemed inert copies of what his critical eye had seen; they needed an infusion of something not taught in the school — illustrative imagination. He set himself to experiment with other ways of drawing. He was then nineteen, his friends were at college or at work. The early seventies were panic years and his father's business was taking some blows. Provident Quakers though they were, the Pyles had to count their pennies more carefully. Howard's help was needed in the business, so he went to work in his father's office. Drawing and writing became spare-time occupations.

He summed up this intermediate period in these words, ". . . being offered a position by my father in his leather business in Wilmington I availed myself of it and during my spare time created illustrations, stimulated my imagination and worked assiduously on drawings I never submitted. My work was idle for several years while I experimented."

That he made an attempt in another direction to utilize his gifts and training is evident from a short paragraph in Wilmington's evening newspaper, *Every Evening*.

Art Instruction: Mr. Howard Pyle, a young Wilmington artist has taken Room No. 8 — Masonic Temple, where he will give lessons in drawing, sketching and painting in oils. Mr. Pyle studied for two years in the Philadelphia art school of Prof. Van de Weilen, and also in the school of anatomy, and is, we doubt not, capable of giving valuable instruction to students. A picture of his in the window of Ferris' jewelry store, at Fourth and Market Streets, of a view of the Brandywine is attracting the public attention.

There is no evidence by which to ascertain the success or failure of this venture, but it shows enterprise and is another indication of what was to become so characteristic of his mature years — the ability to keep many projects going at the same time. Although the writing instinct had been crowded out by the other activities of art school days, it came surging back. Howard tried his hand at some ballads and poems but the results seemed disappointing to him. He also wrote some short stories which he felt, somewhat confidently, were more promising. He was reading widely and had discovered William Dean Howells through *Their Wedding Journey* and *A Chance Acquaintance*. His introduction to these novels marked the beginning of a lifelong admiration for their author that eventually led to a close and cherished friendship. The early admiration stimulated imitation. He began to write in the manner of Howells, trying to train himself to observe the life about him in order to gather material for his short story efforts. Although in time he came to recognize that his talent and Howells' were dissimilar gifts, this attempt at emulation played its part in enriching his powers both as a writer and an artist.

The Pyle household read and discussed. Trollope was embraced, Carlyle rejected after debate. Darwin had exploded a bomb in the Victorian consciousness, and the clarifying and persuasive rhetoric of Thomas Huxley was working on men's minds. The revolutionary implications of Darwinism were a central topic in the family conversations. The Pyles, like other thoughtful and searching people, were shaken by the new and incalculable vistas which the concept of evolution was unveiling. Its stirring implications pressed and pervaded every thought and custom of their lives and even their religion.

Although they had become members of the Swedenborgian faith and attended the new church on 14th Street, their Quakerism was innately bred into their fiber and tissue. It could be modified, rebelled against, but not discarded. The Pyles found Swedenborg's books fascinating but puzzling. His often electrifying and mystifying words led them on and on, through discussion, doubt and revelation, but the generations of Quakerism in their ancestry prevented complete surrender to his inspiration. They were immersed in an experience that plumbed their deepest convictions, and to the end of his days, Howard read, pondered, experienced exhilaration and caught glimpses of visions but never penetrated through to the ultimate understanding he had hoped for in his youth.

But life was not all solemnity in Wilmington. The older Quaker families, who, with unconscious snobbism, assumed that their circle was all that mattered, were lively enough. However, the infiltration of the southern Delawareans with their traditional plantation gaiety had helped to leaven the decorous Quaker majority. There were rounds of parties, formal and informal, picnics, dances, sleighrides, hayrides, sing-times, charades and amateur plays. Howard was drawn into these pleasant pastimes and was soon an enthusiastic member of Wilmington's gay young set.

The days, weeks and months slipped away although at intervals Howard had qualms about the passing of time and his temporizing ambitions. At these moments he fell back on a fury of work with all its hopes, little triumphs and frustrations. He was groping for themes, hopeful when new subjects and patterns seemed to emerge and dejected when he fell prey to the old clichés. Occasionally he turned out some short tales or verses for children which had an ingratiating and artless touch that seemed to offer promise. His mother, a fond but somewhat stern critic, thought they did and her judgments were not at the mercy of her affection. Her opinions carried great weight with Howard, but his own critical sense was gradually developing. Both agreed that his attempts at adult fiction were immature, but that some of the children's scripts were more than routine amateur efforts and that the factual articles for adults showed signs of professional skill. They were constantly reading the current magazines from cover to cover and using them as standards of comparison. What they found there caused Howard to destroy many pages of written script and many drawings too.

A happy conjunction of events brought to an end his long period of vacillation and self-doubt. In the spring of 1876, partly for pleasure and curiosity and partly in search of possible subject matter, Howard made a trip down the Eastern Shore peninsula of Delaware and Maryland, to the islands of Chincoteague and Assateague off the Atlantic coast. They were low sandy islands and one of them, Chincoteague, was locally famous for its wild ponies. Presumably the descendants of the survivors from some early wreck, the ponies had adjusted to the island environment, multiplied and become a source of income for the settlers of the adjoining village of Assateague. Each spring a roundup was held, the ponies were branded and auctioned off. It was a picturesque and unusual event to discover on the Atlantic shore. Young Pyle drank it all in, talked to the natives and sketched. Back in Wilmington with his material and his imagination aroused by many impressions, he set to work to reorganize and complete some of his sketches and amplify his notes.

At about the same time he had dashed off a set of verses about a magic pill that turned an aged and fretting parson into a terrible boy. With some outline drawings to illustrate it, he mailed his hopeful efforts to *Scribner's Monthly*. Back came his first letter of acceptance with a check. Suddenly his hopes shot up and his confidence returned. He then wrote a little fairy tale for children and sent it to *St. Nicholas*, the most flourishing children's magazine of the time. That too was accepted. The family was elated.

Now Howard pinned his expectations on the article drawn from his trip, "Chincoteague, The Island of Ponies." It was his most ambitious venture to date, and the eleven drawings for it were done and redone. The article was accepted for the *Monthly* with the proviso that the drawings be reworked by a staff artist to fit them for reproduction. Howard's father on a business trip to New York stopped at the Scribner offices and had a long and pleasant talk with Mr. Roswell Smith, who was an editor as well as one of the owners of the publishing house. He heard many complimentary things about his son's work, what a bright future he seemed to have and how the publishing world was in need of young writers and artists. Mr. Smith advised the senior Pyle to send Howard to New York where he would be in close touch with the publishers, his fellow writers and illustrators. He also gave Mr. Pyle the impression that Scribner's would find enough work to keep a young man busy.

This news carried back to Wilmington brought the whole problem of Howard's future into focus. The family council talked of nothing else. The move to New York was debated from every angle but the move was so obvious and right that the only real problem to be discussed was how it should be accomplished. Naturally the family would feel the separation, but New York was only three hours away and Howard would be able to come back at intervals. The more serious problem was one of finances. Naturally, the Pyles hoped that Howard would soon be self-supporting, but they knew he would need their help at least at first. The leather business was struggling to weather the panic years but the thing had to be managed.

In mid-October of 1876, his bags packed, letters of introduction tucked in his pocket, Howard drove with his parents to Wilmington's downtown station and climbed aboard the New York express.

VI

NEW YORK APPRENTICESHIP

NEW YORK was the place where young untried talents such as Pyle were judged. This recklessly growing city was sucking in the adventurous and the ambitious from the length and breadth of the land as well as from all the countries of Europe. The young man from Wilmington was just another hopeful and quaking atom in the maelstrom.

He rode across to the crowded island of Manhattan on the Jersey City ferry and experienced his first assault by crowds and noise as the boat bumped into the ferry slip on the New York side. Fortunately he had some addresses and letters of introduction and was able to find a comfortable room in a boardinghouse managed by the Misses Marshall, who were former neighbors of his mother's. The house was on East Forty-eighth Street, a longish distance from the publishing houses downtown, but it was suitable until he could find a more convenient place. The first rattling elevated line on its single pillared supports running up Greenwich Street from the Battery to Cortland was of little use to him, and the two new lines running up the island were just nearing completion. Later he was to find the long walk, or the jolting ride in the horsecars down Broadway tedious and boring. He was eager to explore a host of new activities and amusements and the theater immediately caught his interest. As a young adolescent, Pyle had developed a fever for the stage, but Wilmington had only limited dramatic fare to offer. Luckily, however, his parents had relaxed many of their inherited Quaker restraints and the theater had never been a forbidden place for him, although many of his friends and relatives raised their eyebrows at the mention of it. Like many young persons springing from a Quaker background, Pyle rebelled against the ancestral tendency to starve life of its embellishments. He hungered for color and movement, the intoxication of optical imagery — he yearned for immersion in the sensuous world. The natural tendency of his picture-shaping mind was to crave the spectacle and he found what he sought in Wallach's Theatre, a fusty, crowded, downtown building which presented a wide variety of old classics along with the newer trivia. It was almost the only extravagance he allowed himself out of his limited funds. Without his realization, the theater played an important part in his artistic education.

Gradually, Howard grew accustomed to the foreign voices and faces that were an important part of the New York scene. The immigrants from Europe were pouring through the greatest port of the country. Some only passed through on their way to the open West, others remained. As he walked the streets, exploring, he passed from one racial enclave to another. Almost half the population of the city was foreign-born, and their faces constituted a wide gallery of racial types for an artist to study.

Like most of the city's inhabitants, he walked downtown to see the rising piers of New York's latest wonderwork, the Brooklyn Bridge. The site had become a favorite sketching spot for artists as were the miles of piers along the Hudson and the East rivers with their cluttered shipping docks. On these strolls he could economize on food by patronizing the new quick lunch counters or the saloons where a schooner of beer entitled one to some snacks of free lunch. Being an alert youth, he soon learned the streets of the metropolis and how to find his way about. He came to know the entire city from the Brooklyn ferry slip at the tip of Manhattan to the newly opened Metropolitan Museum on Fourteenth Street, which housed a growing collection of plaster casts, Audubon engravings, Cesnola antiquities and Kensett landscapes.

But he never lost sight of his main objective. He had come to work as an artist and to win a niche for himself in the publication world. First he went to see Roswell Smith, the chief editor at Scribner's, and came away somewhat disappointed. Mr. Smith had been kindness itself, but it seemed that the amount of work that could be given to a young novice had been exaggerated in the hopeful minds of the Wilmington circle. Smith could only offer him occasional small items, but the older man was most generous with advice and criticism. Upon learning that Howard had a good tenor voice, he offered him a paid position in his church choir. However, Pyle's conscience would not permit him to accept money for a church activity. Mary Mapes Dodge, the editor of *St. Nicholas* magazine, offered better opportunities to a struggling artist. *St. Nicholas*, the most important of the children's magazines, was growing rapidly, and needed a generous amount of material. Mrs. Dodge discerned a certain charm in the young artist's work and encouraged him to submit writings and drawings.

Howard wrote long detailed letters to his mother about his interviews and the reactions of the editors, and by the middle of November, a month after his arrival, he could report that he had sold a group of fables with drawings to *St. Nicholas* the previous week for seventy-five dollars and had prepared another group for which he expected to receive not less than sixty dollars. The editors of the magazine were somewhat disappointed with the way some of his pen drawings were showing up in reproduction and Howard reported that he was being sent down to the photoengraving companies for coaching in how to prepare his drawings.

Howard's mother apparently had more confidence in his ability as an illustrator than as a writer, and, as always, he was very heedful of her opinion. He now had the opportunity to see something of the large body of both drawing and writing talent that had converged upon New York and he had no illusions about the competition he faced. Nevertheless he had a combative confidence in his innate gifts. ". . . it's in me and *shall* come out," he wrote home.

As the year drew to a close his self-confidence was tested. *St. Nicholas* and *Scribner's Monthly* accepted fewer and fewer of his drawings and fables. At first, he concluded he had lost favor with the magazines, but presently he discovered that it was merely because they were overstocked and in a few months they would be in the market again for new material. Spurred by the many admonishments from Drake, the art editor, and Smith about his drawing, he joined a sketching class at the Art Students' League to gain more facility in drawing the human figure. His work showed improvement almost immediately and his progress reinforced his confidence. He made some new drawings for his portfolio and began the rounds of all the publishers with some good results, particularly at Harper. Charles Parsons, the art editor there, liked the boy and his work and began giving him assignments from time to time. Thus a famous association came about which was to last to the end of Pyle's life.

His alliance with the Harper publication family housed in their two large buildings in Franklin Square was most fortunate for young Pyle. His relationship with them placed him in close touch with the busiest, most enterprising and best-staffed center of pictorial reproduction in the country. He had only to work and keep his eyes and mind open to benefit from the best education a young illustrator could hope for. His avid brain and consuming ambition made the most of it.

He was not a salaried member of the staff but a frequent contributor and as such could come in contact with practically everyone in the organization. He could watch the entire publishing process from original manuscript and drawing to the printed bound copy. The organization was the largest of its kind at the time, but it was still small enough to preserve a family atmosphere which allowed each individual a measure of importance. The members of the firm were accessible and Henry Mills Alden, the editor of the *Monthly*, although a quiet man was not aloof. Pyle, in a letter to his mother, described him as,

> . . . a strikingly handsome man of about fifty. He has an unkempt look though, his hair and beard are shaggy and look constantly tousled. He has very regular features and deep brown eyes deep set under rather

heavy brows. He speaks very little, and when he does talk he contorts his face as though the act of talking was a painful labor and effort with him. Last time I was down there he rather surprised me by coming into the art rooms and joining Mr. Parsons in talking with me for nearly half an hour about American art and artists and what not. Rather a complimentary thing for a poor devil of an artist like me.

Parsons, the art editor through whose hands all of Pyle's work had to pass, is described as distinctly American in appearance, ". . . not the lanky, cadaverous American cast though. He has a bald forehead, and gray hair which he brushes back, a gray beard, and wears glasses. He is kind, cordial, and in every way encouraging . . . He is a gentleman, and a gentleman of refined tastes."

Both Alden and Parsons were men of exceptional ability and they played important roles in the rapid development of the American periodical. They entered the field early enough to witness its first, groping efforts and before they retired, they saw the magazine industry grow toward giant size until it became the largest and most varied business of its kind in the world. Parsons was a shrewd, practical man of taste with a flair for discerning illustrative talent. He had been trained as an artist and was a watercolorist of no mean ability. His task had been to build an art department from scratch — a department for which there was little precedent — a job for a wise opportunist. He had to find artists possessing excellence, but of a new and special kind. They had to combine the ability to execute rapidly, to be resourceful in pictorial ideas, and at the same time, they had to have the knack of communicating to large audiences. It was a new breed of artists he was trying to raise.

Gradually he gathered a team of these new talents about him. They were headed by senior artist, Charles Stanley Rinehart, lately back from the European art schools, a fine figurative draftsman and a pen artist with a sensitive but decisive line. His easy treatment of complex compositions, crowded with figures, aroused both admiration and envy. Pyle was beginning to master the one and two figure compositions but the spatial and gesture relations between six, eight or more was a toilsome and uncertain problem. Fortunately he could often watch Rinehart's designs take form, and learn.

Next in ability came Edwin Abbey, a young man of Pyle's age. His short, cheery figure already hinted of future plumpness. Abbey was a prodigy. He had studied at the Pennsylvania Academy of the Fine Arts about the same time that Pyle was toiling under Van der Weilen. Although Pyle is on record as saying he spent several weeks in the Academy classrooms, he does not seem to have met Abbey until they came together in Harper's art room. Abbey's work at this point had begun to find its ease. It had, at first, a kind of backwoods quality that made it fairly akin to the work of Arthur B. Frost, another young Harper artist, but was shedding this rapidly and moving toward the crisp and engaging elegance of maturity. His command of gesture and the aura of style he cast over his figures were the admiration of the Harper's circle, and Pyle was aroused to emulation. The two became fast friends and each contributed something to the other's art.

The others whom Parsons favored were J. W. Alexander, Frank Vincent Du Mond, Arthur B. Frost and the veteran A. R. Waud. Waud had been a Civil War artist correspondent and Pyle had pored over his pictures as a boy. Alexander considered the Harper art room as a way station in his career. His hopes were directed toward Paris, and in time they would be realized and he would return to achieve a deserved reputation as a painter. Du Mond, too, would move on to become an important muralist and celebrated teacher. The most famous of the artist contributors to Harper was the redoubtable Thomas Nast whose biting cartoons had broken the corrupt Tweed Ring and sent its principals to jail or into exile. Nast worked at home but bustled in and out of the editorial offices with a few friendly words for the admiring art staff.

Frost and Pyle developed an instant liking for each other and became lifelong friends. Frost would one day enjoy a reputation almost as great as Pyle's. He had a disarming sense of humor that crept into almost everything he drew. It reached masterpiece stature in his drawings for Joel Chandler Harris' *Uncle Remus*. Frost could never be mistaken for anything but an American artist. He was unaffected, sometimes ingratiatingly naïve, interested in the life of the small town, the farm, the roadside, the sports of the new opulent America and occasionally the showy self-consciousness of the new rich. Never profound or pretentious, he reported, with a chuckle of appreciation, what his eyes had discovered.

Pyle could not have been more fortunate in the choice of his two new friends, Frost and Abbey. They differed in temperament as their pictures differed in execution and message. Abbey was moving rapidly toward his charmingly sophisticated style and developing his interest in the historical; Frost never lost his homespun affection for the life around him while his technique became ever more delightfully spry and spontaneous. Between them they opened artistic doors for Pyle and played an important part in his education.

Above the art room where these men bent over their drawing boards was the engraving room and here, too, Pyle pursued his education. It was quiet by comparison with the art room which was usually filled with ebullient artists. The engravers, eyeshades tilted over their brows, bent over their boxwood blocks, the rounded handles of their short gravers nestling against their palms. The fate of every illustrator's drawing was in their hands.

Here was the bottleneck that constricted the flow of pictorial material for rapid publication. No matter how quickly a drawing was prepared, it had to be translated into a printing surface and wood engraving was the only feasible method for the periodical production of the day. It was a slow and tedious method. Nick by nick and threadlike line by threadlike line, the drawing had to be translated into an intricate arabesque of tiny printing shapes. The shapes that the graver cut out would show as white paper when an impression was made, the untouched areas would receive ink and print black. A drawing in simple black line was relatively easy to execute but tonal pictures in oil or watercolor meant interpreting simple gray tones by means of a laborious network of dots and hairlike lines.

It was a highly skilled craft and experts were rare enough. The American publishers had begun with a woefully inadequate force of engravers, but a considerable number of British craftsmen had found it profitable to migrate. By Pyle's time a younger body of American engravers had been trained but those of superior ability were still in the minority. There was much competition for these men among the publishers and their wages were constantly going up. Somehow Harper seemed to get the pick of them, although in a combined complaint and boast they announced it was costing them about five hundred dollars to engrave a typical full-page block.

The engravers were a cocky and independent company, proud of their skills and high salaries and quick to take offense at being thought of as of lower caste than the artists. The two groups had plenty of opportunities for feuding; in fact, there was a long history of contention that went back to the earliest days of white-line, facsimile engraving. The artist's frequent complaint had always been that the engraver had botched his picture and how often that must have been true. The slightest hairline deviation of the graver's stroke and the expression of a face could be changed or its construction marred. Faces were usually the critical areas in an engraving and chances of bungling were very great. No wonder there was considerable maneuvering among artists to have the top engravers work from their drawings. In the earlier days the drawings were made on the block, and when the engraver had finished, the drawing had been chipped away. No direct comparison with the original was possible, only a memory remained. A good deal of misunderstanding originated just there. Later, tracings from an original were sometimes used and finally, with the improvement in photographic techniques, the block was sensitized and the picture photographed on it. Once this process was perfected the original could be saved — the engraver could consult it as he worked and the art editor could place picture and trial proof side by side and make just comparisons.

Some of the engravers' complaints were justified, one of their main contentions being that the artists often gave them impossible problems to solve. It was true that many artists showed not the slightest interest in or understanding of the mechanics of wood engraving and blandly expected miracles from their poorly prepared drawings. There were also lazy illustrators who gave the engraver only a few jottings and expected him to fill in and amplify certain areas and reviled him when things were not to their taste.

These intricacies were part of Pyle's education as a practical illustrator. Across the courtyard in the adjoining manufacturing building he could see the recently installed giant Hoe presses, the fastest and most efficient of their day. In his dreamy Wilmington days he had had no conception of the complex stages through which his drawings would pass before their facsimiles would reach the hands of the public.

Beyond the practical sense he was beginning to develop, he was forming a vision of what this great new enterprise might mean. He could leaf through the earlier files of the *Monthly* and *Weekly* and trace the changing styles of the pictures. The clichés of mid-Victorian drawing were gradually fading from the pages. He could see the figures beginning to show muscles and unstiffen their joints. Skirts began to heed the wind and the pipelike trousers were breaking into folds and wrinkles. But even more intriguing to Howard than the new grip and bite which he saw in the pictures themselves was the challenging thought that they were speaking to thousands and millions of readers. Nothing comparable had ever happened before. Almost everybody could now be in touch with events, could sample the thoughts and opinions of many minds and indulge his appetite for pictures. Howard sensed that America was beginning to command a place in the publication world concerned with dissemination of the printed page, and that its illustrators were assuming a position of power and responsibility as pictorial interpreters for a great nation. Over the years this sense of great opportunity and responsibility deepened and came to form one of the rock-founded motives of his life.

Part of the responsibility, as he came to see it, implied the cultivation of identifiably American art that would draw its flavor from the native soil. It must have been his ancestors speaking to him. Although he had been immersed in English literature from his young years and deeply admired the work of Holbein, Dürer and the little German masters, and later was to devote a considerable part of his writing and drawing to medieval subjects, he would always have an underlying suspicion of European influence. He saw that the media of magazine and book illustration might help America's art discover its own accent. He was right, although almost a century later the critics have yet to discover it.

*

Early in 1877 Pyle was ready for the next step in shaping his career. For the first time in New York he felt reasonably secure. He was now committed to illustration.

Parsons liked his picture-making mind and was accepting many of the sketches he submitted. But always they were assigned to one of the other artists for development. Pyle was disturbed by this and resentful. He could not but feel humilated at not being considered professional enough to make a finished drawing from his own sketches. He now felt he knew something of the wood-engraving process of reproduction and was capable of preparing a drawing suited to its requirements. He also realized that his drawing needed to be fortified by reference to the model. His boardinghouse bedroom was not a suitable place for posing a model, so he began a search for a proper studio. He found a large and comfortable one that he could afford by sharing it with two other artists, Durand and Le Gendre. He set to work making a series of pictures in gouache that were more complete and painstaking in drawing. The results gave him confidence and led to a major victory in his battle for professional standing. He has described it himself.

> I took one day to Harpers an idea-sketch which I had called "A Wreck in the Offing." It represented an alarm brought into the Life Saving Station, a man bursting open the door, with the cold rain and snow rush-

ing in after him, and shouting and pointing out into the darkness, the others rising from the table where they were sitting at a game of cards.

I begged Mr. Parsons to allow me to make the picture instead of handing it over to Mr. Abbey or to Mr. Reinhart or to Mr. Frost, or some other of the young Olympians to elaborate into a real picture. With some hesitating reluctance he told me I might try, and that, in the event of my failure, Harpers would pay me ten dollars, I think it was, or fifteen for the idea. I believe I worked upon it somewhat over six weeks, and I might indeed have been working upon it today (finding it impossible to satisfy myself with it) had I not, what with the cost of my models and the expense of living in New York, reduced myself to my last five cent piece in the world. Then it was that my fate or my poverty, or whatever you may choose to call it, forced me to take the drawing down to Harpers, instead of drawing it over as I should have liked to have done.

I think it was not until I stood in the awful presence of the art editor himself that I realized how this might be the turning point of my life — that I realized how great was to be the result of his decision on my future endeavor. I think I have never passed such a moment of intense trepidation — a moment of such confused and terrible blending of hope and despair at the same time. I recall just how the art editor looked at me over his spectacles, and to my perturbed mind it seemed that he was weighing in his mind (for he was a very tender man) how best he might break the news to me of my unsuccess. The rebound was almost too great when he told me Mr. Harper had liked the drawing very much and that they were going to use it in the Weekly. But when he said they were not only going to use it, but were going to make of it a double-page cut, my exaltation was so great that it seemed to me that I knew not where I was standing or what had happened to me. As I went away I walked on air . . .

This was indeed a turning point. It was now late in 1877, for it had taken him about a year to climb a watershed. Now, he could put behind him the almost incessant worries, struggles and the heartache and the hours of self-examination and look back at what was, after all, a period of considerable growth and adjustment. His work as a creative artist had been accepted, and rightfully Pyle felt he had reached a ridge from which to look more knowingly into the future. He could now feel that his decision to come to New York had been justified.

Pyle's previously accepted sketches do not exist. Thus, there is no way to compare them with the versions reworked by other hands. We cannot do other than assume that the first drawings displayed crudities and lacked a professional look, and that the editors were hoping for the development that would permit them to entrust him with completions. Parsons and the other editors were experienced persons of judgment and their ability to discern potential talent was uncanny. They all liked young Pyle as a person. In fact it is easy to see how Pyle's friendly, engaging and intelligent personality must have won him the approval of his new associates.

Pyle's picture of the shipwreck provides the viewer with a much better insight into his abilities at the age of about twenty-four. A lot of good things can justly be said about it, but the picture was scarcely the work of a prodigy. Those who had come in contact with the young man's magnetic personality could probably detect the great powers of growth that were beginning to show themselves. His powers ripened surely but not in haste.

The drama of the picture is immediately evident. The engraved block is rich in a pattern of dark, mysterious shadows. The halo of light from a source hidden by the central rising figure casts glints of illumination into the turned faces of the group and spreads softly up the walls. This palpitating design of dramatic light and shadow is one of the finest characteristics of the picture and shows unmistakably Pyle's early command of the emotional potentialities of light. The startled group is extremely well controlled and unified by a common impulse of surprise and alarm. It isn't until the eyes encounter the incoming figure in the shadow of the open door that there is a pronounced letdown. Here the struggles and fumbling and frustration of execution show themselves. Nevertheless, it is evident that the problems of a picture of considerable complexity and unmistakable power has been nine-tenths solved on a commendable level. The editors had a right to be pleased.

Of course, the young artist was elated and proud. The drawing was seen by all the editors and his fellow artists. It was an advertisement of his new rank as a professional. But he was not satisfied with the engraver's work. From this point on he would often complain of what the incising tools had done to his pictures. And the more individual and accomplished his style became, the more his pictures would be vulnerable to the trite, leveling technique of the average engraver.

He sent off a block proof of his picture to his mother and seemed amused and a trifle chagrined at her calm, Quaker acceptance of his momentous achievement and her dry words of comment. But he could say: "Work is beginning to roll in upon me at last . . . My work is beginning to pay better too and I think before long I shall be able to pay off my debts to father *in toto*. I have just finished a picture for Harpers Monthly . . . It was quite a success and they are going to put it into the hands of the best engraver in New York City, Mr. Smithwick."

He satisfied his mother's curiosity about his new friends and associates with descriptions that reveal his artist's sensitive eye.

> Mr. Abbey is a little man about twenty-six years old. He is a comical little fellow, but quite the gentleman; he wears glasses, and being troubled with dyspepsia, has a habit of grinning in rather a ferocious manner.
>
> Dr. Drake of Scribner's . . . is almost the antitype of Mr. Parsons. He is a very youngish man of about thirty-five or forty, but as bald as a bat, with the exception of a few thin scraggly hairs about the nape of his neck. His head looks like an egg, and sits with a sort of pendulous ease on a skinny neck. He has a thin, scraggly beard and moustache. He has a habit of dropping his lower jaw and scratching his chin in a vague uncertain way. Yet, in spite of this vagueness and uncertainty, he always manages to get things cheaper than what the artists ask for them.

Abbey who had a good deal of the actor and mimic in him used to stage a little act of a poor devil of an artist bringing a picture to Drake.

Drake: "How much do you want for this?"

Artist: "Twenty dollars."

Drake: "Well — a bit too much. How about eighteen?"

Artist: "Oh yes, yes; it really was eighteen."

Drake: "Well, we'll make it fifteen."

The years '78 and '79 were a productive period. During this time Pyle became established and grew in the esteem of his peers. His circle of friends and acquaintances was enlarging, and they were a group of artists eager for lively debate and bristling with new opinions. In addition, he was enjoying the composition class at the Art Students' League — it was crowded with able men and the sharp competition was stimulating. They were a young, ebullient group, full of themselves and their hopes, argumentative and dogmatic in their presentation of new ideas.

William Chase was one of Pyle's new friends. He had come from his years of training in Munich with a great reputation which was now mounting rapidly in his native land. Pyle was agog over and envious of Chase's studio which was crammed with tapestries, Renaissance frames, majolica and old European furniture. Chase's virtuoso technique was something to marvel at, for it was a natural extension of his showman personality. His trimmed beard and handsome face fortified the effect of the romantic artist. Although Chase's dexterous brushwork was the talk of the New York artists, Pyle never seems to have expressed himself on the subject and there are no clues to show that he tried to emulate his colleague's style. Very early in life, he showed an antipathy to technical display; he seldom used the very word "technique," and with typical Quaker reticence shied away guiltily from obvious display. He was beginning to demonstrate what would prove to be a lifelong tendency to place content and technique in separate compartments. This in spite of the fact that dramatization was natural to him in his pictures and was to become an electrifying element in his later teaching lectures.

Pyle's description of the volatile, boon-companion Chase and the informal "Artist's Club over the Beer Saloon," seems to have aroused his mother's concern. He reassured her that inspiration was their principal object, the beer and pretzels were secondary. Although obviously dazzled by Chase's talent and personality, Pyle was more drawn to Walter Shirlaw, another former Munich student, whom he described as, ". . . one of the best-hearted men in the world, kindly to a fault . . . His criticisms and hints have been of the greatest use to me."

Association with men like these, and with Julian Weir, the young impressionist painter with a poet-painter's eye, opened vista after vista for Pyle. He would never have met their like in Wilmington. This was a moment of happy conjunctions of talent, time and place. These young missionaries, although differing widely in their innate visions and their ultimate contributions, were united in their zeal to ignite the pictorial mind of America. Inevitably Pyle felt the ardor of this crusade. In his letters home he talked of it. His exuberance and excitement bubbled over, but occasionally there was a note of questioning doubt or withdrawal. There was sometimes the feeling that he might become engulfed and lose his highly valued independence in a group. He had broken out of the enclosed society of Wilmington and tasted the flavor of a wider world. The experience was intoxicating and essentially a strengthening one but there was a touch of suspicion that it might contain a threat to the essential Howard Pyle, the creature of his ancestors. He was not completely happy in the atmosphere of debate; he needed the reassurance of familiar faces and places.

He was proud to be included in an informal group of about thirty artists who were to choose the ten most accomplished artists in the city. He wrote that the ten, ". . . will in all probability be Ward, the sculptor, possibly Church, the landscape artist, Chase, Shirlaw, Weir, George Inness, Swain Gifford, Louis Tiffany, Winslow Homer, John La Farge, possibly Abbey, or if he goes abroad, Rinehart. The outside honorary members will probably be Eikens of Philadelphia, Hunt of Boston, Boughton and Hennessey of England with Abbey if he goes there, Bridgman of Paris, and Duveneck of Munich . . ." Mingling with many of these men was often his pastime on those evenings not spent in the Art Students' League classes or when he was free of the encroaching deadlines which kept him at his easel. When possible he would slip away from his daytime tasks to visit the increasing number of New York exhibitions. Both Rinehart and Abbey were exhibiting in the annual shows of the young American Water Color Society, against a background dominated by the pale controlled washes of the English tradition and where the bite and breadth of Winslow Homer was a warning of the might of American aquarelle that was beginning to follow him. Chase, Shirlaw and Inness were showing at the National Academy where the younger painters were mostly Paris or Munich trained.

Meanwhile Harper kept him busy and he was developing a following among its readers. He was looking about for a studio where he could be by himself. A large room in the university building was tempting but adding up the rent, janitor's fees and stove-coal costs made him hesitate and finally he found a nearly ideal room at 788 Broadway, at the corner of Tenth and Broadway. It had a fine north light and two side windows overlooking Broadway. Steam heat and running water were included — all for twenty-three dollars a month with an allowance for painting and some other touches. Best of all, it was only two blocks from Scribner's and less than a fifteen-minute walk to Harper.

The demands of the *Weekly* and *Monthly* spurred him to his best efforts and he doggedly drew and redrew, often discarding the work of many days in his desire to reach for his own ideal of competence. He knew that these two publications were show windows to the literate American public. He was beginning to get letters from some of that public and he was beginning to feel closer to a body that had at first seemed impossibly remote. He no longer felt he was working for the editors alone.

Along with some of the more routine assignments, the success of his "Wreck in the Offing" had made him a candidate for other double-page "showpieces." Parsons asked him to submit a sketch for a double-page

Christmas piece for the *Weekly*. He chose to make a picture of "Christmas Morning in Old New York," pre-Revolutionary New York. The idea was accepted and he went to work filled with his usual intoxication of hope. The composition was crowded with figures of many types and conditions and with a wealth of accessories and architectural detail — probably the most ambitious piece he had attempted. He had his troubles but he fought through them. One of his exasperations was to find authentic costumes for his models. He ransacked the costume houses of the city and finally found one that seemed to have some fairly suitable material, but when the stuff was delivered to his studio he examined it and his temper exploded.

He tells his mother of it in a letter of November 16, 1878:

> . . . my disgust giving way to anger. I kicked the boottops into one corner, the coat into another and the hat on top of the closet, in consequence of which I tore said hat. This morning the costumer — a big, flabby, meek man, came to my studio. "How did you like dose soldier clothes?" he said. It was Sunday to be sure, but in spite of that I took him by the buttonhole and so retained him while I reproached him bitterly. He took the costume and torn hat meekly away. In consequence of this I shall probably have to have a costume made.

This was the beginning of what was to become his large and valuable collection of authentic costumes which included both originals and reconstructions from research material. Throughout his life he would continue his research into the history of American costume and his intimate knowledge of it became greater than that of the scholars in the field. The result would be that his pictures would implant a concept of early dress and life in the American mind.

Appraising the picture by its wood-engraving reproduction, both its success and lack of it can be noted. It was an ambitious, complex and taxing effort. It lacked the dramatic, unifying shadow pattern of the shipwreck picture, and the figures were still stiff and self-conscious. In fact, the picture's charm lies in a certain naïveté of drawing and composition. Compared to the work produced by Abbey and Rinehart in that same year of 1877, Pyle's picture lacked the authority that was already evident in that of his two associates. Compared to his own work of four or five years in the future — for example, his picture of "Alexander Hamilton Addressing the Mob" — the giant strides that Pyle would be taking in the next years can be measured.

Picture making was now his major interest but he had not abandoned his writing. He was still writing little tales accompanied by pen drawings of an ingratiating quality for *St. Nicholas.* His most important writing effort was a long article, "A Peninsular Canaan," which dealt with the life and customs of the Eastern Shore of Delaware, Maryland and Virginia. This article was published in three installments by the *Monthly* and was accompanied by a liberal number of illustrations.

Although his place in the magazine field now seemed secure, he was concerned about the next step. He realized that an illustrator's life meant working from assignment to assignment, that the opportunities were very great in this swiftly expanding field but that growth meant change, and change meant uncertainties. His nature yearned for a steadfast course, but there were too many possibilities tugging him in too many directions.

Parsons suggested that he take a trip to Texas and he blew hot and cold over the idea. It would have involved writing and illustrating several articles or a single one in installments over a period of four or five months. Pyle, at first eager, named a salary of forty dollars a week and expenses. On second thought he demurred about the writing part of the assignment and Harper agreed to send a writer with him. Some of his friends advised him against the trip. Pyle's final, considered reactions reveal some of his basic characteristics; he was not a born traveler and he liked a comfortable, habitual life. He said, "Here I enjoy myself; I have found at last congenial companions among the more considerable artists. There I shall have a hard life." And perhaps most revealing of all, ". . . and introductions to total strangers, which I hate." So nothing came of the project.

His innate involvement with the history, the shape, feel and flavor of his own land was to lead him into frequent disparagement of foreign influences, but behind all his defenses he was vulnerable to the recurrent pull of Europe. Several times in his letters he spoke with regret of Abbey's impending departure for England. It meant parting with a close friend and Pyle envied Abbey his opportunities. ". . . I only wish Harpers would send me to Antwerp. Yes, Antwerp or Brussels is my latest fad." Then a short time later, he told of an acquaintance, a rich man whom he does not identify, who offered to send him to Paris with two hundred dollars a year for five, six or seven years, the only repayment being a painting at the end of his studies. The idea excited him, but apparently he would have had to make up about five hundred dollars a year himself to live comfortably abroad and that was beyond his means. His indecision and search for direction showed his perplexity.

His indecisions were not apparent in his own work. He had become a man of work, happy only when immersed and he remained so until ill health robbed him of his strength. His pictures were now, in the later part of 1879, showing an accelerated improvement and so was his writing. His short story, "The Last Revel in Printz Hall," written for the *Monthly*, he considered his best writing to date. The illustrations for it and for two articles by other writers, "The Old National Pike" and "Sea Drift from a New England Port," had marked him out as a knowledgeable and convincing portrayer of the early American scene, and he began to taste the pleasant flavor of growing success. Now that he had passed through the anxious stage of struggle for recognition and could feel the waxing strength of his creative powers, New York began to be a less necessary and exciting place.

Almost overnight his cherished circle of friends was breaking up. Abbey had gone to England and talked of staying there. Rinehart had left the Harper's staff and was pursuing his own creative ends. Frost had moved back to Philadelphia. Others were married, moving to the country or less inclined to congregate and talk the evening away. There was a new, green shift of younger artists coming in and they had their own private language and set of enthusiasms. It was late '79; he was twenty-six and in that Victorian climate he was sensing middle age on the horizon.

He was discovering that his roots were in Wilmington and the valley behind it. New York had prodded him, had licked him into shape for what promised to be his lifework. He had seen an America changing rapidly before his eyes, and now he found himself craving a snug coign of vantage where the evolution was less headlong. New York was the nation's publishing center, among other things, but the train and ferry journey of less than three hours would put it within commuting distance, should he choose to return to Wilmington.

He sounded out the Harper's editors and they were sympathetic and willing to send him stories and articles. He had been almost completely a Harper's man for about two years and now he was more than a little apprehensive about having all his eggs in one basket but he was hopeful of reestablishing relations with Scribner's and other publishers. He felt certain he would find it possible to be more productive in the quiet of Wilmington, particularly as he had planned in his mind a children's book on the old Robin Hood theme with abundant illustrations. He left New York with some qualms and regrets but with high hopes.

VII

MOVING TOWARD FAME

BACK IN WILMINGTON, Pyle felt rooted again. The New York experience had quickened him, expanded his horizons and equipped and shaped him for the steps ahead, but it was not the source of whatever strength he might have. He had to touch earth in his home valley. Like his friends, Frost and Abbey who had left too, he had experienced the attractions and repulsions of the metropolis. Frost had settled in Ardmore, a small suburban community outside Philadelphia, where the country was only a few steps away. Abbey had been drawn to England, eventually to the hills of Gloucestershire.

A room on the top floor of the Pyle house was easily converted into a studio. His mother, happy to have him back, fitted it out with odds and ends of the household furniture and saw that it was kept clean. Howard set up his easel and drawing table and since his principal mediums were still ink and gouache, there was no smell of turpentine and linseed oil to seep downstairs. He settled in to work.

Parsons kept his promise to send him work from time to time and a few assignments came in from other sources. The winter of 1879–80 was busy and fruitful. The illustrative assignments kept him reasonably occupied but he found more time for reading and study than he had had in the New York interval. His tentative days were over; he now saw his goals more and more clearly and how to move toward them. He was beginning to come to terms with his versatility, which he now accepted as an ingrained and unchangeable element of his nature. He was prepared to allow this capability to function and find its release through work. He was also beginning to sense his limitations though not without regrets. His confidence increased as he became aware of his extraordinary capacity for work, fortified by unusual powers of concentration. He was beginning to move into a pattern of work and formidable productivity that would persist until his last months of illness.

From his continued reading in American history Pyle found material that he craved to picture; yet since it was obvious that receiving such assignments was chancy, the answer was to furnish his own text. Besides, he was coming upon many little-explored areas of our history that he felt should be better known. So he experimented with an article on the early Bartrams of Philadelphia, a family of pioneer botanists who had contributed a great deal to the knowledge of the flora of the new continent. It was an excellent article that pleased Parsons very much. He accepted it gladly for *Harper's Monthly* and suggested another of a similar nature.

Once permitted a wide choice of subject matter, Pyle chose a topic close to his heart — early Wilmington. There was little digging to do for this article; in his head were a hundred tales and anecdotes of kith and kin. Many of the old familiar landmarks were within walking distance; some that had disappeared were recorded in prints or paintings in the local historical collections and libraries. He called it "Old Time Life in a Quaker Town" and, together with the Bartram article, it not only spread his reputation through the country but also prompted Harper to give him more roving assignments to likely places in southeastern Pennsylvania and southern New Jersey.

He saw great and inviting possibilities in a succession of such articles, and this plus his illustrative assignments would have satisfied most artist-writers but, in addition, he was giving most spare moments to sketches and tentative scraps of text for his projected *Robin Hood*. He was engaged in experimenting with a prose style that would convey the flavor of the old tales to children and at the same time was trying various types of pen drawing that would achieve the same end.

Not all his time was spent in his third-story studio; he slipped back into his old friendships and the social round of the hilltop circle. He was a bit of a hero, now that his pictures and prose were appearing in the popular magazines — at once an oddity and an enigma. The tight little society of affluent Wilmington, where old family names meant everything, reacted somewhat self-consciously to having an artist and writer in its midst. This small world was not without experience with eccentrics but expected these to appear among the southern families which were accepted as a leaven in the Quaker crust. More than southern leaven was working to crack that crust. The meetinghouse benches were no longer crowded, more and more Friends were seeking ritual in the Episcopal Church — some were even singing "The Blood of the Lamb" in the Methodist and Baptist chapels. For many this was a great and grave change, but the new labels did not erase the seriousness, the self-discipline and sense of responsibility which were the core of inherited characteristics that were not to be shed as readily as the Quaker dress.

The youngsters of Pyle's age were a rebel generation. As children they had experienced the upset of the Civil War, and become an inquiring, reading, debating group. Though cushioned in modest comfort they were eager for trials and tests and tempted by the galloping industrialization of their day.

These young people had an appetite for the fruits of the arts and nibbled at the culture-labeled sweets of Europe, from the accredited Tennyson to the brow-raising Swinburne, Pater and Rossetti. In a year or two (1882) Oscar Wilde would be coming on his famous lecture tour. Gilbert and Sullivan were becoming fashionable and could be safely admired but Wagner was considered dangerous. However, the young Quakers could now lift up their voices in song. They formed a Lyceum, a gathering where they could sing, talk, debate and listen to invited lecturers. A Lyceum picnic was planned and this brought young Pyle into the young people's fold and shortly afterwards into matrimony.

The picnic plans called for some choral singing but there was a serious vacancy in the tenor section. Pyle had a tenor voice of local reputation so he was invited to join. Easily persuaded, he set off dutifully to his first rehearsal. It was at the house of the Poole family, a name vaguely familiar to him, and he was early. The Pooles' young daughter, Anne, opened the door and that moment saw the beginning of regular visits. Their engagement was announced shortly after, in July of 1880.

Now his income became an issue of prime importance and he went through the usual calculations of a head-of-a-family-to-be. He was busy enough at the moment and he allowed himself to have high hopes for *Robin Hood* when finished, but he needed reassurance from the publishers. So he made two trips to New York to query the sources of his bread and butter. His friend Parsons was openly glad to see him, but spoke glumly of the mounting costs of publishing and of the need for retrenchment. Nevertheless the Harper's editor made it clear that the magazine looked upon him as a regular contributor. Pyle indicated that he felt the need of assurance in the form of about twenty-five hundred dollars of work a year, and Parsons commented that this seemed entirely possible. Pyle felt some trepidation in approaching Scribner's, fearing that they might feel he had abandoned them for *Harper's Monthly*, but that publication received him with open arms, and Drake made it plain that he looked forward to seeing more Pyle pictures in the magazine.

Encouraged by his success in New York, he made a trip to Stroudsburg, Pennsylvania, to gather material for an article on that hilly and mountainous country threaded by the broad Delaware River and its tributaries. He worked long hours in his upstairs studio on this project and on *Robin Hood* and wrote almost daily, in great detail, to his future wife. She was summering with her parents in the family cottage at Rehoboth Beach, on Delaware's Atlantic shore about eighty miles south of Wilmington. Whenever possible, Pyle took the long train ride down for a brief visit.

The Stroudsburg article, "Autumn Sketches in the Pennsylvania Highlands," turned out so well in text and pictures that Harper suggested he spend some time in the Pennsylvania German country of Lancaster, Berks and York counties. He made the trip in mid-November of that year (1880), and his letters to Miss Poole not only paint an amusing and discerning picture of his experience but also are a revealing portrait of the young twenty-seven-year-old artist. They disclose his reactions to a new experience, his first distaste at encountering a life and types so different from his own cozy circle, his puzzlement but rapid adjustment and his final appreciation.

November 16, 1880

. . . I went around to a Dunker minister to talk things over. The minister seemed quite an intelligent man, but said that one Jacob Pfantz, living near Ephrata, would be the one to give me the most information, since he was both very intelligent and very well-informed, beside being a man of such entire leisure that to give information and to toddle about the country with me would be a positive luxury to him. Said Pfantz is a Dunker and knows all about the interesting spots. I want to stay with him if I can while I am gathering my material.

November 17, 1880

. . . You see where I am (Ephrata) and the name spelled right thanks to being printed. But I am not going to stay here — oh no! I am going back to Lancaster tonight. And I am going to stay in Lancaster and am going to get one meal at least in Lancaster. The unpronounceable proprietor of this Mount Vernon House told me today that this was a Dutch house, kept in Dutch style, and that I must help myself accordingly, which I did, to fat pork, turnips, diminutive sweet-potatoes, dried peaches and an indescribable pie, but oh my! — never mind, I won't say anything about my poor stomach just here . . .

And now for my absolute news. I found the natives here as hard to open as an oyster without a knife. Your mother was quite right. They do not expand with the genialty one might expect from the bucolic German. On the contrary they shut with the most persistent tenacity . . . Mr. Bare had given me a letter to John (not Jacob) Pfantz, whom he represented as a man of great intelligence and knowledge of the German Baptists. I found at home a pleasant-faced German woman and a man with a long beard and a pendulous wen on his cheek. John was in the work-house; she rang the bell and he came. He turned the letter over and over in his hands with a vague look on his face that gradually broke with some intelligence as he said that he remembered Dan Bare. He maundered on about his having books and things, but happened to forget what was in them. I confess I felt rather helpless when I considered this as a sample of extra-intelligence, but the pleasant-faced woman (his daughter) ex-plained that the old man was getting childish — which made the old man mad.

I had to give it up, so I walked up the road a piece to where one of the Bishops of the church lives, but he was not in. His wife informed me that "he'll generally be here till (at) ten o'clock. I don't think he'll be gone till very long." I waited an hour for him but no signs of his approach appeared — still, his wife every now and then dropped in to tell me that "he's generally here till ten o'clock or a little after. I guess he'll found somebodies down to the drain to talks," or something of the kind. I left at eleven o'clock and went up to see another man in reference to the sister-hood, who referred me to another man who was not in town. So I went down to the Cloister to look at it. It was stunning. It would make an article of itself. I shall certainly devote most of mine to it.

Then I went down to see the Bishop but found him as oyster-like as all the rest. But by that time I had my knife, so to speak, patience. I talked to him patiently and persistently, and he finally opened up quite succu-lently, so to speak. He gave me whole gobs of information, told me of many books of reference and wound up by taking me over to the big meeting house in his queer, rickety little rig, opening the place and show-ing me through generally. Just think of it! If I had been here last week I could have seen a love-feast, but I missed that and there won't be an-other until next spring.

Then I went down again to unintelligently intelligent friend Pfantz, applying to him also the oyster-knife of patience, and he opened also in as great a degree as he was capable of doing, promising to show me through the Sisterhood Cloister tomorrow . . .

November 18, 1880

. . . Ye Gods! What a time I have had! I came back and found my friend Pfantz waiting for me at the station according to promise —

and very much good he did me. Item to be booked for future use: Never take a man to be a fool when he seems anxious to represent himself as being one. To use an expression of your mother's, "These people are smarter than they look." At least, that is what is beginning to dawn on me. When you begin to enquire of a Pennsylvania Dutchman about things with which he thinks you have no business and which concern him, his face assumes a stony "expressionless expression," so to speak, most exasperating and most helpless to an impatient nature. My aged friend Pfantz showed himself quite agile and intelligent this morning. He talked to me and gave me quite an amount of information.

He took me up to the Cloisters and pointed out the different buildings, giving quite a little lecture on them. He took me in and introduced me to the chief sister, pleading in the most engaging fashion for permission for me to sketch. He took me around and introduced me to the minister, also pleading with him and finally got full and limitless permission to make all the sketches I wanted.

I think I can say without vanity that I made a complete "mash" of the chief sister. I talked to her in the sweetest way I was capable of doing, and she answered me in English as broken as an ancient Italian china. She was a very fat, dumpy specimen of humanity about sixty years old. She showed me all about the chapel and the cookhouse at the rear where the soup is cooked for the love-feasts. She took me upstairs and downstairs, into crumbling cubbies and moulding pantries. We ascended grasping a rope in lieu of a bannister. She introduced me to the other sisters of which there were three, exhibiting my sketches and assumed complete ownership of yours truly. She showed me old spinning machines, reels, dilapidated chairs, clocks inhabited by earwigs and things, flat wooden legs for stretching stockings upon, wooden candlesticks and Providence only knows what else.

The minister who lives near asked me to dinner and a right good plain dinner it was. He was another I took to be stupid at first, but who turned out to be quite an intelligent and not a badly informed man.

"Do you speak German?" said he,

"No, sir."

"Also not at all?"

"No, sir."

"Then I might scold you well without your knowing, ain't," said he. I think I must have stared at him with the most absurd blankness, so surprised was I at his joke . . .

I have only one regret — I asked the old sister to sit for her portrait but she declined. I begged, I implored, I argued with her for half an hour — but no go. She smiled, looked sheepish, and declined in the best Pennsylvania Dutch.

November 19, 1880

Bur-r-r-ruh! but it was cold today. I managed to potter along tolerably well in the morning, sitting in the sun and sketching the old buildings of the Cloister. But when I undertook in the afternoon to go around and get another view, sitting in the shade, I had to resign. I worked along for some time with stiff fingers and chilled bones, but when I got to painting and the water I was using froze in little cakes all over the picture, I absolutely could not go on.

. . . I went in to warm my hands and the strict head sister took them into her own puffy palms in the most motherly way, saying with a surprised air "dey is golt," just as if it were a land of Egypt out in the shadow of the woodshed. I though it a good time to bone her again about having her picture taken, but she still firmly declined in Pennsylvania Dutch . . .

As I could do no more at the buildings I went over to see my ancient friend Pfantz. I showed him the sketch I had made and he was interested. Then I asked him to sit for his picture. Here his daughter put in her word, objecting most strongly. I think the old man rather liked the idea. He had the queerest old trowsers that might have been worn by Noah anterior to his cruise — yellow with age and patched with parti-colored remnants — oh! so picturesque! His daughter thought it would be ungodly to have his picture taken. I thought she meant ungodly for me to draw it. "I'll take the responsibility," I said. "You better be responsible for yourself," said she, "one soul ought to be enough for you." Then I quoted Scripture and she answered with twice as much. Then I appealed to the old man. "She will scold at me," said he, "and make it onpleasant." To make a long story short I finally prevailed, provided I would not sketch more than his head.

The old man followed me out of the house when I was done. "Vos you going to publish that in Harper's Weekly?" said he.

"Harper's Monthly, if you will let me. I hope you won't object?"

"Ho-no-no," said he — then after a pause, "but don't tell my daughter."

"Oh, no."

Again he hesitated. "You'll put my name, won't you?"

"Why, I don't know."

"I t'inks you petter — ain't my name's John B. Pfantz — John Bauer Pfantz — aigh? (with a rising inflection). And you might send me one of the papers — aigh?"

The article turned out to be one of Pyle's better pieces but in the mysterious way of the publishing world, when items are first delayed and then forgotten, it rested in an editorial drawer for nine years before it appeared in print.

There was a steady flow of assignments coming in, mostly from Harper and Scribner's. His worries about his ability to support a family were groundless. He was able to put money aside for his approaching marriage. A new magazine for children, *Harper's Young People*, proved a welcome outlet for his stories and pictures. His first picture in that publication appeared in April of 1880 and soon his name was in almost every issue. He began a series of rhymed anecdotal fables, with a hand-lettered text surrounded by pictorial incidents from the rhymes, all interwoven with swirls and clusters of naïve ornament. Each panel was drawn in pen and ink and designed for full-page reproduction. The effect was artless, engaging and strongly suggestive of medieval manuscript illumination with infusions of a vaguely Art Nouveau tendency. It is likely that Pyle picked up some suggestions for his page design from Walter Crane who was becoming a strong influence in British bookmaking for children, but he was not tempted to imitate Crane's innocuous figurative draftsmanship. Pyle's full-page panels were by no means of even quality, but even the less successful showed his innate urge to delineate character and his ability to inject an almost peasantlike sense of humor into his pictures for children.

All things were working well, he was on the crest of a wave of happiness, and he was entitled to feel the intoxication of success, hope and affection. When he and Anne Poole married each other in the Quaker way at the Poole home, on April 12, 1881 with A. B. Frost as best man, they could not have helped being aware that Wilmington thought of them as a striking couple, well-endowed and popular. Anne was a true beauty, a girl of personality and character. Howard was tall, handsome, with an active frame and strong, well modeled features although his hair was beginning to thin and by his mid-thirties he would be quite bald. His demeanor was one of quiet competence — a naturally impatient nature was disciplined by a strong will bequeathed to him by his Quaker ancestors. Neither he, Anne, nor their friends had any doubts of a radiant future.

The young couple moved into the large new Poole house at 607 Washington Street and a room was fitted out for a studio. The Pooles were accustomed to spending the long summer months at their vacation cottage at Rehoboth Beach and their newly married daughter spent part of the summer with them. At first there was no proper studio space for Pyle to work at the resort so he usually only joined the family for weekends. But later, as children arrived, a many-roomed house facing the ocean was acquired and a studio built behind it. There, with John Weller, the handyman, to attend to chores and occasional stints of posing, Pyle could work steadily through the long summer days, except for an occasional trip to Wilmington or New York.

In the year of his marriage he saw the results of his first experiments with color illustration: two thin, squarish picture books for children filled with his illustrations were published under the Dodd, Mead imprint. The books were attempts to emulate the remarkably successful work of the great English color printer Edmund Evans. Evans' delightful color books, exhibiting some of the best work of a trio of well-known English artists — Randolph Caldecott, Kate Greenaway and Walter Crane — had received world applause and deservedly so, for they are now considered milestones in the history of early mass color printing. Pyle's two books, *Yankee Doodle* and *The Lady of Shalott*, were not in the same class technically. We have no way of knowing how much or how little Pyle's designs were botched, but the *Yankee Doodle*, in spite of poor printing, had great flavor and an ingratiating charm. *The Lady of Shalott* was less successful.

With continued prosperity Pyle could soon afford to build the studio that had been in his mind since his return from New York. He bought a plot of land then on the city's edge on the west side of Franklin Street between Delaware and Pennsylvania Avenues. The studio was placed well back from the street. It was a sturdy structure of brick with a wooden front porch and a gable-end second story, framed in with wooden beams and plastered between — a faint echo of Victorian-Elizabethan architecture. From the porch one entered a small reception room with a series of casement windows occupying one wall and a long bench another. Then one passed through to the large high studio with its corner fireplace and north-facing skylight. To the left was an extension of the studio with a lower glass roof so that sunlight would stream down on a model posing for a sunlit picture. To the left were also a small office, a washroom and a narrow stairway leading to a small bedroom that occupied the space over the reception room. When the architect asked Pyle how he wanted the interior walls finished, he replied, "I want them to be the color of a telegraph pole." So they were lined with soft gray weathered shingles.

This studio was the center of his creative life for more than twenty-seven years except for those summer intervals in the little studio behind the cottage at Rehoboth Beach or the big upstairs space in the mill at Chadds Ford. There was an interval, particularly when Pyle was working on the verses and decorations for *The Wonder Clock*, when his sister Katherine occupied the studio extension under the glass roof. But for most of those years Pyle stood before his easel under the downfalling light while his secretary typed in the office or read to him as he painted. Sometimes, for a change of pace, he moved from the easel to his stand-up podiumlike desk where he would work on a manuscript or draw in pen and ink.

In the same year the studio was completed, *The Merry Adventures of Robin Hood* was published by Charles Scribner's Sons in America and by Sampson, Low, Marston, Searle and Rivington in England. Pyle had put his best effort into it and had kept a sharp eye on the printing, the engraving and quality of paper stock. It was a work of conspicuous distinction in an era of slack book design. The care lavished on its production had pushed its price above the usual level and that curbed initial sales, but it was praised by all discerning reviewers; the artists acclaimed it as well and slowly but surely its fame spread. In a few years it had become a favorite and a classic and well over a half century later it is still in print and a landmark in children's literature. When Pyle learned that William Morris had discovered it with surprise and delight and had paid the chauvinistic yet astonished compliment that so excellent a book could come out of America and wished it had been the work of a Britisher, he was inordinately pleased. Behind the passion for his own country lurked a reluctant Anglophile, sensitive to English opinion.

The 1880's were years of abundance. Pyle's mind was teeming with projects, and he was driven by ambition and by the glittering promise of a constant parade of new ideas. His productivity amazed those close enough to him to witness its steady flow. His family and friends watched him work without confusion on several things almost simultaneously. He might have been tense and anxious from pressure but whatever seething may have gone on inside, outwardly he was almost always serene, assured, alert and completely in command. He seemed to have the precious knack of organizing time and effort.

Two years after *Robin Hood*, in 1885, his first novel, *Within the Capes*, appeared. It was an adventure tale of shipwreck and treasures told with a matter-of-fact conviction that was refreshing after the frills and posturings of most of the romantic books of the time. The characters rang true, they were believable, drawn in the round. The story demonstrated what a pictorial mind could do in print: Pyle could convey the feel of the weather, the aura of place, the sight, smell and sound of common and uncommon things. The drama of it was enhanced by the straightforward quality of the prose with no straining for melodramatic effect. It was an excellent yarn without any other pretensions.

A year later Pyle produced a completely different kind of book. The decorated verses that had appeared in *Harper's Young People* were collected, some fables added to them and the whole was published under the title of *Pepper & Salt or Seasoning for Young Folk*. It had a lighthearted, casual look; it lacked the cohesion of *Robin Hood*, but it appealed as a "dip-in" book to be picked up and dropped at whim.

Even before this book was published, Harper encouraged him to begin a new series of tales for their children's magazine and these grew into *The Wonder Clock*, his best book of fairy tales. It seems to have been written with the greatest ease and drollery and is happy and unaffected in picture and text. His sister, Katherine, embellished it with twenty-four charming verses with accompanying decorations. It, too, would take its place on the shelf of children's classics.

The year of the "Wonder Book," 1888, turned out to be a banner year — Pyle published two other books. *The Rose of Paradise* was his first pirate story, a forerunner of many a tale and picture. His relish of the pirate theme never failed to communicate itself. Saturated with tropical color, blood, death and villainy, his tales never slipped into melodrama or stock types. His pirates were believable human beings and they did believable human things; "This is how it was," his readers said. Something had cracked his shell of Quaker decorum and permitted him to live vicariously in a hot, robber's world of risk and greed. His report of it in picture and prose quickened the pulsebeat of thousands. The third book, *Otto of the Silver Hand*, was one of his greatest. The story is grim, sad, brave and touching, a complete contrast to the insipid pattern of its day. The pictures are bold and monumental. Three very different books, three kinds of prose, three types of picture making came from his studio in a year. The country had an opportunity to ponder the rich multiple talent it had produced.

His star was rising steadily, his name had become familiar to the reading and picture-loving public and he had slipped into a secure and self-chosen pattern that would persist until the last year of his life. A letter to his old friend, Edwin Abbey, disclosed Pyle's evaluation of his own habits and the nagging questions that thoughts of Europe so often aroused:

> What jolly times you must have in your English life, with the right fellows you meet at your club and elsewhere! I wonder whether two lives could be more different than yours and mine: the one full of go, novelty and change; the other humdrum, mossy, and — no, I will not say dull or stagnant, for it suits me to perfection. Yes, it suits me so perfectly that I doubt whether I shall ever cross the ocean to see those things which seem so beautiful and dream-like in my imagination, and which if I saw might break the bubble of fancy and leave nothing behind but bitter soap-suds. I have always had the most intense longing to see some of those jolly bits which you are always throwing out as sops to us less fortunate mortals — by the bye, *do* you see them or do you only carry motives of them around in your, "nut," the same as I do the old German castles?

Pyle's own words clearly define his ambivalence: his hunger to confront the real Europe about which his imagination had played since childhood and his dread of having his dream conception destroyed by reality. He seems never to have reasoned that the Early American pageant of his imagination had been nourished, not shattered by his acquaintance with its existing monuments. Abbey wrote a reply which, alas, was never mailed. It might have given food for thought. In part he wrote:

> If, as you say, you wax miserly of your time, don't waste any more of it trying to imagine what has already been imagined. Your German and Dutch castles are much less picturesque than they really are. One month

in Nuremberg, Ghent, Middelburg, or any other North German Han-
seatic town would open your eyes wider to the possibilities of your ability
than twenty years toiling through the translations of them other eyes
have given you. You can't invent any more curious architecture of the
period than exists in these old places. If you could you would be the
greatest architect living today. The first fortnight I spent in England
. . . made me wish back all the English drawings I had ever made . . .
This little village, of perhaps five hundred people, has, I daresay, only
half a dozen houses built within the century. The casements in every
house are leaded ones. Here are one or two drawings. I can't get it all in
a sketch these days. Our dear old Charles Keene manages to somehow
— and old Menzel. This latter is a perfect example of industry, drawing and sketching everything even now in his seventy-first year . . .

Pyle's questioning letter reveals some of the doubts which he usually
suppressed — doubts that were never resolved even when the Old World
was faced, too late in life. The last two sentences of Abbey's letter are of
interest, too. Abbey in mid-career is musing on two of the men he, Pyle
and their young Harper circle had so greatly admired and been influenced
by and still looked up to with undiminished respect: Keene, whom Degas
had called the greatest of the English draftsmen, and Menzel, the prodigious German, both unwisely forgotten. If to these two the name of
Daniel Vierge is added in the case of Abbey, and Vierge and Dürer in the
case of Pyle, we will have the major influences that formed their respec-
tive pen-and-ink styles.

By about 1890 Pyle had made himself master of three fairly well defined pen-and-ink styles. The pen fascinated him and he experimented
with all kinds, from the goose quill to the flexible steel-point Gillotts.
The goose quill suited his bold, rich-line, medieval-inspired drawings
that owed so much to the study of Albrecht Dürer and the little German
masters. Some hints were gathered from the more decorative British illustrators of the sixties, Leighton, Rossetti, Sandys and Burne-Jones. This
was the style that embellished the *Robin Hood, The Wonder Clock, Otto
of the Silver Hand* and the King Arthur set. Even within the confines of

this style he played variations — no one of these large sets of pictures possesses exactly the same characteristics as another.

Differing widely from these was the style strongly influenced by Daniel Vierge, the Spanish master of the pen. Using a flexible thin steel point, this style was characterized by a nimble, lighthearted line. It was ideally suited to the delineation of sparkling light, outdoors or indoors — the shadows were open crosshatchings of fine line, and a minimum of line was used in the lights — the effect was lively and buoyant. A great many of his incidental drawings for historical subjects in *Harper's Monthly* were done in this manner, as were some for *Harper's Young People* such as "The Talisman of Solomon" and the book illustrations for *The One-Horse Shay.*

A third and less easily defined style was partly an amalgam of the preceding two, partly an influence of Adolf Menzel's powerful work in Kugler's *History of Frederick the Great* and partly the result of an admiring study of several of the freer draftsmen of the British school such as Charles Keene and Boyd Houghton. In this style the exaggerated contrast between light and shadow of the Vierge influence was diminished by more insistence upon detail and local color.

In practice none of these styles was precisely defined and there are a fair number of maverick pen drawings that conform to none of them. Technically, pen and ink was the medium in which he indulged his most far-ranging exploration and experimentation and in which some of his most characteristic work was done. Oil paint, the major medium of his later years, displays little of the same sense of search and discovery.

As Pyle's abundant output continued through the nineties, it is easy to see the effect of the rapidly changing technology of reproduction and printing upon the art of illustration. The time was not quite ripe for dependable and widespread color printing but the halftone had now largely replaced the wood engraving, although the uncertainties of the new process still required considerable handwork by the now diminishing company of wood engravers. Pyle was now painting his black-and-white tonal illustrations in oil and this practice was an echo of what was happening throughout the illustrative fields.

The change was controversial and even today, well over half a century later, critics still take sides. The artists of that day almost to a man were enthusiastic about the new inventions. The artist could now count upon a much more faithful reproduction of his drawing — be it tonal or linear, subtleties of tone were more easy to come by and illustration making had become more flexible. But there was considerable criticism of the general softness and mushiness of the new halftones and regrets at the passing of the crispness of wood engraving. The blandness of the halftones eroded the sense of page design and the book field suffered particularly.

One of Pyle's medieval tales, *Men of Iron*, published in 1892, when compared with his slightly earlier *Otto of the Silver Hand*, points up two contrasting conceptions of bookmaking. The illustrations for *Men of Iron* are excellent but they are tucked into the book and give the appearance of afterthoughts. The gray halftones are printed on glazed paper (an unsympathetic surface at variance with the text stock) and tipped in at suitable intervals. The book is an example of bookmaking by rote. *Otto of the Silver Hand*, on the contrary, is a fine example of integrated design; text and picture pages are in harmony with each other, the pen drawings have reach and power to stir the youthful mind — the book is a unified product. Except for *Stops of Various Quills*, a book of poems by William Dean Howells in 1895, and the four King Arthur books in the early years of the new century, Pyle's interest in book design seems to have lapsed. Most of his later books were put together in the routine ways that had become prevalent in American publishing.

Pyle's early vision of a flood of American publications that would find its way into almost every home in the land, and carry with it a vital illustrative art that would spring from native sources and stand independent and individual, was largely coming true. He was conscious that the abundance had brought with it a great deal of the meretricious, but some of his hopes for a distinctive American illustration were being realized. American illustration had now captured the grudging attention of Europe.

Art students returning from Europe had told him how the international coteries they had left behind dismissed American painting out of hand but eagerly awaited the latest American periodicals to study their illustrations. For them, American art meant American illustration. Joseph Pennell's monumental volume on *Pen Drawings and Pen Draughtsmen* had appeared in 1889, and it devoted a great deal of space to the American pen artists, who now held their own with the best of Europe. There were several pages of text and six reproductions devoted to the work of Pyle, while generous examples of Abbey, A. B. Frost, Alfred Brennan, Remington, Rinehart, Smedley, the new rocketing star, Charles Dana Gibson, and others were included. In a footnote, Pennell writes, after a careful examination of the drawings and engraving at the Paris Exhibition of 1889, "American pen drawing, the Exhibition conclusively proves, is the best . . ."

The tepid Walter Crane, in his useful survey of book decoration, *The Decorative Illustration of Books* (1896), included only two Americans — Will Bradley and Howard Pyle. Pyle is mentioned in several complimentary sentences and two drawings from *Otto of the Silver Hand* are reproduced. American illustration was beginning to disturb the British complacency.

Pyle and most of his thoughtful fellow artists were deeply conscious of the power of the instrument they were helping to shape and which was shaping them. It was both intoxicating and sobering to realize that their pictures were being seen by hundreds of thousands. Whether those thousands engaged in calculated study or cast no more than a glance at their pictures, it was evident that the work of their hands had touched an amazing circle of lives. That contact would have consequences, trivial or perhaps important. Pyle felt the responsibility of it acutely. It drove him to be severely self-critical and equally critical of the work of the growing body of American illustrators. He was depressed by the preponderance of mediocrity. In his thoughtful moments he turned over in his mind the possibilities of attracting more brilliant talents into the field and the ways and means of developing them. Despite the writing and illustrative assignments that continued to pour in on him through the years of the nineties, he was preparing himself for still another major activity — teaching.

VIII

THE ARTIST BECOMES A TEACHER

IN HIS INTROSPECTIVE MOMENTS, and they were many, Pyle would retire from the immediate and importunate self and with cool detachment regard Pyle the brilliant, still young artist, Pyle the talked-about picture maker who was attracting large audiences to his work, Pyle the writer with his growing and demanding young following. He would measure this composite self against his fellow artists, against the expectations of his own ambitions, against the background of the bustling American scene.

He felt a sense of security in the niche he had climbed to. He was part of America, a land of prodigious appetites, which could not resist the temptation to taste everything but was young and vital enough to draw nourishment, from even injudiciously chosen food. Its strong gastric juices could triumph over the strangest brews and most cloying mixtures. The country hungered for pictures and was beginning to devour them at an extraordinary rate. As a consequence, a vast mechanism was assembling itself to deal with this demand. Daily, weekly, monthly publications and books of many kinds were pouring from the new, power-driven presses. Engravings, halftones and linecuts were being improved almost daily, being locked in printer's forms to multiply the artist's drawings by the millions.

Pyle contributed to this world. In his quiet studio in Wilmington he was out of its bustling center but his work fed into it. He knew that the illustrator was the artist of the people. He and his fellow illustrators confronted an opportunity no artists of the past had enjoyed. Through their pictures they could speak to thousands and millions — the mechanism of the industrial revolution had furnished them with multiple voices. The new opportunity was staggering, frightening and invigorating, and Pyle was fired to make the most of it.

He could not help but be keenly conscious of the inadequate number of creative picture makers who were attempting to cope with the mounting demands. These artists were recruited from various sources. Many who had attended the art schools and been trained as painters were often unable to adjust to the disciplines of reproduction. There were many who were only copyists, secure when facing the posed model and inert objects but baffled by any demands upon the imagination. In these earlier days as now there were hacks, incapable of breathing life into their listless forms. As for possessing that sixth sense of sympathy with the written text and giving it pictorial enhancement and understanding, it was a rare gift.

There were few days that Pyle was not brought face to face with the inadequacy of the average illustrator. The poor quality of the available talent was an ever present concern of the New York editors and they talked over their problems with him. Several urged him to accept pupils. Letters both from young people hopeful to enter the new profession and from older artists, who often had an art school training and even some experience in the publishing field, came in constantly.

With eighteen years of professional experience behind him and a high and secure place in the field, fortified with unusual energy and ambition, Pyle made the decision to teach, a decision that was to leave its mark on the future of American illustration and was to become history. There was no art school in Wilmington, but in Philadelphia, which was within commuting distance, there were four: the venerable Pennsylvania Academy of the Fine Arts; the School of Design for Women; the newer and rapidly growing Pennsylvania Museum School of Industrial Art and the recently opened Drexel Institute of Art, Science and Industry. It was natural that Pyle should think in terms of the Pennsylvania Academy, for it was the oldest art school in the country and famous throughout the land. The School of Design was only for women, the other two were newcomers by comparison, but actually more likely to be sympathetic to Pyle's way of thinking, for they were, at that time, pioneer schools that had risen to meet the challenging demands of the new industrial society.

Pyle offered his services to the Academy and was refused. There seems to be no record of whether he made application in person or by letter, but several of his students have passed on versions of Pyle's account of the affair. The Academy's reason for refusal was reported to be that it was solely a school of the fine arts and that illustration was not recognized as such and therefore was beyond their interests. The sequel seems to be that some time later, when Pyle's success as a teacher had become apparent to all, he was invited to become a member of the Academy faculty on his own terms. This time the refusal came from him. His comment was, "He who will not when he may, when he will he shall have nay."

If he smarted from the Academy refusal, his hurt was alleviated by an offer from the Drexel Institute. There seems to be no direct record of the approach but a later letter from Clifford P. Graycon (Director of the Department of Fine and Applied Arts at the time) says, "When Dr. Mac-Alister [then President of Drexel Institute] asked if I could suggest anyone . . . I told him we had one of the ablest illustrators of the country practically right in Philadelphia. Howard Pyle, living in Wilmington, would probably be interested in such a class."

An appointment was made, Pyle came to Philadelphia for a talk with Dr. MacAlister, and an agreement was reached for Pyle to take complete charge of a class in illustration. It was a propitious time. Trained illustrators were needed and no truly adequate course was to be found in the country. The Institute was a new and alert educational center, attuned to the unexpected problems engendered by a volatile industrial climate. Pyle felt that he could be certain of understanding and enthusiastic backing from the Drexel administration and faculty.

The building was new and spacious. Three stories of classrooms, offices and galleries surrounded a glass-topped courtyard well. The illus-

tration course was allotted adequate classroom space on the third floor.
The class was to meet on Saturday afternoons at 2:00 P.M. and to begin
in October of 1894. The following announcement appeared in the catalog of the Department of Fine and Applied Arts for the academic year
1894–95:

ILLUSTRATION

A course in Practical Illustration in Black and White, under the direction of Mr. Pyle.

The course will begin with a series of lectures illustrated before the
class by Mr. Pyle. The lectures will be followed by systematic lessons
in Composition and Practical Illustration, including Technique, Drawing
from the Costumed Model, the Elaboration of Groups, Treatment of
Historical and other subjects with reference to their use of Illustrations.
The student's work will be carefully examined and criticized by Mr.
Pyle.

The class was open only to advanced pupils and an examination in
drawing was one of the requirements. Pyle's reputation and a modest fee
of twelve dollars for the year's sessions brought many applications but the
requirements kept the numbers down to thirty-nine. This was a tidy
number but a demanding one for the instructor. The simple mathematics
of dealing adequately and intimately with nearly forty students in about
two hours' time adds up to an allotment of about three minutes to each.
Consider the mechanics of the routine that subtracts precious seconds
from the criticisms — the hundred and one little happenings that can defeat the prompt opening of the session, the lifting of the pictures to the
easel, the retreat to viewing distance, the precious seconds of appraisal
while judgments are being formed, the replacement of the picture on the
table or floor. In such a situation even clearing the throat seems to squan-
der time. If the student is queried about obscure intentions or any other
factor, the resulting dialogue can run into many minutes and of course
should, if it is to lead toward clarity. Experienced critics know the con-

tinual struggle to compress understanding and enlightenment into tiny segments of time. Theoretically every word should count and yet all this must be done as an impromptu act. This was a school for Pyle as well as his students.

Pyle may well have felt some inner hesitations as he faced his first classes, but they vanished quickly as he began to feel his magnetism exert its power upon his audiences. He was fluent and simple. He might pause for a moment's reflection but he did not fumble. He made no attempt to build an exotic vocabulary; he preferred the short, direct Anglo-Saxon words.

In a short time he developed a number of characteristic and telltale mannerisms that became signals to his students. After placing a student's picture up on the facing easel, he would always pause. Then, if he wrinkled his brow and slowly brought his hand up to stroke his cheek and nose, the first words were likely to be, "I feel in this . . ." and the student braced himself for a hard time. If during the pause there was a gentle inclination of the head and no stroking of the nose, the first words were likely to be, "I like this and I'll tell you why." Then the student released his held breath and relaxed.

Pyle developed rapidly during the first year at Drexel Institute. He had prepared mentally for his classes, sorted out his thoughts, formulated something he could call his philosophy and determined what demands he might place upon the students. He encountered nothing that changed his basic outlook or his approach to pictorial art, but the daily, person-to-person dialogue between teacher and student constantly produced the unexpected. In the composition classes this dialogue scarcely disclosed itself, for the master spoke and the pupils listened. But to a sensibility as aware as Pyle's, small signals would often give important clues — a shift of expression, a small movement, a change of atmosphere. He realized that there was more to the art of instruction than announcing his own opinions — he had to be aware of their reception as well. A glint in an eye, a sullen mouth could tell a great deal. Ideal criticism should be infinitely flexible. There were always the devices of asking questions, inducing a spoken response, trying to touch a significant chord. He learned to encourage the students to come to him with their problems before and after classes, in his office away from other ears. And in the other classes devoted to the posed model he was able to come more closely in contact with each student on a conversational level.

After all, his native wit and innate interest in the human character solved most personal problems. His major pictorial concern was with the human image and what better way to study and cope with it than with the raw material immediately under his nose. He learned to avoid blanket formulae and to assess each situation in its own light and against its own background. He developed flexibility, not of purpose, but of ways and means.

The fact that he had largely educated himself conditioned his thinking more than he was aware. He had learned to draw by drawing, to paint by painting and to compose by composing. And those long hours, days and months of self-apprenticeship had not been a span of monotonous drudgery but a period of enthusiasm, an excursion into the world of the imagination. Enthusiasm and imagination became key words in his philosophy — he felt they held the solution to most pictorial problems.

Two years under his Belgian drawing master had given him a taste of conventional academic education but that was all. He had no first-hand experience of the art school routine of his day, but he had observed many who had worked their way through it. He had ambivalent feelings about it. He deplored its being almost entirely an imitative exercise which seldom actively involved the imagination. In fact, the gift of imagination was scarcely in good standing. Usually it was ignored, the emphasis was on seeing and recording accurately. But at the same time Pyle was fully conscious that training armed one with the techniques to implement the imagination which needed raw material and skills of the hand. So he asked that his students acquire a grounding in the basic tenets of academic training but he left this to other teachers.

The class was an instant success. There was immediate respect and admiration for the new instructor. Some students were galvanized into productive creative activity; others were brought face to face with their own inadequate talent or purpose. The praises of the course spread by word of mouth and when the 1895–96 school year opened the numbers of applicants had grown. By the following year illustration was the most important course in the department, and it became necessary to restructure the curriculum. The course was promoted to the status of a School and the catalog for 1896–97 carried this announcement:

School of Illustration

After two years of experiment in conducting a class in Illustration at the Drexel Institute, under the direction of Mr. Howard Pyle, the results have been such as to warrant the Institute in extending considerably the scope of this branch of its work in the Art Department.

The work in Illustration has therefore been reorganized and will be carried on in two parallel lines of study and training.

This reorganization meant two full days of teaching for Pyle instead of the half day on Saturday, but it had been thought necessary to meet the increasing demands. Now on Mondays and Fridays he caught an early train to be in his office by 9:00 A.M. For an hour he was available to students for consultation and advice. Often this was the most important and taxing hour of the day. The classes in drawing and painting from the draped and costumed model were conducted from 10:00 to 12:00 A.M., while the classes in composition and practical illustration took place from 3:00 to 5:00 P.M. Evening classes in model study were also scheduled for Mondays and Fridays but these were abandoned after a year.

These changes placed Pyle in firm command of the training of his students. This routine attracted the diligent and dedicated and discouraged dilettantism, but it placed a heavy burden of hours and energy-drain on the master. Two days of the week were spent at Drexel; during the winter months he rose in the dark and came back home after sunset. But he was in his prime and took it in his stride. During the daylight hours of the rest of the week he was usually in his studio. He still had his contract to furnish Harper with three pictures a month and there were usually other pictorial commitments to be slipped in. Then there was always some book, story or article manuscript to be finished, usually in scraps of time such as during the train ride to Philadelphia and back and in the evenings at home. Pyle's natural faculty for concentration had an opportunity to be sharpened by constant practice.

Frank E. Schoonover, who was to become one of his teacher's favorite pupils and friends, has told of his early experience in the Drexel classes. He was studying Greek through hot summer hours, preparatory to training for the Presbyterian ministry, when a full-page advertisement in the Philadelphia *Inquirer* announcing the Howard Pyle classes in illustration fell into his hands. That advertisement changed the course of his life. He gathered his drawings and rode to Philadelphia for an interview. He was enrolled, but told that he could attend the composition class only as an auditor and would not be privileged to submit drawings for criticism until he worked his way through a series of preparatory classes. From drawing cubes, cones and spheres he progressed to the inevitable whitewashed casts, with Michelangelo's "Slave" as a final showpiece. The charcoal stick sharpened to the finest of points was the sole instrument for these exercises. Under the watchful eyes of an excellent teacher, James Wood, he was made to hunt for the precise line — the thick or indecisive line was taboo.· After the completion of these drills came the painting in oil and watercolor still life — jugs, bottles and pans, with an occasional clump of flowers. The life and composition classes were open only to those students who had successfully completed the preliminary classes.

Young Schoonover performed the whole drill faithfully, but he lived for the hours when he sat in the back row of the Monday composition class. He could look over the heads of those qualified to submit pictures (many of the heads had high pompadours, for the majority of the class were women) to the picture under discussion on the high easel and the tall frame of the instructor standing beside it. In the first row were a number of youngish to middle-aged women who always preempted the same seats and knitted without pause during the session.

One of the values of Pyle's method was that any alert student, whether he had submitted a picture or not, could apply any one or all of the criticisms to his own condition. Pyle sometimes made comparisons or in the midst of a criticism he would hark back to the difficulties of other students who were currently struggling with the same problems.

Always there was the incentive to raise oneself to the level of the more gifted students. As in most classes in most art schools there was a small core of the gifted and ambitious and a large body with modest talent or virtually none. The conspicuous star was Maxfield Parrish. He had studied at Haverford College and has left behind a chemistry notebook crammed with whimsical and imaginative sketches which today is treasured in the college library. He had spent some time at the Pennsylvania Museum School of Industrial Art (now the Philadelphia College of Art) and had painted a monochrome mural panel on the plaster wall of the cast-drawing room. For almost a half century it was pointed out to incoming freshmen, and each summer when the dirtied walls received a fresh coat of paint the workmen carefully painted around it. But the day finally came when a heedless new janitor pulled his brush across it.

Parrish already had the beginnings of a reputation and Pyle was a little nonplussed by his excellence. He felt the occasion of the first class demanded a little extra fanfare, so he introduced Parrish to the others in a brief, laudatory speech. Parrish rose to the occasion and replied with a small, grateful speech of his own. This sent thrills through the lesser ranks of the class.

Four particularly gifted women, Violet Oakley, Jessie Wilcox Smith, Elizabeth Shippen Green (Elliot) and Margaretta Hinchman were members of this class. Miss Oakley, positive, determined and self-sufficient, possessed of excellent draftsmanship and design sense, made only a brief excursion into the field of illustration. She craved space and the opportunity to communicate a large message and found abundant scope for her talents in two splendid sets of murals in the Pennsylvania State Capitol at Harrisburg.

Jessie Wilcox Smith achieved a reputation early as an illustrator of children's subjects. She espoused a consistently late-Victorian outlook — her children were charming, scrubbed, unrumpled and always on the side of the angels, no glint of little monsters — a spinster's dream of childhood. Two of her finest books were Stevenson's *A Child's Garden of Verse* and *Little Women*.

Elizabeth Shippen Green (Elliot) was one of the most accomplished of Pyle's women students. Her work was most consistently on a high level — gracious but firm, and always delightfully composed, calm rather than lively — and it always cast an independent light upon the text. All these women used a similar technique — charcoal for black and white, heavy but fluid outlines for the principal forms with an interesting distribution of flattish tones within the outlined areas. For color reproduction the black-and-white drawing was sprayed with fixatif, and washes of transparent watercolor were laid over it with body color sometimes used for some final touches. Margaretta Hinchman often followed this procedure but she was more inclined to experiment. Judging from the limited number of pieces she finished, she had as much potential as any, but she never pressed it home.

It was natural for Pyle to take a personal interest in each of his students. Only in that way could he hope to penetrate their outer layers and to understand their dreams, purposes and potentials. The conscientious Quaker in him set up standards of a rigidly impartial treatment of all, but the susceptible romantic in him was seduced by his pupils' intelligence, talent, charm and character. He had his favorites in spite of himself. He had his revulsions in spite of himself. His apparent contradictions often worried him but they bound his students to him.

He felt a fatherly concern for two of his younger students, Frank Schoonover and Stanley Arthurs. He found they had talent, driving ambition, faithfulness and an unremitting capacity for work. Every day young Schoonover came on the early train from Trenton and left for home long after the classroom had emptied. Arthurs, a Wilmington boy, rode up in the same train as his teacher. Pyle had a need for unfettered conversation about the class too, and he often invited one or the other or both to join him at lunch. He not only enjoyed opening their minds but also satisfying their appetites, and as a lover of good food he would recommend new dishes. When he discovered that neither boy knew of Philadelphia pepper pot, he took them to the Hotel Bartram where that old Philadelphia soup was supposed to be at its best. Schoonover and Arthurs never forgot the lunch and both became addicted to that local specialty. Pyle had the knack of turning even a small occasion into an adventure.

One noon he asked Schoonover to come with him for lunch. Pyle was in an irritable and touchy mood and at the table he exploded, "I can't stand those damned women on the front row who placidly knit while I try to strike sparks from an imagination they don't have."

There were other things he couldn't stand — stupidity, listlessness, dilettantism. He was patient and impatient at once. If one had imagination and was willing to support it with diligent work, Pyle could give of his unremitting best; if not, he found it difficult or impossible to preserve his interest.

As the school moved into its third and fourth years certain developments became evident. Quite a number of the earlier students were now out in the professional world and their work was being exposed to the public eye. For most people, this was the most convincing proof of the value of Pyle's teaching. The enrollment of the course was constantly mounting although the enrollment of the Department of Fine and Applied Art as a whole was shrinking. Pyle's classes were obviously holding up the department. Pyle now knew the extent of his teaching powers and he felt a sense of waste; the enthusiastic knowledge and inspiration he flung out so prodigally were empty words to some of his dullards.

He had tried several more innovations in the curriculum and one excited him with its promise. He had managed to obtain a scholarship fund of ten thousand dollars which was divided into ten awards of one thousand dollars each for summer study with him at Chadds Ford. This covered board, lodging and all except personal expenses. The awards, of course, had gone to the cream of the classes and the summer sessions of 1898 and 1899 had been unqualified successes. Pyle had experimented in working with a small group of the unusually gifted; he had lived with them from day to day in an outdoor environment that stimulated both teacher and students and seemed to enhance the impact of his words. He began to feel that he had come close to the ideal teaching conditions.

Returning to the fall and winter classes made him more aware than ever of their limitations and his own accumulating exasperations. Reluctantly but purposefully he decided to withdraw, for his mind kept automatically evolving plans for a school of his own. His letter of resignation was dated February 14, 1900, and said in part:

> 1) My time is very valuable, and now that I find myself quite matured in my art knowledge, I think it both unwise and wrong to expend my time in general teaching. (2) The great majority of a class as large as that which I teach (35) at the Drexel Institute is hopelessly lacking in all possibility of artistic attainment. (3) There are only one or two who can really receive the instruction which I give (4) to impart this instruction to these two or three who can receive it appears to be unfair to the others who do not receive such particular instruction. (5) This apparent favoritism upon my part must inevitably tend to disrupt the Art School or to make the large majority discontented with the instruction which they receive in contrast with that which the few receive; nor is it possible to assure such discontented pupils that that which I give them is far more abundant and far more practical than that which they could receive from any other Art Institute . . . the fact remains in their minds that they are not given that which I give to other pupils and that apparently there is favoritism in the Class.

By trial and error Pyle had discovered that the sheep must be separated from the goats and he was not qualified to teach goats.

IX

OPEN COUNTRY — CHADDS FORD

AT THE EDGE OF WILMINGTON on the Montchanin road (Route 100) the sign says Chadds Ford — 10 miles. The mileage dial on the car reads 9.8 miles. Pyle's students used to say it was about twelve miles, but they thought in terms of leg or bicycle miles. It is the kind of road one wishes were even longer. It twists and turns, often within sight of the Brandy-wine, and slips out of a pleasant suburb of Wilmington without passing through any of the usual commercial clutter and defacement that rim al-most every American city. It is a charming, unhurried road and has prob-ably changed very little from the days of the Pyle summer school.

Summer school or not, Pyle and his young people traveled the road incessantly; it was their favorite escape into the open country. Whether on foot or more often by bicycle or occasionally by horse and carriage or more rarely by the new automobile, this group knew every foot of the way. They sketched the slow curving hills. The more handsome trees turned up in their pictures. They learned to depict running water by studying the currents of the Brandywine. The old road was one of the favored extensions of the classroom.

Pyle had known this valley road intimately since his early boyhood days and by the time he had attained his manhood and picture-making years he realized that the sights and sounds, smell and feel of the open country were essential to him as a person and an artist. In turn, he felt these things must be essential to the young minds he was attempting to ignite. Moreover, blessed as were the days at the easel in the studio, he knew that unremitting hours in that steam-heated cube under the cold northern skylight could invite a creeping claustrophobia. The studio dare not become a prison, for beyond the door was the moving world.

So his instinct for the open country caused him to found one of the happiest and most rewarding creative enclaves in the story of American art education. His frustrations with the mediocre minds and spirits of most of his students at Drexel contrasted with the joys of finding creative sparks in a handful of the truly gifted, guided him toward forming a little congregation of talent in the summer outdoors.

With the approval and financial help of the Drexel administration he was able to select ten of his most promising students for his first experimental class. He knew the ideal place, had known it from his boyhood. It was the little village of Chadds Ford which straggled along both sides of the Baltimore Pike and up the intersecting West Chester road that ran close to the banks of the Brandywine. Mile after mile of flooded meadows, plowed fields, wooded slopes, stone barns, houses and mills provided pictorial delight. The answer to the mundane problems of housing and studio space was also at hand.

The old Painter house could be rented to accommodate the large Pyle family. It was perched partway up a rounded hill and, from its broad veranda, one looked down on the Baltimore Pike and across a stretch of meadow grass to an old gristmill beside a brook. This building was ideal for a classroom and studio. On the hill near the Painter house were two old and historic farmhouses. The one nearest the village had been Washington's headquarters during the battle of the Brandywine. Here were accommodations for the men students. The other building, the so-called Lafayette headquarters, could house the women. The setting's natural beauty and its aura of history made it a place especially attractive to young, imaginative natures. Thus began five, happy, thriving summers of development that would be warmly remembered by everyone who took part. Through the summers of 1898 and 1899 the school tested and proved itself under the Drexel auspices.

Working farmers also lived in both the old Washington and Lafayette headquarters and the students lodged in each sat down to meals cooked by the farm wives. The boys, in Washington's former headquarters, tossed for choice of rooms and the losers took the attic. There was no running water; the inevitable pitcher and washbowl were supplied from the hand pump in the kitchen. There was an outside pump too, and off to the side was the outhouse, drafty and leaking. A poster of "Barker Bone and Nerve Liniment" fastened on the side toward the prevailing west wind mitigated discomfort a little on rainy days. The Lafayette headquarters' facilities were similar.

The two buildings looked down on the Philadelphia to Baltimore pike, one of the oldest roads in the country and one of the most important north and south routes. In that day it was considered a busy artery, but it was easy to stroll across it in the usual long intervals between the slow farm wagons, the faster surreys and buggies and still faster bicycles. The occasional automobiles were still something of a curiosity.

A path down to the mill ran through the broad meadow on the far side of the road. The mill was walled with Pennsylvania stone of random sizes, the roof timbers were hand-adzed and the warped wooden shingles were dark with age. The mill was a working mill with its stones, wheel and gate intact, but the heyday of the small gristmill had passed and the miller found it more profitable to close down the machinery during the summer months and rent it for studio use.

The mill was open to the summer breezes, but even so, there were torrid days when Pyle in his studio space on the second floor under the high roof could hardly work. He could always escape to criticize the students on the floor below where the temperature was a few degrees lower or hunt out the Sybarites who had fled to the basement beside the cool millrace and the motionless wheel. Upstairs Anna W. Hoopes, "Miss Anna," stuck to her secretarial duties at her old desk between the filing cabinets.

There was ample space on the first floor for those students who chose to cluster about the posed model and for the independent spirits who preferred to work on their individual problems in isolated corners. The greater number of working hours were spent out-of-doors, for Pyle believed in taking advantage of every opportunity to paint the shifting light of the open air. The winter sessions tended to instill a concept of the figure always lit by the cold overhead light of the studio. The adjustment from this stereotyped light pattern to the flickering rebounding illumination of direct or indirect sunlight was always difficult and taxing for students. Pyle taught them to see light flooding and enfolding every form, and every form relaying its received lights onto other forms — he inspired his students with an awareness of the complex interplay of reflected lights that required organization and simplification by the artist if he hoped to capture it on canvas.

Naturally there was a period of confusion and perplexity. The eye received a bewildering number of light, color and form messages while the mind struggled to sort them out and reduce them to a workable order. Many pupils tried to cope with the myriad-faceted problem by adding colors to their palettes, sometimes twenty or more. In fact, this only added to the confusion. Pyle, in a drastic move, removed color from his students' palettes and limited them to black and white only. This simplified the problem; the search was now for *values*, the equivalents in the monochrome scale to the colors under study. This was by no means an easy search, but gradually the eye learned to make accurate distinctions and, one by one, the students were allowed to resume the full color range.

The search for the understanding of outdoor light was not new, but it was a matter of neglect and indifference in most conventional art training. The classroom skylight set the light pattern for many generations of studio painters, for to paint by it had become an ingrained custom and only the adventurous dared to attempt a new and arduous way of seeing. Moreover, the summer art school with its opportunities to paint under the sky had yet to come into its heyday, and Chadds Ford was a pioneer.

Pyle must have felt the lively influence of French impressionism although his writings seemed to ignore it. In his earlier years in New York he had met the first wave of Americans returning from Paris and impressionism was in their conversation and on their canvases. True enough, the French schools were almost equally indifferent to the new vision. but it was an inescapable topic of controversy and young painters could scarcely avoid taking sides. The pastel tints of the plein-air school were no longer a rarity in nearby Philadelphia and in New York. Not many miles up the Delaware at New Hope, the nucleus of a landscape group was forming and it was beginning to coalesce into an authentic school of American outdoor painting. However closely or remotely Pyle followed the work of this new breed of painters, he was not willing to follow their objectives to the extremes, to the point where the passion for light saturation obliterated solid form. His most basic and natural commitment was to form and he believed it was the mission of light to reveal and enhance form.

A very practical reason lay behind this bred-in-the-bone predilection. Pyle's commitment was to illustration and this communicated most emphatically in terms of form. When color was possible, four process plates — red, yellow, blue and black — were employed for reproduction. This was no longer the experimental and chancy method of a few years before, but it was least reliable with intense colors or light, bright tints. It was most effective in the middle or dark color range and this accorded with Pyle's native taste for rich, medieval pigmentation.

The material for studying the endless ramifications of natural light began at the mill door and extended for as many miles as the seeker cared to travel. There was subject matter for a lifetime of study down the mill brook to the Brandywine, down the Brandywine to its mouth or up through the valley into the Welsh Hills. The eye could feast on flat meadows, tilted pastures, woodlots, tilled fields, old stone houses and some new ones, barns, mills and quarries. Just behind the two headquarters' buildings, over the brow of the hill was a small, humped-up region of little mounded hills and amphitheater dells, the gentler slopes under plow, the steeper ones well wooded. This was a favorite sketching ground for those, like N. C. Wyeth, who were sensitive to the enchantment of these sheltered nooks.

Pyle often selected a definite spot for the class to sketch. A favorite place was Brinton's Mill, a mile or more above the pike on the Brandywine. Students were expected to be on location by eight o'clock. One morning Frank Schoonover overslept. He gathered up his painting traps and in a guilty panic jumped on his bicycle. As he neared the mill he could see, with a sense of relief, that H. P.'s bicycle was not among those racked along the fence. He ran down the lane, set up canvas and easel and began to lay out his colors. Up the road he could see his teacher pedaling toward him. He smeared up his palette in a few seconds and began on the canvas. He managed to cover it as Pyle came down the lane. While trying to give his best imitation of the dedicated student, Schoonover could hear approaching steps and sense his master's presence over his shoulder. "Try to be on time tomorrow," was his criticism for the day.

The students looked back upon these as Spartan days — exhilarating Spartan days — filled with a sense of growth and hope. Pyle was no unheeding martinet; he knew when to relent, relax and divert. He realized minds and muscles had to be allowed their unharnessed interludes.

For example, he liked to organize picnics. Some were impromptu midday lunch affairs but others were all-day excursions. For the summer months he hired a horse and carriage, a vehicle large enough to carry the whole family, with William, the Negro jack-of-all-trades, for driver. Pyle also bought a new tandem bicycle with a front section without the horizontal support bar so that it might be ridden by one of the girls. Pyle had noticed that one or two of the girls had to walk their bicycles up the longer hills, so he planned to place a strong boy in the back seat to furnish the major part of the power for the girl in the front. On the day after the long excursions to Valley Forge, which was one of the favorite trips, there was always one gallant boy with aching legs.

Saturdays were free days. Most of the students played or relaxed, some worked. There was an improvised baseball diamond in the meadow beside the mill. There were seldom enough players to recruit two nines, although sometimes a few neighboring boys would join, so usually "movings up" was played — a game that would accommodate a flexible number of players and which now has almost become a thing of the past. There were some tennis players and a few fishermen.

Pyle, with his amused, concerned eye and keen nose, detected a need. He organized a weekly swimming and bath party for the boys at the end of the sweaty Saturday afternoons. He would appear punctually at a certain hour with a chip basket filled with fresh towels and clothing and a bar of soap placed conspicuously on top. His party thus equipped would follow him down the brookside to the Brandywine and through the thickets of pollarded willows down to its bank. This length of the Brandywine resembled a bit of France, for in the early days of the Du Pont powder mills, which needed the charcoal burned from willow twigs, the farmers had been encouraged to plant willows and crop them regularly for the new growth of green twigs.

Once at the swimming hole, Pyle disappeared into a screen of willows to change, then emerged in his swimsuit, threw his bar of soap into the water and jumped in after it. This was one occasion when he expected imitation and got it. Young Schoonover, who recorded so much of the school days with his camera, was hopeful of photographing Pyle in his bathing trunks but always met a stern frown. His best effort was a snap of Pyle's glistening bald head sticking out of the water.

Properly freshened up and cleanly clothed, the swimmers then made their way back to the headquarters on the hill, ate their farmer's supper and then put on their high stiff collars and bow ties or wide four-in-hands. The more sophisticated parted their hair carefully in the middle. Except for Sunday church it was the one time of the week for dressing up, for it was the custom to gather for some hours of talk and impromptu entertainment at the Pyle house. The girls brushed up their best pompadours over their rats (coils of false hair) and broke out their better shirtwaists with the high stiffened collars. Some pinned small gold watches over their hearts.

A number of the men and women had good voices and several were musicians. Some of them were mimics and ham actors like Philip Goodwin whose rendition of a bear fight was received with enthusiasm. These young people belonged to a generation that still enjoyed charades; they were an inventive group and improvised entertainment easily.

All this usually took place on the broad front porch of the Painter house. But in cool evenings everyone moved inside to the large front room and set the logs going in the big fireplace. Pyle was usually part of the gathering and could be persuaded to talk about his experiences with the New York editors whom the students hoped to face in the near future and the artists, worshiped from afar, who were his old friends. Sometimes Pyle was in the mood to get out his drawing board and work on a pen illustration while laughter and conversation went on all about him. His pupils never ceased to marvel at his powers of concentration, for not only did the drawing seem to suffer no impediment from the hubbub but also he was aware of the conversation and would enter it when so moved.

Any number of instances of this quality of concentration have been reported by those who were close to him. Thornton Oakley told of crossing the lane to the Pyle house on a summer day to ask some questions. "On the stairway landing I found my teacher at his easel working on a canvas for his 'Travels of the Soul,' his young children cavorting about his knees, a model posed nearby in costume to give him some detail of texture, Mrs. Pyle sitting beside him reading aloud for his correction proofs from King Arthur, he making comments for her notation."

This capacity to concentrate became one of the qualities that fortified the Pyle legend. The students, inspired by the example of a man who immersed himself totally in his pictures, who knew by repeated experience the tremendous psychological focus it required and the ease with which such an imaginative climate could be shattered by outside distraction, watched their teacher's brush bring compelling shapes into being while his voice pronounced one vital decision after another. They could only marvel and admire. None possessed this dual concentration inherently or could cultivate it except in a limited way. But they could talk and brag about it and add luster to the legend that was beginning to take form around a greatly endowed human being.

Actually, at the very beginning of the creative impulse, Pyle needed to shut out all outside distractions. When the first beckoning images were emerging toward the light, he withdrew into himself and became oblivious of the outside world. Those close to him knew the signs and left him to his inward solutions. This was why his morning stroll from home to studio was so precious to him. This interval of incubation allowed half-glimpsed images to coalesce and sharpen into an exciting pattern. Once a picture had taken form in his mind's eye, he felt secure, for then his conscious intellect, keen and disciplined, would take charge and shape it into graphic realization.

The idea for one of his finest series of panels was born on a bicycle ride that grew out of a thirst for lemonade. Pyle had an innocent passion for lemonade made with Apollinaris water. Sometimes on hot summer afternoons at Chadds Ford the thirst would begin to torment him, and apparently homemade lemonade was not the answer. The brew at Anscow's Restaurant and Oyster House opposite the public library in the heart of Wilmington was famous. No one seemed to think of the long miles to be pedaled into the city and back. So, one August afternoon Pyle with a few of the ambitious boys set out for Anscow's. He chose his new tandem bicycle with the ever-willing young Schoonover in the front seat. Pyle had on his well-worn tweed knickers and an ancient turtleneck sweater, faded from its original crimson to a dusty purple and stretched in every direction, its distended neck hanging in a roll across his chest. At Anscow's the lemonade was ordered by the pitcher.

On the slow ride back, Schoonover was conscious of complete and unusual silence behind him. When he reached the first long hill and rose in his seat to bring more weight and effort to bear on the pedals, he heard Pyle's sharp voice, "Frank, sit down and stop swaying from side to side!"

He obeyed and knew that a mood had come upon his teacher. When they reached the gristmill, Pyle bounded inside and called up the stairway, "Miss Anna, Miss Anna, are there any academy boards up there?"

By the time he reached the floor above, Miss Anna had a pack of them in her hands. He selected six, set his palette and began to paint. Schoonover and Anna Hoopes watched as one by one the lay-ins for "The Pilgrimage of Truth" series, came into being. In a little over an hour the essential rough pictorial statement of the six small panels had been made and the palette was laid down. The next morning the stock of old mahogany wood was picked over and six panels cut to size, and with the lay-ins before him he began to paint, panel by panel, one of the most imaginative groups he ever conceived. Together with a short text he wrote later to accompany them and a number of pictorial headpieces and initials, they appeared in the December 1900 issue of *Harper's New Monthly Magazine*.

The hours of work alternated with play and the other businesses of life, while his alert, absorbing mind, apparently occupied with other things, was unconsciously storing up a great reservoir of images. Then there were the shorter intervals of reverie when the unconscious toyed willy-nilly with its plunders and brought them into strange and unpredictable conjunctions. Finally came the electric shock of recognition that creation was taking place, and the conscious mind focused intently on its subconscious partner and watched a new conception emerge. When the moment came to pick up pen or brush, the image was implanted in the mind's eye and the task was that of translating it into two-dimensional forms upon a flat surface. This was Pyle's lifelong pattern of creation.

In many ways Pyle felt at his peak during the Chadds Ford days. The open air, the freedom, the informality were stimulants. He loved to paint the outdoor light and pose the model in the open. When Harper sent him a manuscript that called for a pirate captain to be braced on a heaving deck, he had Arthurs and Schoonover hammer together a tilted platform that would simulate the slanting deck, and the ever-willing John Weller, in seaboots and long cloak, mounted it and struck a fierce pose. All this took place under an old sycamore beside the mill — the cloak was wired out to the tree to suggest the tug of the sea wind and the boys sloshed buckets of water from the brook over the platform to keep it glistening with reflections.

Master and pupils became very close during those days. Pyle felt he could call upon one of his newest students, young N. C. Wyeth, to hitch up the carriage team on the spur of the moment (for N.C. was good with horses) and drive a group for miles about the battlefield roads. There were always some who were eager to join him when he felt like walking cross-country or climbing on his bicycle. On the Fourth of July he tended to invest heavily in fireworks. The day was a large family outdoor party — a deafening, singing, shouting, eating spree that finally sputtered out with the last Roman candles and pinwheels of late evening. No one was expected to be at his best the next day.

Pyle was naturally the confidant of his students and they brought him many of their private problems. These were always a matter of deep concern; he carried them about in the back of his mind and brought the best of his experience to the solving of them. On the other hand, he could laugh and chuckle at some of his young people's antics. For instance, there was Wyeth's and Harding's race with the bull. Wyeth told about their bemused walk in the Brandywine meadows through the evening light.

On our travels we came upon a huge oak overhanging the river with a black wood forming a background, when in the profound silence of evening a huge snowy white crane rose from the bank as silently as death slowly disappearing from sight . . . We finally got up and started for home across the pasture which was soggy and wet, when we suddenly heard a roar and a thudding of hoofs and what should we see but a huge bull making for us not 20 yards away. We turned and I fell.

Harding made across a pond in the pasture going up to his waist. When I finally got on my feet after much difficulty, I also made my way across the pond. We then sat down and roared at the sudden change of our thoughts, immediately before, thinking of the quiet, poetic beauty of nature and its charms, and then running for our lives.

Often the students' problems concerned money, and Pyle was almost always able to solve these, not by direct charity but by finding an opportunity for them to earn. Often he could do this by locating some illustrative or similar work; if not, there were usually useful chores to be done. For instance, Wyeth tended and milked a cow herd for his board at Chadds Ford and others waited on the table at one of the boardinghouses. Sometimes there were misunderstandings between pupils and parents, and Pyle's wise and tolerant intercessions often worked wonders. There were always the students' depressions and discouragements. Pyle was an expert in this area, for he had been through the ups and downs himself.

After the summer sessions were over, Chadds Ford continued to lure the students throughout the other seasons, for midwinter sleighrides or spring sketching picnics. Pyle was particularly fond of the spicy fall days and of the pleasure of gathering chestnuts. The stream banks and wooded slopes were dotted with the handsome native chestnut trees; probably the valley was even more beautiful then than today, since the blight has killed them all.

On frosty fall afternoons Pyle liked to lead his band to his favorite nut trees. He carried his longbow, a long coil of light cord and ropes of several thicknesses. To an arrow he attached the lightest cord and then fastened to the cord a heavier one which was secured to a light but stout rope, sturdy enough to support a body. He would then shoot the arrow over one of the heavily laden branches and pull until the rope could be reached from the ground. One of the lightweight boys could then put a foot through a loop in the other end and be hauled up into the tree. Holding to one limb and dancing and jumping on another, he could rain chestnuts on the group below.

Sacks of chestnuts were carried back to the studios to be roasted in the open fireplaces along with popcorn on winter evenings. Shellbarks were the second-choice nut. The meat was good but small and a nuisance to come by. The shell was adamant and had to be cracked by a heavy hammer with the nut held on a stone or brick. The toll of damaged fingers was often too heavy a price to pay.

These were some of the little experiences of the Chadds Ford days that implanted lifetime memories in the minds of the students. And blended with these were the more significant experiences of awakened perceptions, ripening pictorial resources and visions of a dazzling future of endless picture-making. All these things crept into the students' pictures and fed their imaginations for the rest of their lives. In turn, some of them tried to pass this spirit on to their students.

They could hear Pyle's words, "Look on this, study it, absorb it. Never again will it be the same. If you see it tomorrow, the light will be different and you will be different. This moment is unique." So their minds were attuned to the hundreds of everyday visual accidentals. Each day became a pageant of pictorial opportunities. Their eyes acquired a special sensitivity to the wayward effects of the moment and then, closing their eyes, they had access to the procession of the imagined. Almost all the students have left records of their Chadds Ford memories. As Wyeth said, many times, stretching his long arms, "Those glorious days!"

There were five years of that outdoor growth and study. The two summers of 1898 and 1899 were experimental, when Pyle worked out his ideas with the Drexel groups. Those years confirmed him in the direction he had taken. The two summer's-end reports to Dr. MacAlister with their quiet, straightforward record of accomplishment contain a sense of mounting satisfaction and triumph. There was no class during the summer of 1900 while the student's studio was being built and the new school planned. Then came the three consecutive summers of 1901, 1902 and 1903, when the most brilliant company was assembled and Pyle was at his best. The span of time was short but it left an imprint.

There were no regular summer classes after 1903. Pyle and the students frequently returned to Chadds Ford to sketch and paint, explore and picnic up until 1910 before he left for Italy. But in 1903 Pyle was fifty, his incredible energy was giving the first hints of diminishment and his commitments to picture making could not be reduced.

Wyeth took a nostalgic trip to Chadds Ford in the early summer of 1904. He went through the Pyle house. "It seemed so queer to go into that house and not hear the voices and romping of children or not see Mr. Pyle standing in the doorway beaming all over with joviality."

X

SCHOOL AND COLONY

CERTAINLY Pyle had found his mind working on the problem of establishing a school of his own long before he sent his letter of resignation to the president of Drexel. The results of the first summer's work at Chadds Ford clarified the reasons for his discontent with his winter classes and forced him to come to some positive conclusions about a school which would conform more closely to his ideals. He felt deep satisfaction with the results of the summer work. A great deal had been accomplished in the form of tangible paintings and drawings, and in every case there had been marked individual development. His pupils had flourished under the warmth and magnetism of his personality. He could sense their outgoing response but he now accepted the fact that success had been possible only because the group was a handpicked company. Each student possessed not only talent (all in all, not too rare), but also the supporting attributes that make for a creative life; imagination, purpose, courage and health.

Once back at Drexel, his ingrained antipathy to institutionalized instruction flared up. He now had sufficient experience with the products of enough of the country's art schools to make some considered evaluations. The mortality rate, creatively speaking, among art students appalled him. Of the many who entered the school doors, a large percentage dropped out in a few months or a year. He recognized the inevitability of this — always in art, many have been called, few chosen. The greater number of those remaining, sustained by the approbation of their instructors and visibly progressing in the skill of depicting the posed model, finally reached a point where they could paint and draw competently and accurately the figure before them in the accustomed cold, overhead light of the northern skylight. That point often marked the limit of their capabilities. Year after year they might pursue the routine of copying the model but they were rarely able to make any creative use of their skills.

He realized that he possessed a gift for stirring young imaginations, something seldom found in the art school faculties. He felt that his gift was wasted on unreceptive material, but he also knew that he had a trustworthy instinct for recognizing the responsive student. He wanted young, flexible material not yet rigidified by adherence to dull conformity, and yet he was not equipped to teach the step-by-step kindergarten lessons of art. He could not do without the schools — they would have to teach his students to take their first steps.

The second summer's work completely convinced him. He was committed to return to Drexel, for the course had been announced in the catalog and advertised, but shortly after the turn of the year he composed his letter of resignation. It was dated February 14th, 1900.

Just a few weeks before, he had begun to spell out his plans. He had written to his friend and publisher, J. Henry Harper,

> It is a great disappointment to me that my teaching at the Drexel Institute has not done more than it has, and I have given the matter no small consideration. The first thing, obviously, is to resign my position as teacher of the School of Illustration, for I cannot waste my time teaching mediocrity . . . It now remains to turn my acquired knowledge of teaching to some real account. To this end the following plan has suggested itself to me.
>
> That I build here in Wilmington a studio or set of studios adjoining my own studio; that I gather together in these studios some six or nine pupils, singling them out, not from Philadelphia alone, but from the larger schools in other cities, such as New York, Boston and Chicago.
>
> I propose giving my instruction gratuitously, expecting the students

to pay only a small rental to cover the interest on the money invested in the building. They would, besides, have to pay for their models and for heating the building in winter. Beyond this there would be no expense for instruction and I think that from seven to ten dollars a month (exclusive of the hire of models) would be all that they would be called upon to pay.

In the meanwhile I shall endeavor to throw in their way all the illustration of the first class I can obtain, thus endeavoring to instruct them first of all to make their art useful before turning it into the direction of color work. I also think that by doing such illustrative work they would not only be able to pay their expenses of studio rent but even provide their living expenses as well . . .

Less than two months later he amplified his thoughts in a letter to the artist Edward Penfield who was acting as art editor for Harper,

. . . My final aim in teaching will not be essentially the production of illustrators of books, but rather the production of painters of pictures. For I believe that the painters of true American Art are yet to be produced. Such men as Winslow Homer and Fuller in figure painting, and a group of landscape painters headed by George Innes as yet are almost the only occupants of the field. To this end I regard magazine and book illustration as a ground from which to produce painters.

My plan of teaching, as it grows in my mind, is something as follows: the students who come to me will be supposed to have studied drawing and painting as taught in the schools. My first object shall be to teach them to paint the draped and costumed model so that it shall possess the essentials of a practical picture. To teach this requires considerable knowledge not usually possessed by the artist-teachers in the schools, and this knowledge I feel myself competent to impart. I believe I am not devoid of a sense of color and I trust that I will be able so to instruct the pupil as to preserve whatever color talent he may possess.

My experience is that within a year of such teaching the pupil will be sufficiently grounded in a practical knowledge of painting to be able to embark upon illustrative work.

I shall make it a requisite that the pupil whom I choose shall possess, first of all, imagination; secondly, artistic ability; thirdly, color and drawing; and I shall probably not accept any who are deficient in any one of these three requisites. It is needless for me to say that my opinions as to the requisites of color and form may not be the same as those entertained by the art schools.

My instruction . . . would embrace not only daily criticism of the work done in class, but also instruction in composition, Facial and Figure Construction, Anatomy, Perspective, and Proportion. I shall give lectures perhaps twice a week in the evenings . . .

As the weeks passed these plans began to come into sharp focus and presently he was conferring with builders and architects and fitting their estimates into the capital fund he could spare for the project. His income had risen over the years and was a generous one by contemporary standards, but financing the large studio building was a serious and responsible undertaking and meant curtailments of other expenditures.

Ground was broken and the building began to rise in the summer of 1900. It was of red brick with wooden trim and thus similar to his studio. Three studio units with separate entrances were housed under the same roof. The gable end faced the street, beginning a few feet inside the property line and the long front face ran down the length of the brick walk to the original studio. This left a small square of courtyard at the rear bounded on two sides by the end wall of the new building and the side walls of the older studio. A larger plot of grass and shrubs and a few trees ran down to the street from the front porch of the original studio. It was still possible from the upper windows to see fields and strips of woodland to the west.

The new walls looked raw by comparison with the older structure which was beginning to weather and over which the ivy was beginning to thicken. Some of the neighbors were pondering the impact of young art students in their midst.

Even before the new studios were finished, Pyle's eager pupils moved in. The first students, now warm friends and proven talents, were almost entirely recruits from the Drexel classes and accustomed to his ways. They were proud of the new studios smelling of damp plaster and fresh paint. The new steam pipes leading up from the large coal furnace in the basement often gave off too much or too little heat, but that was considered the natural fluctuation of a welcome new invention. Pyle, who had learned, as every artist does, of the chill seeping down from the slanting glass of a studio skylight on a winter's day, had made the architect frame each skylight with a line of heating pipe. The students were told that no big city art school had this special comfort.

Each studio had a steep and narrow stairway which led up into a small second-story room. At times these rooms were used for sleeping quarters by some of the impecunious pupils, but they were not popular. Too poorly lit for proper working areas, they gradually became catchalls for the usual accumulating lumber of the artist's life. Only the models seemed to appreciate them for dressing rooms.

Odd bits of furniture appeared from here and there. Some of the students shopped for bargains in the second-hand stores and after a lucky find, two or three of the strong boys could carry a sofa or chest a mile or two from the shops on lower Market Street uphill to the little enclave on Franklin Street. Contributions came from some Wilmington attics and the inevitable easels, palettes and canvasses collected. In no time at all the prim, immaculate interiors began to look livable, inevitably soiled and cluttered.

Pyle now had his ideal school organized. He had formed a snug little colony close about him, and he was in absolute command — a despot, kindly but exacting. He had learned the extent of his powers; they had been tested under fire and they produced results. There was no mistaking his ability to kindle creative fire in others. There was no mistaking his ability to bind others to him. At last he had a proper stage to perform upon, for he possessed latent talent as an actor.

In a sense his pictures depict the history of an actor. In the same sense his teaching was a long series of performances. Acting, with its sense of immersion of self, empathy, and revelation was at the heart of his philosophy, and his entire creative life. When he exhorted his students to "live in your picture" or "throw your heart into your pictures and leap in after it," he was calling upon them to act out their pictures, in the hope of igniting their dramatic sensibilities. Unless he could touch those responsive chords, he knew his teaching was lost.

This strong histrionic strain was the motive force that breathed life into his pictures, but it was scarcely a rare possession for an illustrator of ability. The gifted illustrator usually finds it working for him involuntarily — an instinct of his genes so native that he accepts it as a matter of course. At times the artist may become conscious that he is grimacing as he works, his face is contorting with all the passing emotions he is trying to depict, or that his muscles are twitching into the shapes he is trying to form on the canvas. The analytical artists like Pyle deliberately encourage this. The performance might well seem odd and dubious to an uninitiated spectator, but the artist knows he is tapping a source of power that will help to sweep him through and over many obstacles. If he can feel and act out in his own muscles the movement that concerns him, he is likely to be able to animate his drawing, impart a swing or rhythm to it and lift it above mere mechanical competence. Many an illustrator's studio has a large mirror reaching to the floor, in which the artist can peer and draw from his own contortions.

Pyle was trying constantly to summon up just such latent powers in his pupils. It was one of the important gifts that he tried to discover in each of the young applicants who aspired to enter his classes, and he made few mistakes. Before his assembled students he was able to turn on this ready force and dramatize each moment of his lecture.

Teaching, painting, writing, he had many channels for his abundant talents. The little nagging chores of life which annoyed him were largely taken care of by many pairs of helping hands. There could be no school without some problems of administration, but at Wilmington they were kept to a minimum. There were no formal records, no tuition fees, no marks, no attendance charts, no diplomas, no catalog, no advertising. Pyle made all the important decisions but there was always a succession of minor details to be disposed of. He could leave a great many of these in the hands of two of his former Drexel students, Frank Schoonover and Stanley Arthurs. They were gifted, devoted and reliable, and he installed them in the rearmost studio nearest his own. They became his unofficial monitors, ready to cope with the inevitable little emergencies as well as certain regular duties such as model hiring and posing, setting up chairs and easel for the regular criticisms and carrying official messages to the other students.

In a sense each student was a scholarship holder, since Pyle charged nothing for his instruction. The interest charge on the capital investment for the students' wing was prorated among all. It varied slightly from year to year, but was always a minimal sum — in 1902, for instance, it came to approximately four dollars and ninety cents a month per student. In addition, the model fees were prorated and art supplies were available at cost. In fact, the student expenses worked out to a smaller figure than Pyle had originally estimated.

Willing students were always available to put their hands to the inevitable chores. One or two of them took charge of the art supply closet, and saw to keeping the stock up, buying new supplies and charging up the accounts to be paid at the end of each month (sometimes the most difficult part of the job). Walter Whitehead was the first store manager and he was followed by a succession of helpers, including Thornton Oakley and Allen Tupper True. The total yearly supply expense varied from student to student, of course, but it was seldom less than forty dollars or more than sixty. Most of the students found these modest expenses no problem, but a few had to count every penny. Yet, Pyle seemed to learn the needs of each and saw to it, once a student's work attained the professional level, that commissions would be made available to cover all costs.

This open-hearted kindness, the ever-present concern that Pyle displayed not only for the artistic development but also for the well-being of each student, knit these young people to him and brought them closely together in an effort to prove their worth and affection. This attachment was a warmer and closer thing than could have happened had their benefits come from some impersonal source, an endowed scholarship or public grant. They had experience of the master's solicitude daily; they witnessed the long, dedicated hours he spent at his easel or writing desk; they were conscious that the publisher's checks, which his brush and pen had earned, had gone into the bricks and mortar that housed them. The very matter-of-fact and unobtrusive quality of his generosity impressed many of them deeply and committed them to a carrying on of the same purposeful helpfulness in their future lives.

The life on Franklin Street gradually settled into a fairly fixed routine and work was central to that routine. Students were expected to be at work by about eight o'clock and, except for lunch and breathing spells, to continue until five or even six. There were no attendance rolls or time charts, no one spied or supervised; a general sense of purpose and driving ambition kept them to the long hours.

Pyle would be leaving his breakfast table at 907 Delaware Avenue shortly after his students were assembling. He would stroll up the street under the maple trees sometimes followed by his brown poodle, dreaming and planning out his day. It was often an absentminded stroll, if while he paced the brick sidewalks he was reaching within for some elusive pictorial image. Sometimes, when he had mounted the studio steps and closed the door behind him, he would mutter to his secretary with a shake of his head, "Good heavens, I'm afraid I walked past Mrs. Faraday without noticing her. She'll think I am the rudest man in Wilmington."

Usually he looked in upon his students first, said a few cheerful words of encouragement, suggested a change here or there on a work in progress, made an assignment or talked out a conception that was in a sluggish state. This brief early morning interlude gave the pupils an important lift for the day's work and sharpened Pyle for his own.

When he closed the door of his studio behind him, he first addressed himself to his mail which was almost certain to contain pleas to enter his school. The mail would have been opened and sorted for him by his first secretary Miss Hoopes or by her successor, the bright, cheerful young Gertrude Brincklé, who was the daughter of a friend and almost one of the Pyle family. Then the answers were dictated and he put on his painter's smock and faced the easel.

If there was a picture in progress there was seldom much hesitation about picking up where he had left off the previous evening. An atomizer spray of retouching varnish would restore the dried-in areas to their original intensity and the picture could be studied coolly in the candid light of the morning after. Like every other painter, Pyle knew only too well the experience of facing a picture that had kindled a glow when left in the flattering, fading light of late afternoon and which then had to be confronted with the matter-of-fact light of a new day. This was the moment of truth for both picture and painter.

But Pyle was an experienced professional. He would automatically make an objective appraisal. The appraisal might tell him to set his palette and pick up his clean brushes to bring an exuberant canvas to a triumphant conclusion. Or it might tell him to readjust some color relationships, repaint some portion of a figure or even make a radical change. He would follow the behest of his evaluations without further brooding. He knew that pictures begin in hope and at their happiest pass the point of prediction and astound the artist with his own revelation. He also knew of their treacheries, how they coaxed the aroused mind to believe that imagined glories had found their way into the paint layers. He knew the moments of excitement and the moments of appraisal — the warm time when the right relationships flowed naturally from the brush, the cool intervals when the meditative mind scrutinized as though with the eyes of another person.

Like all painters of achievement, Pyle was almost another man with his brushes in hand. The very accustomed feel of them, the touch of hog bristle on canvas grain, the slide of pigment set the pictorial mind in motion and warmed the imagination. Almost against his will, he took pleasure in his competence and resourcefulness. He had technical ability in abundance and he had labored hard to sharpen it, but he was suspicious of it. He tried to brush it out of sight, under the carpet. Mechanical proficiency must have seemed a kind of ostentation which aroused his latent Quaker horror. He professed to have no faith in the wisdom of his fingers, yet that digital cunning helped to carry him through many a pictorial crisis.

He was fearful that technical dexterity might deceive his students. He seldom spoke of technique to them — what he did speak of was of the office of the imagination, the power of the emotions, the necessity for immersion in and identification with the created image. The inner light of the Quaker had identified itself with the inner light of the artist.

He was not a showy painter and his brushwork was without bravura but he painted rapidly, knowingly and with great ease. Once he had visualized a composition, he usually brought it easily to fruition. Those who had the opportunity to witness his beginnings and completions were amazed at his facility.

At midday, instinct or sometimes the distant factory whistle from the banks of the Christiana brought him out of his creature spell into the world of Delaware Avenue's brick pavements and the warm lunch at home. Sometimes he stopped in the studio building for a brief interval.

An hour later he would retrace his steps and in good weather find some of the students eating their sandwiches and sprawling in the sun on the studio steps or on the grass under the trees. Four or more hours in the pleasant studio, retreating from the easel to appraise, advancing to place a brushstroke, watching the picture accumulate meaning and substance was the routine of the afternoon. With the fading of the light came the slackening of effort and the musing over the day's work. If things had gone well, he would think of his students in the next building and feel a desire to communicate his inner elation. If it had been a stumbling day and the picture faced failure, he would be inclined to walk down the brick path, past the studio doors, brooding. Often before leaving he would read for a few minutes. Not infrequently it was Swedenborg's *Divine Love and Wisdom* or the difficult volumes of his *Arcana Coelestia*. This usually struck a spark in him, and he would leave, volume in hand, cross the brick walk, enter one of the studios, read and then launch into comments on the text.

His pupils, warned by the same fading of the light, would begin scraping their palettes and washing their brushes, cleaning the paint from their hands with turpentine and screwing back the caps on their paint tubes. A few perfunctory gestures of tidying up and they would relax and talk with an ear cocked for the soft thud of the Pyle studio door and the rebounding slap of the knocker. If they were quiet enough they could catch the rustle of ivy leaves as their teacher's coat brushed the vine. Sometimes the footsteps passed their door and diminished down the path, more often they mounted the steps and the door opened.

He seldom stayed long, but these informal and impromptu interludes were often studded with the unexpected. He talked and followed the unpredictable course of his current thoughts. Certainly he savored these sessions as much as his students and they filled a need for both. He needed to talk out his thoughts for clarification and the students needed his presence and the sense of joint exploration. He encouraged them to speak out and to open their minds. This sort of session was not a class; it was a bonus, an exchange, a time of give and take, an improvisation on the mood of the moment.

The walk down the street under the gas lamps brought him to home and the wife and children he had seen little of during the daylight hours. After a leisurely dinner and some time with the children, there was only an occasional evening of complete relaxation. More usually he had a story or book manuscript to work on or a pen-and-ink picture to draw. And so to bed, an average day of perhaps ten or eleven hours of teaching, writing and picture making.

*

The nucleus of the new school came from the best talents of the Drexel classes. Stanley Arthurs and Frank Schoonover had now reached a stage of accomplishment; they were loyal and devoted followers and Pyle depended upon them for a hundred small offices from running errands to packing his drawings and delivering them to the New York editors. Also James E. McBurney, Philip Hoyt, Ethel Franklin Betts, Sarah Stillwell and Ellen Thompson were among the first students.

Since no records were kept of comings and goings, there remain for posterity only the memories of former students, these not always certain and occasionally contradictory. However, it is certain that for a very brief period two of the women, Ethel Franklin Betts and Dorothy Warren, occupied the rear studio, but within a year new men had crowded in and for a while the studio arrangements were: Philip R. Goodwin, James E. McBurney, Samuel M. Palmer and Francis Newton in the first studio next to the street; Clifford Ashley, Gordon M. McCouch, William J. Aylward, Henry J. Peck, Ernest J. Cross and Arthur Becker in the central unit; and Stanley Arthurs and Frank Schoonover in the rear.

The word had spread rapidly and applications poured in. Most applied by letter, some in person, and many bundles of drawings arrived without advance notice. A former student has said that during the first year about five hundred made application from which twelve were chosen, and in 1903 we are told that for two to three hundred aspirants, there was room for only three. This demand came from all over the country, from inexperienced hopefuls to trained veterans, but mostly from students in the large city art schools. Never before in this country was there such a concentrated rush to learn the art of picture making under one man. Pyle's opportunities and gifts were in tune with the times.

The bundles of applicant drawings were studied, not for skill, finish or display qualities in particular, but for what might be called *purpose*. Pyle had an innate knack for seeing through the surface demonstration to the underlying intent. As he wrote to one applicant, "When you apply for membership to the school, don't send me 'samples' of your work, send examples! There are no samples of art."

THE COMING OF LANCASTER, Howard Pyle. Oil.
Wilmington Society of the Fine Arts.

THE BATTLE OF BUNKER HILL, Howard Pyle. Oil.
Wilmington Society of the Fine Arts.

PILGRIMAGE OF TRUTH, Howard Pyle. Oil.
Wilmington Society of the Fine Arts.

FATE OF A TREASURE TOWN, Howard Pyle. Oil.
Wilmington Society of the Fine Arts.

BLIND PEW, N. C. Wyeth. Oil.
From *Treasure Island* by Robert Louis Stevenson (Charles Scribner's Sons).
Collection of Mr. and Mrs. Andrew Wyeth.

THE ORE WAGON, N. C. Wyeth. Oil.
Collection of Southern Arizona Bank and Trust Co.

CANADIAN TRAPPER AND WOLF, Frank E. Schoonover. Oil.
Collection of Mr. and Mrs. Andrew Wyeth.

GENERAL HARRISON AND TECUMSEH AT VINCENNES, Stanley Arthurs. Oil.
Wilmington Society of the Fine Arts.

PLOUGHING UNDER THE BUFFALO BONES, Harvey Dunn. Oil.
Collection of the Pugsley Union, South Dakota State College.

La Fée and Bertrand, Elizabeth Shippen Green. Watercolor and charcoal. *Wilmington Society of the Fine Arts.*

MAY DAY, Andrew Wyeth. Watercolor.
Permission Mrs. Andrew Wyeth.

SMOKEHOUSE, Andrew Wyeth. Watercolor.
Collection of Mrs. Clarence B. Petty.

CHICKEN HOUSE, Carolyn Wyeth. Oil.
Collection of Mr. and Mrs. Andrew Wyeth.

N. C. WYETH IN HIS STUDIO, Henriette Wyeth Hurd. Oil.
Permission Henriette Wyeth Hurd.

LANDSCAPE WITH POLO PLAYERS, Peter Hurd. Tempera.
Collection of Clare Boothe Luce.

SPRUCE HEAD, John McCoy. Watercolor.
Permission John McCoy.

If the portfolio seemed promising, the next step was a personal interview. Pyle again relied upon instinct; he had a way of reading a person deeply. No one has given us a more telling picture of such an interview than Newell Convers Wyeth.

Young Wyeth had attended classes at the Massachusetts Normal Art School and the Eric Pape School of Art. Two classmates of his, Clifford Ashley and Henry J. Peck, had gone on to the Pyle classes and had written back such glowing accounts that Wyeth was fired to join them. On a blue and gold day of late October 1902, his twentieth birthday, the tall, strong youth faced the master.

My most vivid recollection of Howard Pyle was gained during the first five minutes I knew him. He stood with his back to the blazing and crackling logs in his studio fireplace, his legs spaced apart, his arms akimbo. His towering figure seemed to lift to greater heights with the swiftly ascending smoke and sparks from the hearth behind him.

. . . I was young, ambitious and impressionable. For years, it seemed, I had dreamed of this meeting. Success in winning this master's interest and sympathy to the cause of my own artistic advancement seemed so much to ask, so remote, such a vain hope. But here was I at last, seated before him in the very room in which were born so many of the pictures I had breathlessly admired from boyhood. Paintings and drawings that had long since become a living and indispensable part of my own life.

And as Howard Pyle stood there, talking gently but with unmistakable emphasis, his large and genial countenance hypnotized me. The mobile mask of his face became more than individual. My rapid reflections were swept beyond the actual man. It was bewildering. I heard every modulation of his voice and I took note of every word. Occasionally I would answer a question. I remember all this clearly. But a searching beyond his countenance persisted.

The soft top-light from the glass roof high above us poured down like a magical and illuminated mist over his magnificent head . . . the entire countenance became majestically severe, forceful, unrelenting. The recollection of the masks of Beethoven, Washington, Goethe, Keats, passed in swift succession before my vision, and in a sudden grasp of the truth I realized that the artist's face before me was actually a living compromise of the men of history and romance which he had so magically and dramatically perpetuated on canvas.

This is an honest and moving report by an imaginative and susceptible youth, seconded by any number of similar accounts.

The studios were soon packed with newcomers. The demand was so great and the talent so promising that Pyle was tempted to overcrowd. Harvey Dunn, George Harding, Percy Ivory, Newell Convers Wyeth, Edwin Roscoe Shrader, Sidney M. Chase, Thornton Oakley, Allen True, Walter Whitehead and Harry E. Townsend were among the new faces. One by one, the newcomers faced the experience of being absorbed into the older nucleus. Each new student received a friendly welcome but each had to undergo the inevitable period of scrutiny and evaluation. As always, proper modesty on the part of the novice was a help to acceptance. In spite of the fact that there were no gradings or class demarcations, the students naturally grouped themselves in approximate conformity with attainment and seniority.

As one of the group expressed it, "One of my vivid recollections of these early days down in Wilmington is of our series of studios. There were three. One was for the babies; another given to the middle-stage students; and another studio, the third, was given to two very august grandees or graduates, Arthurs and Schoonover."

The groupings fluctuated as attainments grew. Wyeth moved rapidly through "baby" and "middle-stage" levels and arrived shortly in studio three with the old guard of Arthurs and Schoonover. Some stayed a long time in number one and a very few never reached two or three. The brand-new pupil received Pyle's explanatory and encouraging talk, was introduced to grandees Arthurs and Schoonover and a few others and set to work interpreting the current model.

Thornton Oakley speaks of his first session in the painting class.

I had been endeavoring with oils and brush and palette to suggest on canvas the spirit of the model that had been posed before us. It was my first handling of the medium — as it was, I believe, of other raw recruits who formed the class and my efforts, I full well know, were terrifying to behold. When H.P. stood before my easel, he was silent for many a minute. At length he spoke. "Oakley," he said, choosing his words with care, "either you are color-blind, or else you are a genius."

As time and practice revealed to Pyle, neither guess was wholly correct. Thornton Oakley never learned the nuances of color but had an ingrained predilection for the primaries, red, yellow and blue.

The intricate problem of guiding an increasing number of ambitious, competitive and resourceful young men and women of diversified temperaments and experiences might well be expected to be a taxing task threatening an unending series of small, nagging decisions. Pyle managed it with his accustomed concern, dignity and aplomb. He was aided by the caliber of his students who were all responsible, intelligent and committed to a purpose, united in their affection and respect for him as a person and an artist. But it was a competitive little society, a breeding place for the ambivalent feelings of admiration and envy. Naturally, there were friendships and antipathies. Disagreements and conflicts arose — some even came to blows. One student spent some of his meager allowance on boxing lessons in one of the Wilmington gymnasiums to prepare for a showdown with a rival.

In spite of Pyle's close rapport with his students, he could not have known all the tensions and conflicts that disturbed the group, but there must have been times when he wisely chose to appear not to know and allowed things to settle themselves. Eventually they did. Group opinion had its influence and the older students, particularly Arthurs and Schoonover, brought their weight to bear. Differences were worked out in a rough and ready democracy, and the unanimous urge to get on with the work at hand kept peripheral flare-ups in their place.

But there were explosives in the young muscles and an overflowing supply of energy that could not be drained off, even by the long, concentrated studio hours. Pyle, who knew this, winked at some activities and promoted others. There were frequent picnics under the Brandywine trees and skating and sleighing parties in winter. Someone was always promoting a party. A lot of artistic ingenuity was expended on ways and means. Costumes, always popular, were put together from the widest medley of scraps and castoffs. Table and room decorations could be concocted in a few inventive hours. Invitations were painted and hand-lettered, attached to small twigs and tossed through open doorways. The sale of a picture was often the signal for an impromptu party. Many students were theater enthusiasts and while the Wilmington repertoire was sometimes limited, Philadelphia was only about a half-hour's train ride away. Wilmington had no art gallery or museum, but again the Pennsylvania Academy of the Fine Arts was accessible as was the Memorial Hall in Philadelphia's Fairmount Park, teeming with exhibits which had been created for the still talked-about Centennial Exposition. Pyle went up to Philadelphia too, sometimes, to see old friends such as Arthur B. Frost, and to pace through the Academy galleries, although he was apparently untouched by the brilliant high-keyed color and slashing brushwork of the rising young school of American impressionism. He might lunch at the Franklin Inn Club with Dr. S. Weir Mitchell, whose historical novel *Hugh Wynne* he had illustrated, or with Owen Wister and other Philadelphia literary figures. Some of his early pupils such as Clyde DeLand, Violet Oakley and Jessie Wilcox Smith were now firmly established professionals in the city, and others would soon extend the colony of Pyle "graduates."

High-spirited capers and practical jokes continued to punctuate the long hours of work on Franklin Street. One episode was hatched by Wyeth, Schoonover and a few others. Dressed in lumbermen's shirts and high laced boots and carrying tapes and surveyor's transit, they moved to one of the town's busy intersections and went through the mockery of surveying a mythical project, holding up traffic and collecting a crowd. They slipped away before the police scented a hoax.

Then there was the celebration of the master's fiftieth birthday with an

ambitious medieval banquet. The students, about a score, dressed as favorite Pyle characters from the pages of his books — Robin Hood, Little
John, Friar Tuck, Lancelot — a whole circle of brightly garbed figures.
There was a banquet table of simulated medieval dishes and after a hilari-
ous and noisy evening of eating, drinking, speeches, parades and ceremo-
nies, the worn-out guest of honor departed in a glow of affection at eleven
thirty. Then suddenly, in Wyeth's words,

> Unbeknown to me how it started, there was a rush and a crash and two
> bodies of fellows clashed together, about nine on a side, each wielding
> a huge sword striking to right and left. Every light was extinguished and
> one could see nothing but continual spatterings and sunbursts of sparks
> caused by the clashing steel. Becker's sword was wrenched from his hand
> and hurled through a window followed quickly by Ashley's.
>
> This kept up for some twenty minutes until fellows dropped out from
> sheer exhaustion. They all dropped out but Pfeifer and I, and the battle-
> royal continued for five minutes under strenuous conditions. I had a
> broad sword and wielded it with all my might and he had a Cavalry
> sabre and did the same. Amid cheers and yelling we fought until by a
> lucky stroke I broke his sword at the hilt sending the blade with a br-r-r-r
> across the room. Thus ended the duel. I arose at 9:30 stiff as a board.

*

The spreading fame of the Pyle School not only posed problems of space
and energy drain but seems to have tempted Pyle to go beyond his
reach. Visitors were constantly dropping in and occasional editors would
come down from New York and Philadelphia. One of the most influen-
tial and knowledgeable of the New York art editors, Joseph H. Chapin of
Scribner's, was amongst the most enthusiastic visitors, and by 1904, Pyle
in the full tide of his success was writing to him,

> The year that has passed has convinced me that I really am of use to the
> younger artists through the advice and criticism which I give them, for it
> has been my happy lot to establish several young lives, and I think it

likely that some of my pupils will reach unusual distinction in their profession. I am speaking very intimately to you when I say that I feel that this is due in some measure, to my instruction — I am sure the ideals with which I have inspired them are both broad and large. It has occurred to me that I might broaden my work by extending it to New York, and I want to ask you as a special favor, to tell me very frankly what you think of such an idea.

In general, my thought is, that I should come every two weeks upon Saturday, and should deliver lectures upon composition as I do here in Wilmington, and that I should take the opportunity of criticizing and advising with young artists concerning their pictures. It occurred to me that I might give an hour to such criticism and an hour to a composition lecture — the one, say from four to five and the other from five to six. I should like to make such lectures free to all who care to attend, and to give my services without charge, though I think such a class should pay my travelling expenses, which would amount to not more than fifteen dollars for each trip from here to New York.

If such a plan is worthwhile, and if it could be put into operation, I would like it to be conducted under the auspices of the Art Students' League.

Chapin put his back to the plan and in no time at all the League had arranged a schedule and Pyle was making the biweekly journey to New York. The series continued through the winter months and into spring but by May 8, 1905, he was writing to Chapin in a different vein: ". . . I am about closing my series of lectures before the young artists of the Art Students' League, and I think you will be interested to know that the effort has not been a success — indeed, I think it has been a decided failure."

There were many who attended the series who attested to their great value, but Pyle had made no allowance for the curiosity seekers who came just to hear the famous man, or for the inevitable horde of those naïvely hopeful that without effort on their part merely being in the same room with the great teacher would transfer some of his endowment to them. He had to learn anew that his great teaching success was predicated upon selection, upon his uncanny instinct for sorting out those natures that would be naturally attuned to him.

Meanwhile, back in Wilmington, his school was adding another dimension. The studio classrooms were filled to capacity and until some of the advanced students were pushed out into the professional world, there was no room for any of the hundreds of eager applicants. But the professionals had discovered the school and one by one they applied for help. They came to consider it a kind of finishing school, equipped to push them up a notch or two in the scale of professional attainment. Many were artists of considerable experience and high reputation. They did not need the daily drills with the model or imaginary head construction but aimed for the evening composition class or a special individual criticism. They rented studio space in and about the town, pursued their regular professional assignments and brought in their work for comment at opportune times.

Anton Otto Fischer came, with his deserved reputation as an informed painter of ships and the sea. He was a former seaman turned artist and Pyle helped him to transform his firsthand knowledge into pictorial drama, but had little success in enlivening his lead-colored palette.

Ernest C. Peixotto, another illustrator, also came with a reputation. He was a follower of the Daniel Vierge–Martin Rico school and his brilliant pen drawings of architectural subjects had often appeared in *Harper's Monthly* and *The Century*. He was conscious of his limitations and sensed the change in taste about him. There was a decreasing use of architectural backgrounds, so he hoped to acquire a competent skill in drawing the human figure. Also, the mechanical improvements in halftone had created a taste for tonal painting, and pen delineation was suffering from a turn of fashion. In spite of Pyle's best efforts, Piexotto was never able to develop a competence with the figure that would match the authority with which he drew inert forms. And the change from the steel pen to the paint-loaded brush was not successful. As has been the case with many graphic talents, oil paint was completely uncongenial. Gouache was a bit more sympathetic, and if he had persisted he might have conquered it.

John Wolcott Adams was another who profited greatly from his stay in Wilmington. Inspired by the early history of the country, he drank up the knowledge of Revolutionary costume, life and manners that Pyle was able to impart and also perfected his pen technique which he built upon the method of his mentor. Henry J. Soulen, in later years, spoke of the needed push Pyle's enthusiasm had given him. Pyle encouraged him in his flair for rich color and sumptuous composition, and he moved to his home in the Pickering Valley of Pennsylvania and developed the tapestrylike style that was seen for so many years on the pages of *The Saturday Evening Post*. Edward Wilson, whose book *Iron Men and Wooden Ships* was to become almost as famous as Pyle's *Book of Pirates*, left Wilmington fortified by Pyle's philosophy for a long lifetime of distinguished illustration including a series of the classics executed for the Limited Editions Club.

The group grew in numbers and reputation, among them Harold M. Brett, Will Colby, Charles De Feo, Douglas Duer, Edward Edwards, Herman Pfeifer, Olive Rush and Remington Schuyler. Some like Gale Hoskins, Herbert Moore, Charles A. MacLellan and Howard E. Smith made Wilmington their home for long periods of time or for life.

Pyle now had, in effect, two schools on his hands. To the original group of young, growing talents under his eye were now added the mature, independent and professional newcomers. Since many of his young group were now doing professional assignments he had obtained for them, the small city of Wilmington was now, and would continue to be for a number of years, an important center of American illustration.

XI

THE CRUX OF INSTRUCTION

THE CRUX of all Pyle's philosophy of pictorial education centered in the Monday evening composition classes. Necessary and important as all other studies were — the drawing and painting classes from the draped and costumed model, the exercises in drawing imaginary heads and figures, of depicting the emotions of the human face, the outdoor sketching trips, the perspective and proportion lessons, the talks on historic backgrounds and accessories — all these were types of knowledge and skill that were means to an end. The end was the picture itself.

It was here that Pyle was at his best and it was from these classes that his pupils carried away their deepest and most lasting memories. Monday evening at seven-thirty the pupils gathered at one of the studios. There were several lines of chairs and stools of every size and kind, from heavily carved Baroque copies to slab-seated benches and collapsing Victorian wicker fantasies, facing a pine board fastened to the wall and lit by an overhanging electric bulb. A tall painter's stool was beside the board where Pyle could lean or from which he could leap and stride about.

The compositions, mostly in charcoal on standard sheets of French charcoal paper, had been handed in at noontime and Pyle had taken an interval to review them and make up his mind. Sometimes he only chose ten for criticism, treating with silence those that seemed to project no gleam of life or message. By trial and error over the years he had convinced himself that he was incapable of summoning up interest in any picture that showed no sign of vitality or enlarging emotion. He was patient with clumsy construction and fumbled technique as long as an inner spark was discernable, but he needed that spark to trigger his own imagination or else he could not find voice.

Standing under the overhead light, stimulated by the ring of young expectant faces, the spirit would usually come upon him and he would speak from the heart. The fire he kindled transferred itself to the listeners, sometimes leaving only a passing warmth, sometimes igniting a light that lasted a lifetime.

The impact of a Pyle lecture is typically expressed in Wyeth's sentence from a letter home after his first experience, "The composition lecture lasted two hours and it opened my eyes more than any talk I ever heard."

And Ida Daugherty Aylward has painted a word picture of these evenings:

Pyle stood under a strong light usually with one leg on the rung of a stool and he thumbtacked on the wall one composition at a time (big charcoal drawings, covering a sheet) and took it in. Then he asked the maker if what he had gotten — he stated it — was what the maker had intended to show.

If that wasn't it, it was unsuccessful. But that was all to the good, for then he turned toward us in the darkness outside that ring of light, and as we listened, enthralled, he dove into his own profound imagination, and described to us what *he* saw in its depths, as portraying that thing we had tried to show. A wonderful word picture grew before us. We were fired with it . . . He had gone so much deeper than we could, yet had such a sure grip upon reality, and added mystery and beauty and feeling we hadn't dreamed.

Only a scattered few of his actual words have come down to us. Some of his phrases — "Live in your picture" and "Your subjects have had a history — try to reveal it in your picture" and "Feel the wind and rain on your skin when you paint it" — stuck in the minds of his pupils and were repeated to other generations. Several students took notes.

Allan Tupper True used to hasten home after class to set down the words before his memory blurred.

Project your mind into your subject until you actually live in it. Throw your heart into the picture and then jump in after it. Don't take my criticisms as iron-clad rules but more as suggestions, because while you are there (pointing down) and I am here (holding arm horizontal) nature is away up there (pointing up).

Art is not a transcript of nature nor a copy. Art is the expression of those beauties and emotions that stir the human soul . . .

I criticize these compositions by analysis but an illustration cannot be made that way — it must be made by inspiration.

Make your pictures *live;* there are fifty-thousand artists but how many make their pictures living?

Olive Rush and Ethel Penniwell Brown also took notes, reporting the artists and the actual pictures that were criticized. But without the actual pictures or a reproduction before us, Pyle's words lose much of their pertinence; however, there are sentences that have meaning for all pictures.

Make real things, real surroundings, real backgrounds. A tone for a background will not do.

Paint your picture by means of the lights. Lights define texture and color — shadows define form.

The student learns rules but all the rules in the world never make a picture.

A valuable supplement to the composition lectures and criticisms were the Saturday evening sessions devoted to imaginative drawing from a given theme. These were linked directly to the composition class, for the students in a short session together tried to put into practice the insights given them by their teacher. The sessions were only an hour in length, and they were held in different studios; each week a different student acted as host. He announced the theme for the evening — it might be Consolation, or the Fugitives or Rebellion. Then all set to work in pen and ink, each attempting to clarify pictorially their own interpretation of the theme. Pyle worked with them, not as mentor but as participant. At the hour's end the drawings were collected, placed around the walls and evaluated by the class. A vote was taken to determine the most apt and striking solution and the winner was given Pyle's drawing of the evening.

This practice made for rapid thinking and rapid execution. The pen-and-ink medium made for forthright handling. It is not a vehicle for hesitant or indecisive minds; it preserves the marks of vacillation and bungling, a challenging test for a student to pass. A collection of such an evening's work is in the files of the Historical Society of Delaware in Wilmington and it shows the remarkable maturity and assurance of the students' work.

These were the methods that Pyle worked out over the years to condition his students for professional life. They were tested methods and they produced abundant results. But it was not the methods that worked, it was the man who worked them. In other hands they could have turned worthless.

Only those who have struggled through the beginning years of picture making can truly feel the rock bottom despair of having reached the end of one's woefully inadequate resources, or experienced the dim realization that there is much beyond which one may be helpless to achieve. The artist's early years are a succession of such despairs, and it was Pyle's genius to sense these intervals and, with the alchemy of verbal sympathy and sometimes demonstrations with pencil or brush, clear the path for the student to advance a few more steps. Pyle was a builder of futures. He put new courage into disheartened minds and made them believe in possibilities. He peered into the inadequate pictures before him and read a new future into them: "Talk about life in your own way," he said. "Paint ideas, paint thoughts." Under his persuasions his students discovered that their minds had thoughts and that their eyes looked out at life in a way of their own. He had led them into the ways of self-discovery. Undoubtedly he invigorated some natures that might well have remained dormant.

Coupled with this was the authority with which he spoke — the authority of one of the greatest, probably *the greatest* illustrator of his day. His pictures were all around them. Every month there were new Pyles in the magazines, his books were in all libraries and many homes. And the students were in the center of things, often in the very studio, seeing the new pictures grow under their eyes. No art school in the country had such an instructor; in most cases any comparisons would have been ludicrous. They knew they were privileged. It was natural that they bragged and strutted a bit. They were a picked company and their pride in it was enormous.

XII

THE YEARS OF FAME

FAME COMES SUDDENLY to some but for Pyle it came by steady ac-
cretion. By the middle of the eighties, he was working into his stride —
ease, and power and confidence were showing in his pictures. In spite of
the varied facets of his pictorial work, his personal imprint was on each.
The promising, gifted young illustrator had become the artist of growing
distinction and his name was becoming a household word. Even as his
black-and-white pictures were becoming famous, his pictorial powers had
to wait upon a technological advance to attain their richest fulfillment.
Color reproduction for mass distribution was developing; progress came
by fits and starts, but with the turn of the century new improvements
followed rapidly. Within a few years the four-color process, achieved by
means of red, blue, yellow and black halftone plates, was a dependable
and accomplished operation.

No artist was more involved in this period of color experimentation
than Pyle, and with the solution of acceptable color reproduction came
the opportunity he craved, to express himself in terms of his rich and
deeply personal color sense. He did several sets of pictures for these early
stages of color reproduction, and although, from the technological point
of view, they were incomplete and no more than stepping-stones, aesthet-
ically they had excellence. Somehow he managed to get the best from an
experimental and faltering method and the pictures belong among the
finest of his work. They were all deeply imaginative, and the very imper-
fections of the method seemed to work with his intent. The pictures have
the aura of a more remote age, the impression of a vanished style.

The first set to exhibit this experimental and transitional stage were the six pages with incidental decorations for "The Pilgrimage of Truth," which appeared in the Christmas 1900 issue of *Harper's Monthly*. For these Pyle made handsome black line compositions for a master plate and then indicated the color within the enclosing black shapes in rich, flattish pigments. These pioneering reproductions emerged as glowing, decorative panels, both stately and opulent. Then came a series of eleven color pages and panels accompanied by decorated initial letters and subtitles. These were published in *Harper's Monthly* in January 1902. They complemented Pyle's text for his *North-Folk Legends of the Sea*. This was Pyle at his best in picture and text. The printing was in three colors — red, yellow and blue — the black plate omitted, perhaps for economy's sake but more likely to enhance the elusive, recurring green rhythms of the ocean. The theme of deepwater patterns is splendidly maintained and, as the reader turns page after page, he journeys through a remote and tantalizing world of gray-greens accented with jewel-like reds. A comparison of a number of copies of this issue reveals discrepancies of color and impression. The registration is often insecure. But except in a few of the worst examples the lack of conventional sharpness does not detract from the mood and spell of the artist's conception.

A year later, when *The Century Illustrated Monthly Magazine* published four magnificent colorplates with accompanying decorations for Pyle's "The Travels of the Soul," it was plain that the new process had reached a triumphant level. The four impressions of rapid, periodical color printing are extraordinary examples of their kind for such an early date. They have an enamel-like richness of color that wraps the figures in the light and shadow of another world, to make the group one of Pyle's happiest excursions into the pictorial imagination. Up to that time there had been nothing like it in American illustration.

In another year's time appeared the set of four colorplates for "Peire Vidal Troubadour" with an echo of the early Renaissance minor masters. These four groups, executed within a span of a little over three years, not only demonstrated the last rapid stage of the development of trustworthy color reproduction but also were choice examples of the way in which a great illustrator in his vintage years could seize a new instrument and exploit its best possibilities. These early years of the new century were Pyle's prime years, his productivity was incredible, his energy prodigal. The opportunity to utilize the richness of his palette acted as a stimulant. He goaded himself into making the most of his harvest years.

He had a pattern of work that seemed to give fullest scope to his wide gifts and uncommon energies. He had the support of many willing helpers. His wife with her acute intelligence and common sense, her charm, competence and steadfastness, cushioned the problems of their family and their social circle. Financial problems often hovered on the horizon of his mind but he usually brushed them aside. The students presented a steady series of decisions to be made, but Pyle really welcomed the demands made upon his concern. His pupils were a remarkably understanding and self-sufficient group and they seldom bothered him with trivial matters.

Always at hand was the ever-faithful and resourceful John Weller — gardener, houseman, butler, carpenter, child-watcher, jack-of-all-trades. John saw everything that went on in the Pyle's world. He had posed in the greatest assortment of costumes for countless drawings and paintings. He was the custodian of the costume chest and he knew his dates and styles and could indicate the correct attire to the students who needed to make use of them.

When Pyle lost the services of Anna Hoopes, his dependable secretary, he found the perfect answer to the problem close to home. From the day he had moved his young family into 1603 Broome Street — five children with Miss Golibart, the governess, Katie, the cook, William, the colored handyman, and two fox terriers, Jackie and Jakie — he had found fast friends in his next door neighbors, the Brincklés. The young Brincklé daughter, Gertrude, became the constant playmate of the Pyle children and became almost like another daughter. In 1904 she was nineteen and Pyle saw her as the answer to a prayer.

He wrote to her father, Major Brincklé, in part,

I believe Gertrude has written you about her helping me as a sort of secretary . . . I do not think I should be an exacting taskmaster, but if she should undertake such duties, it should have to be as a matter of business. It would require that she should give me every morning except the usual times. She will find, I think, that her position with me would add to her social pleasures rather than detract, and the earning of spending money in such a way is a thing very much to be desired by any girl. I should be glad to send her to a good school to learn the rudiments of shorthand and typewriting.

With Major Brincklé's approval, Gertrude attended Goldey's Business College and passed her first test: Pyle's dictation to her of the medieval-flavored and consciously archaic prose of the second Arthurian volume, *The Story of the Champions of the Round Table*. From then on, at five dollars a week, she was an important member of the Pyle circle. Her morning activities involved opening the morning mail, taking dictation, typing, reading Thackeray, Swedenborg, Joseph Conrad or whatever Pyle fancied while he painted, posing for all sorts of feminine characters, quietly attending to innumerable petty details, protecting him from trivial nuisances and distractions. Although Pyle seldom felt the need of special character models, his family, Gertrude and John Weller gave him the theme essentials of a pose upon which he could play any variation he desired. There were times when he demanded a more exact counterpart and it fell to Gertrude to arrange this. When Pyle began work on "Lola," a story for *Harper's Monthly*, the characterization of a Spanish dancer, the chief character, bothered him and hearing that the actress Estelle Taylor was in Wilmington, he sent Gertrude to negotiate with her. Finding Miss Taylor in an old-fashioned house downtown, Gertrude was ushered into a small parlor hung with draperies where she was wedged between a large grand piano and the wall and there she waited interminably. Miss Taylor finally appeared in ill humor. She didn't like Wilmington — "It smells of fish," she said. But she was flattered to be asked to pose for the great illustrator and she agreed. Another color painting was added to the growing Pyle gallery.

So the pulse of the Pyle colony throbbed strongly and steadily, richly fecund, little prone to shock or interruption. All the good and desirable things he had worked for and achieved had fortified him and were his comfort, but they had fitted him into their pattern. He was at the command of the man he had made himself into.

The common sense side of him reviewed the day-by-day, bread-and-butter story. The demands for his work were unabated, more than he could fulfill. Inevitably he could call to mind a score of artists who had run out of favor, not from any diminishment of talent but because of a shift in public taste. He had lived long enough to see that the public could become bored with old favorites and install new ones overnight, yet he had remained secure, applauded by an expectant and renewing audience. The children that had been nourished on his *Robin Hood* and *Wonder Clock* grew into the mature admirers of his adult work.

But he felt he was beginning to repeat himself, that his sense of adventure was abating. His dissatisfaction took the form of resentment over many of the texts that were given him. The era still favored the costume story, with its standardized casts and predictable plots. These stories were third- and fourth-generation descendants of Walter Scott and Alexandre Dumas; their authors were a diminished breed. Several times Pyle voiced his irritation at the highfalutin texts and self-admiring characters in James Branch Cabell's stories. Possibly he was simply tired of an author for whom he had illustrated so much. These stories were later gathered into several books with Pyle's full-color illustrations for the giftbook market. But then Cabell embarked upon a new and more symbolic and satiric style that wove through the series of the imaginary Poictesme country and led to the much debated *Jurgen*. By mutual agreement the writer-illustrator team broke up.

All this discontent led Pyle back to the crux of the matter when he said repeatedly, "I am no story illustrator." He was in a position to say "no" to proffered assignments, but that would have meant refusing perhaps nine-tenths of them, which was impossible if he was to maintain his status with Harper. He was usually happiest when he was providing pictures for his own texts. His contract with Harper, calling for three pictures a month, was his major source of income and gave him the necessary sense of financial security, but it had its treadmill aspects. There were times when he would have liked to have escaped its relentless demands.

He needed to feel that he had room to maneuver, to experiment, but he seemed trapped in his own success. His family was large, the children were growing up and he lived in a certain discreet, unostentatious but costly style which was natural to him. But the monthly bills reminded him how expensive all this had become. He had no gift for parsimony and had always been generous. In spite of his excellent income his savings were very modest.

Although there was temptation enough to speed up his painting, Pyle had seldom descended to common manufacture. He had a fierce eye for any shortcomings in his own work. Some of his canvases were painted and repainted while others were cut to shreds. Several of his students had caught him stamping on an unrealized picture or tossing one into the fireplace.

He did manage to slip in additional illustration assignments in addition to the usual Harper's stints. He did a number for *Collier's Weekly*, which, under the explosive direction of the Collier father and son team, had become one of America's most spectacular periodicals. The Colliers had rounded up a splendid corps of artists, and for a number of years the magazine was consistently a showcase for fine illustrative art. Pyle was proud to be in a group that included Remington, his close friend A. B. Frost, Walter Appleton Clark, Smedley and his former pupil, Maxfield Parrish. Then a newcomer broke into the *Collier's* scene and eclipsed all of them in popularity and remuneration. Charles Dana Gibson had evolved a slashing and spectacular pen technique and was using it to exploit a type of elegant and noble-featured young man and girl that had captured the American imagination. For years he had been the magnet that had drawn an impressive number of readers to *Life* magazine. Now *Collier's* was to be another outlet for his work.

Never before had an illustrator exerted such pictorial persuasion upon an American audience, not even Thomas Nast. Most of the young and many of the middle-aged were trying to make themselves over in the image of Gibson's pictures. For almost two decades there was valid proof that nature can imitate art. The Gibson types, particularly the "Gibson Girl" and "Gibson Man," were models for dress, carriage and physical looks. American girls by the tens of thousands tried to coax their bodies into the look of the Gibson formula: the deep but trim bosom, narrow waist and long, shapely legs, the noble, clear-cut features, the aloof, princess look and the healthy, self-sufficient carriage.

All this emulation was fed by the steady stream of Gibson magazine pictures, by his large-paged volumes on most genteel parlor tables and the large-sized reproductions hanging on the walls. In addition, American ingenuity had devised pillowcovers stamped with Gibson heads — the same heads were on water goblets and beer mugs, ashtrays and decorative plates, leather novelties and printed scarves. The "Gibson Girl" found her way into popular songs and onto the musical comedy stage. There was even a "Gibson Girl" wallpaper designed for bachelor quarters. All these absurd phenomena were no part of Gibson's conniving. He was a kindly and courtly man, handsome and dignified, not unlike some of his drawings. He was engulfed by a flood of emotion, unpredictably released by some innocent and sincere picture making. An idol overnight, he never lost his modesty or aplomb. But one of the by-products of his popularity was an upset in the financial framework of the illustrative world. The competition of *Collier's* for the work of Gibson led them to overbid the *Ladies' Home Journal's* previously high price of five hundred dollars a drawing. Hoping to induce him to leave *Life* and sign an exclusive contract with them, they pushed the bidding up to eight hundred, then nine hundred dollars a drawing. Gibson refused to desert *Life* completely, so

Collier's accepted the compromise of sharing him with their rival. This bidding competition was given wide publicity and the Colliers awoke to the value of it. Their bright, original minds conceived the idea of offering a round thousand dollars a drawing, and better still, a contract of a hundred thousand dollars for a hundred pictures. So considerable newspaper space was bought to announce the terms of Gibson's acceptance.

These were unheard-of terms for that day. Pyle's rate was about three hundred dollars for a full-page color painting, and few were getting that much. The whole fuss and furor shook the illustration and editorial world. Every illustrator had a new idea of his worth. Every editor had to gird himself to defend his budget. Gibson, riding on the crest of the financial wave, was innately such a likable and upright person that none could cast personal aspersions, but there were those who envied him.

Pyle's practical side seemed to respond to his financial problems only when they were sharply called to his attention. His mounting expenses tempted him into a short-lived arrangement that was doomed to failure. The temptation came in the form of an offer to become the highest-salaried art editor in the country. With it went the inducement of putting together the best illustrated magazine in the country and the opportunity of offering assignments to capable but lesser-known artists, many of them his own students. The offer came from the aggressive publisher, S. S. McClure, who was ambitious to make his *McClure's Magazine* the best in the land. The salary offered was thirty-six thousand dollars a year. Pyle hesitated. To accept meant spending his weeks in New York and virtually giving up his own picture making. Impossible. But when McClure offered him eighteen thousand to spend three days a week in the New York editorial offices, he agreed. He thought he could still fulfill his Harper's commitment and do a bit more as well.

In spite of his years of experience in the publication field, he underestimated the stresses of an art editor's job. Picking the right and best illustrator for a given text was only a small part of it. There were a hundred and one small, nagging details without cessation, struggles with printers and engravers, the recurring problems of layout, an unending series of conferences with other editors. Things piled up on the days he was absent from his desk, the other editors always needed him when he wasn't there. It was a nagging, pushing, demanding world, quite unlike his Wilmington life. After a year it came to an end by mutual agreement.

He went back to the old life with a sense of great relief. But it wasn't exactly the old life, the pattern was slowing shifting and had been for a time. For one thing, the complexion of the school had slowly changed. The Chadds Ford summer school had come to an end in the late summer of 1903. It was now a talked-about and celebrated memory. Although Pyle often led the students back to sketch and tramp the meadows, Chadds Ford was now a place to visit, not to live in and immerse oneself. Something had been lost. Most of the earlier students were now busy professionals, some working nearby still needing his support, others following their independent bents in New York, Philadelphia or other places. The Brandywine look was beginning to be apparent in the publication field and Pyle's fame as a teacher continued to grow.

A shift in emphasis from the younger to an older type of student was taking place in the school. The younger students who had come to Pyle with only preliminary schooling or occasionally none, and whom he coaxed into artistic maturity, were gradually giving way to a growing group of what might be called "post graduates." These were men and women with professional experience, who, dissatisfied with their level of attainment, craved the stimulation of the master's criticisms. Some came only for occasional visits, but most settled down in Wilmington studios, carried out their professional assignments and brought their work to the Saturday evening composition classes. Pyle also allotted a half hour of most working mornings for a consultation time with these older students. The relationship shifted accordingly. Pyle treated them as professional equals; he imparted to them the insight and vision of a more experienced worker. There was little need for the fatherly, brooding concern that the young had awakened. He was flattered by the growing professional colony surrounding him, but something of the family feeling was evaporating.

There were changes creeping into his own writings and paintings as well. In 1903 his religious novel, *Rejected of Men*, appeared. It was a venture into a new field, although the subject had been in his mind for a long time. He had worked on it intermittently for a number of years, revised it repeatedly, fought his way through alternating periods of discouragement and optimism and even submitted portions of it for criticism. William Dean Howells was his source of greatest encouragement, but when the book appeared it was received by a skeptical and puzzled public. There were a number of reviews which expressed genuine admiration but between the lines was the suggestion that the admiration was for intent rather than accomplishment. The book slipped away into neglect and was the last effort that Pyle made to write for the adult mind.

The Story of King Arthur and his Knights appeared in the same year under the Scribner's imprint. A lineal descendant of *The Merry Adventures of Robin Hood*, *The Wonder Clock* and *Otto of the Silver Hand*, it was an opulent, stirring volume which opened the gate to an imaginary empire of medieval legend. It did not reflect the merriment of the *Robin Hood* or the innocence of *The Wonder Clock*, but it had much of the power, masculinity and impressiveness of *Otto of the Silver Hand*. Its text captured the medieval spirit, yet the book was readable. The pictures reflected the influence of Albrecht Dürer as it had been transformed by Howard Pyle. The story had been a success when serialized in the pages of *St. Nicholas*, and it was both an immediate and lasting success as a book. Today it occupies a permanent place on the shelf of children's classics.

There was a demand for more of King Arthur and over a space of seven years Pyle added three more books to form a famous quartet. He worked at them piecemeal, often dictating to his gifted secretary, Gertrude Brincklé, while painting at his easel. Her quick intelligence picked up the pattern of his medieval-tinted prose and he learned to rely heavily on her sympathetic intuition. When the last of the quartet was published in 1910, he had written his last book and drawn his last picture for children.

Except for the King Arthur series, the pictures of his later years concerned themselves entirely with adult subject material and, as a consequence, they became more factual than imaginative. He was fulfilling his Harper's assignments, but he was impatient at the routine he had established and with the magazine's expectations. He began to face the fact that he could no longer rely upon unlimited sources of energy. Above all, he needed the challenge of new problems.

The wind of change in American art indicated the direction of an answer. "'The White City," the setting of the Chicago Columbian Exposition of 1893, had revealed the nation's new and growing appetite for mural decoration and monumental sculpture. With all its sharply criticized faults, The White City was constructed on a grand scale with impressive vistas and the sound and sight of water everywhere. The dazzle of the white buildings, their glistening reflections in pond and lagoon, the innumerable brightly colored banners had their calculated effect — the onlookers felt their spirits leap. And supporting this sparkling setting were the works of the largest company of American sculptors and mural painters assembled up to that time.

This company of artists, some of them Pyle's old friends, worked under the direction of Francis D. Millet. Charles Rinehart, Walter Shirlaw and J. Alden Weir were there and Gari Melchers, Walter McEwen, George Maynard, Robert Reid, Edwin Blashfield, Kenyon Cox and others. Very few of these men had had previous mural experience; their talents were feeling their way into a new problem. The public's reaction was one of surprise and delight at the promise of what American artists might be able to accomplish if given proper opportunities.

Pyle, of course, had no part in this project except for his showing of work with the large exhibit of American illustration centered around the Edwin Abbey Shakespearean pictures. But the whole conception aroused his considerable interest and he mused upon the possibilities that mural painting might hold for him. Like most artists, the opportunity to cover large expanses of wall with the bold designs of one's creation was exhilarating, seductive and sobering all at once. Mural decoration seemed the ultimate challenge to his ambitions.

Pyle was well aware that the great shift in scale was likely to be a taxing one and that it was not to be solved merely by enlarging a sketch by mechanical means. The problems of lighting and angle viewing would be vastly different from those of decorating a page, and there would be many knotty technical adjustments.

An early possibility for painting a panel in the Massachusetts House of Representatives in the capitol building came to nothing in spite of the efforts of a group of his Boston friends. His suggestion had been to paint some notable event in Massachusetts history, but the governor and committee were adamant in their desire for an allegorical decoration symbolizing some abstract virtue. Pyle was not interested in this and the commission went elsewhere.

Meanwhile, more mural projects were being launched throughout the country. Edwin Abbey was working on his Holy Grail frieze for the Boston Public Library, where John Singer Sargent was executing his frieze of the Prophets, and Puvis de Chavannes his chalky, allegorical figures in their chill landscape. A little later, Abbey was awarded the enormous assignment of providing the decorations for the new Pennsylvania Capitol at Harrisburg. Edwin Blashfield's studio was now a busy workshop for the production of drapery-swathed female figures bearing a variety of symbols that might hopefully differentiate Civic Virtue from Freedom, or Beauty from Massachusetts Crowned With Plenty. All over the country artists were cultivating their architect friends who might have funds for decoration in their budgets. In the curious underground way of such things the gossip of mural decoration seeped from studio to studio through the land.

Pyle found he could experiment with the mural problem in a modest way. His home on Delaware Avenue was large, with some inviting wall areas. He made some sketches for wall decorations, planning to furbish up the downstairs rooms for his daughter's coming-out party. Working in bits of time snatched from his regular commitments, he painted seven panels of various sizes. The themes were in the decorative fashion of the day, "The Birth of Literature," "The Gems of Art," "Music," "Drama." They were lively and charming and avoided the stiff impression conveyed by tired, posing models that began to be a familiar trademark of so many hopeful efforts. But they scarcely solved any mural problems. They were too small and rightly intimate for the exploration of the dynamics of large spaces and unusual viewing points. The technique, the paint quality, the atmospheric aura were those of an illustration somewhat enlarged. The largest panel, "The Gems of Art" (twelve and a half feet by five feet and five inches), was exhibited at the Society of Architects in 1905 and attracted a good deal of attention.

While these panels were hanging on the gallery walls, Pyle was busy on his first authentic mural commission. Cass Gilbert, the architect of the Minnesota State Capitol, had given him the commission for a panel in the governor's reception room, the subject, "The Battle of Nashville." It was a large painting and not a decoration — a fine battle piece. It was completed and put in place in 1906 and Cass Gilbert was delighted, so much so that he asked Pyle to design a much larger panel for his new Essex County Courthouse in Newark, New Jersey. This was another horizontal space, six by twenty feet. The subject chosen was "The Landing of Cartaret." Increasing experience made itself evident. It was a less complicated and more static subject than the previous battle picture, and the design and technique were adjusted more satisfactorily to the architectural volumes of the building's interior. There was much less attempt to convey the myriad incidents of naturalistic lighting, the tonal and color areas were simplified and although realistically drawn, there was a certain muralesque cohesion of design that moved horizontally across the panel. Pyle's ability to cast an aura of conviction that this was just how it might have happened was there, as it was in most of his illustrations. There was general agreement that it was his most successful mural to date.

As he became more immersed in the hopes and possibilities of mural painting, there seem to have developed a succession of tentative plans, hoped-for intended projects, rumors of possible commissions, promises or half-promises from architects and public or institutional authorities. One concrete contract emerged from this multitude of possibilities — the commission to paint five panels for the Hudson County Courthouse in Jersey City, New Jersey.

This project was more ambitious than the others: five panels — three large horizontals and two small verticals — the largest thirty-five by seven feet. The subject matter was again historical. The largest panel depicted "Life in an Old Dutch Town," the two somewhat smaller rectangles showed "Hendryk Hudson and the Half-Moon" and "Peter Stuyvesant and the English Fleet." The small upright panels each presented a single soldier's figure, one English and one Dutch. For this larger assignment Frank Schoonover and Stanley Arthurs were called in as assistants and they transferred the cartoon drawing onto the canvas surface and painted in many of the color areas; in fact, they painted some portions in completely. Pyle gained experience and discovered that mural painting presented more difficulties than he had suspected. He finished with an incomplete sense of satisfaction.

With the completion of the courthouse panels came time for reexamination and decision making. Pyle would have to come to terms dictated by middle age. Old questions, suppressed by the activity of incessant creation, began to work to the surface. Europe — would it be a disillusion or would it renew his forces? Dissatisfied as he was with his mural efforts and with few opportunities to make just comparisons with great mural works in his own country, Pyle craved to see the acclaimed masterworks of the Renaissance and read their lessons.

He had reason to expect more opportunities to paint murals and he was prepared to make a major effort in that direction. His Franklin Street studio was not of a size to accommodate larger decorations, but he had heard of studios and vast high-ceilinged chambers available in Italy for a pittance. Then, too late in life, he was finding himself with meager financial reserves, and Italy was a cheap place to live.

So the arguments went on in his mind, and when he finally shared them with his wife, the plans for the journey took shape. The family began to choose the things necessary for a year's stay. With them would go indispensable Gertrude Brincklé. Arrangements were made for Olive Rush and Ethel Penniwell Brown to rent and live in his studio during the absence. The student studios were also rented. Then, to raise funds, mortgages were placed on both buildings but nothing was said to his wife of this, lest she be alarmed.

Although he counted upon the certainty of mural contracts, he did not burn all bridges behind him. Harper promised to send him illustrative assignments from time to time as he asked for them, and the possibility of writing articles about the old Italian cities was discussed. Gradually all preparations were made for the second major move of his life. On November 22, 1910, the party sailed from New York.

XIII

ITALY — THE LAST YEAR

WHEN PYLE watched the *Sant'Anna* move out from the New York dock, it was probably the first time in many years that there was no immediate task to his hand. No accustomed tools were in his grasp, there were no familiar studio problems for his mind to attack. The old problems that had been kept at bay by creative work now crowded into his disengaged mind.

He was carrying with him the accumulation of a life's experience with its myriad of unanswered questions. Some of these questions were acute and central to his whole nature and professed philosophy. From his early days he had been sharply aware of his native roots. He took pride in his Quaker ancestors and asked nothing better than to celebrate in picture and text the nation they had helped to mold. He had dreamed about an indigenous American art and had preached it, and his convictions had led him into some disparagement of foreign influences. Yet the pull of Europe was clearly visible in his work, and that pull still exerted itself in spite of his ardent patriotism.

He was facing his season of doubt. At this point of no return he looked back to review the crossroads at which, perhaps, he might have taken the other turn. Not an unusual perspective for a reflective older man. But it rankled that Europe's civilization had been experienced only in word and picture. Once in Italy, he would be meeting Europe face to face and with the confrontation went fears. What he encountered might upset some lifetime convictions; yet, at the same time, there was an elusive hope that he might experience a miracle of rejuvenation. He was aware of possible stagnation and concerned that the grooves of habit were too deeply worn and dictating his path.

The money problems which he had always pushed to the back of his mind were now becoming insistent. After many years of extraordinary productivity and excellent income, it seemed incredible that no financial reserve had been built up, but Pyle had been generous and extravagant. He had often said laughingly that when he and his wife went shopping, he invariably chose the most expensive, his wife the most economical items and then they compromised. The block of studios that he had built for his students represented a generous altruistic investment but the school's extraordinary cultural dividends were not negotiable into hard money. His family was large and costly. The children were well educated and two of the boys had entered Yale. The girls were given coming-out parties, and as the Pyles were proud of their friendship with Theodore Roosevelt, young Phoebe was sent down to some of the White House parties. Pyle delighted in his social circle and certain things were expected of him. Economy would have been difficult considering the life he led.

Italy promised a possible escape and solution. Friends who had visited Europe frequently or had lived there had convinced him of the economy of European living, with its abundance of servants and had stressed the advantages of gaining perspective on America.

He meant to keep his concern about money to himself and so made little of it to the family. Certainly he would not have his Wilmington friends know about it. His brother, Walter, was aware of his worries and Pyle relied upon him to keep an active eye upon his affairs while he was gone and to forward to him any incoming monies. Theodore, Howard and Godfrey, the three older sons, remained in America; Phoebe, Eleanor and Wilfrid, the youngest son who was destined for a private school in Switzerland, accompanied their parents. The three older boys were to rejoin the family in the early days of the following summer after the closing of school. Pyle was anxious that the entire family share the new experience.

The *Sant' Anna* was one of the smaller of the French Line steamers, slow and economical. For the children, and the parents too, the voyage was a new and exciting adventure. The steamer stopped in Boston and many returning Italian immigrants trooped aboard and filled the steerage. Pyle became deeply interested in them, saying, "One of the finest things he had ever heard was the way these poor things felt about coming home." The weather was cold and indifferent and seasickness somewhat dampened their spirits, but as they approached the Azores, the weather improved and the air became balmy. There was a welcome opportunity to go ashore at Terceira and Pyle felt better in the warm sun and under the stimulus of new sights. For the children and Gertrude Brincklé, it was the first experience of stepping on a foreign soil — the elder Pyles had only once before left their native land for a short voyage to Jamaica in the early years of their married life.

Gertrude Brincklé's letters and diary notes have documented the trip quite thoroughly. Dec. 4 — Gibraltar. "Poor Mr. Pyle looked so ill, soon went below, his eyes have a blue glassy look; ill two hours in the night. French doctor; Phoebe had enough French to translate symptoms and remedies." Dec. 7 — "Doctor prescribed opium. Mr. Pyle's illness no better. French doctor good. Even a mustard plaster. They even thought of stopping in Naples, but he got up early, with light of determination in his eyes. Rough — passing Sardinia. Floods of rain, circle of light, Naples harbor. I was busy paying bills and tipping. Baggage off, 14 bags and as many trunks."

Pyle's mind was clouded by his unaccustomed illness and he responded only fitfully to the new sights. They went on to Rome by train, but he seems to have looked at Rome (what little he saw of it) with bitter eyes. He wrote to Stanley Arthurs,

As for Rome, I hate it. I was in my room all the time except twice, and when I went out, then I saw the Roman ruins, and not St. Peter's and the great pictures and statues. The "Moses" was the only thing I saw. As for the Roman ruins, they are without shape, weatherworn, and channeled by the rivulets of centuries of rain. They are black in some places and white in others, and are, I think, ugly and disagreeable. I saw nothing beautiful in them, but only the weatherworn remnants of a past and forgotten age.

When he was well enough to travel he and Mrs. Pyle journeyed up to Florence to rejoin the others who were already installed in their pension. Here he began to recover some of his health and his usual spirits but he grumbled about the pension life. He wrote,

> We are just now in a pension or boardinghouse, and I am not very fond of boardinghouse life — in fact, my long domestic life has unfitted me for it. I get along pretty well except at mealtimes and in the evening. At meals we form a part of a long *table d'hote* of uninteresting people, and though they are now more interesting than they were at first, they are not yet thrillingly so. In the evenings we have a very uncomfortable sitting room where the family gathers and where Mrs. Pyle reads to us. But we have now found a furnished apartment which I think will be very nice.

The furnished apartment proved to be a blessing and they came upon it by happy accident. When the children and Miss Brincklé had arrived in Florence, they hired a cab to take them and their baggage to the pension. Crossing one of the squares of Florence, Gertrude had caught sight of an old friend, an American girl, whom she had often visited at Bryn Mawr. Finding an old friend in a strange foreign city gave all of them a sense of security and when the girl introduced them to her uncle, Dr. Charles R. Parke, a resident American physician in the city, one of their major problems was solved for them. The doctor and his family occupied a small palazzo on the Via Garibaldi. The ample third-floor apartment was vacant and was made available to the Pyles. They moved in and were comfortable and, taking into consideration Pyle's poor health, it proved a blessing to have a physician and newfound friend who spoke his language so near at hand.

By the first of the year he was writing more cheerfully,

> We are getting more and more settled here in Florence. We have left the pension and have taken an apartment at 6 Via Garibaldi, which I trust

will be our address for the next year and a half to come. The rooms are very comfortable, and at one time were occupied by Lord Byron when he was here in Florence. We are in the third story of the house, which is not so fashionable as the second, but it suits us admirably.

I have only to say in closing that I think I have entirely recovered from my illness, and I feel better and stronger than I have ever felt; but only blue because I have not yet got a studio, and because I think it will be expensive to get one . . .

With a return of health, his buoyancy returned and he saw things with appreciative eyes. He could write, "I like Florence very much . . ." and "It seems to be a wonderful place . . ." and ". . . the old masters certainly were glorious painters and I take back all that I ever said against them."

To Ethel Pennewill Brown he wrote,

You know I did not think much of the Old Masters, seeing them in black and white, but in color they are so remarkable that I do not see how any human being painted as they did. You stand among them and you feel that you are surrounded by a glow of soft warm ardent colors in which the yellows and browns are the predominating tones and the wonderful blues and crimsons are the relieving note. Two pictures of Botticelli I saw yesterday are the most remarkable pieces of color work that I have ever seen in my life. One of them in particular, a rich, dark gray with a crimson tone is so remarkable a piece of color that I do not think of anything to parallel it. All the time I was there, I kept thinking of my pupils and wishing they could see these pictures. It would be such a great and splendid lesson to them . . .

With the first hint of spring his spirits rose more. "Already the spring is beginning to approach — one feels it in the air. It is not like the spring in America, when the south wind comes up from the Caribbean Islands and makes you think of foreign parts; but it is just a balmy glow that seems to cover and embrace everything."

And to Stanley Arthurs, to whom he wrote quite regularly and who kept him informed of interesting things that were happening in Wilmington, he wrote in late April, "We do not know in America how beautiful fifty generations of culture will make a country. You have to see the surroundings of Florence for that . . ."

In this way he discovered some of the beauty of Europe and came to terms with some of the doubts that had always plagued him. He discarded some of his mistaken notions and frankly admitted his change of heart to several of his favorite students. There are hints in his letters that he began to feel a sense of creative rejuvenation, sparked by his discovery of the glories of Renaissance painting. His talent might have moved into an impressive late flowering had his health held and a challenging mural opportunity presented itself. Both failed him.

The prospect of abundant creative work, both illustration and the writing of articles as a bread-and-butter resource and the alluring opportunity of one or more expansive mural commissions, never became a reality. He had written to Editor Wells of *Harper's* several times outlining themes for possible articles with accompanying pictures but he was disappointed in Wells' intermittent replies — none of the suggestions was approved. Apparently he then turned to Century and Scribner's, again without success.

It is difficult to know upon what facts the mural hopes were based. Certainly there were no contracts; all expectations must have grown from conversations with and letters from various architects, and those verbal and written promises must have been convincing. A letter of June 1, 1911, enumerates these hopes without filling in any details, "There was Post, with his pictures for the West, and there was Hornbostel with his big pictures in Pittsburgh, and there was Schweinfurth in Cleveland and the hotel in Chicago and Gilbert's library in St. Louis and of everyone of these I have had hopes and have had to give them up. The only one that matured has been the Court House at Jersey City, which I lost money in painting."

This steady succession of disappointments depressed a mind already alarmed by unaccustomed ill health. The one commission that came to give him purpose and replenish his diminishing funds was from the Du

Pont Company. They asked for a large panel (it was eventually eighteen feet, three inches wide by fourteen feet high) that would depict a procession of powder-laden Conestoga wagons moving from the Brandywine mills at the time of the War of 1812. Pyle speaks of asking $2500 for the panel, but there is some doubt that he received that much. It turned out well and is a good example of his historical work, painted in a color scheme somewhat akin to the golden glow he had been admiring in the Botticellis and other Renaissance paintings of the Uffizi.

The powder-train picture was painted in the studio he had rented and liked. It was a large, high-ceilinged room with a pleasant garden attached. He used the garden a great deal, to walk in and to paint the Italian models in the sunlight. Finally he induced an Italian carter to drive in his team to pose for the Conestoga wagon horses.

Miss Brincklé's letters itemize the busy but pleasant days when ill health was not nagging Pyle.

Feb. 4, 1911 — We seem to eat a great deal, 2 courses and fruit at lunch, tea at five and a course dinner. Today Mr. and Mrs. Pyle are going to the Bargello, which Mr. Pyle likes the best of everything. We read Tauchnitz editions; long gloves cost only $1.20. Mr. Pyle enjoys teasing the maids, especially Lina, just how he wants his eggs, due minuti mezzo; he will not learn Italian, found that inchiostro is Italian for ink, and adds *ostro* to everything. Feb. 26 — Mr. Pyle's model reluctant to cut off his mustache to pose. March 5th was Mr. Pyle's birthday, he was 58. We three girls gave him a cake, made him a flat wreath of laurel for the table. Parkes in for dinner. Mrs. Pyle and I had low necked dresses. We had truffles for dinner as a delicacy. Mr. Pyle said they tasted like sewer-gas. Mar. 14 — Have been posing all day, am tired; dreadfully bad weather. Mr. Pyle hates it because he wants to paint horses for DuPont Powder wagon in garden. Eleanor reading Pendennis to father at studio. Mar. 27 — Quite social now, so many people have visiting friends, Hopkins, vanWagenens, May, Maynard, Milligans. I have been posing for sketch. Mr. Pyles' DuPont painting just finished. We went to the Davanzati Palace and the Pitti Apartments. The sketch I posed for was to be a present to Dr. Parke. It looks like me only I have not red hair.

The sketch was presented to Dr. Parke to whom Pyle felt greatly indebted. Dr. Parke was not only his physician and landlord but had become a devoted friend. The Parke automobile and chauffeur were often placed at the Pyles' disposal. Mrs. Parke, with a cook and two maids, was frequently performing various kindnesses, making use of her knowledge of Italian to order food, or take care of other needs and, in general, smoothing the way for the strangers.

The Pyles had been looking forward to being reunited with their son, Howard, and enjoying a period of well-being; they had planned to meet him when his ship docked in Genoa. But the summer heat had descended, the train journey was long, tedious and stiffling and Pyle suffered a severe and painful attack of renal colic in Genoa. Only slightly recovered from that, he experienced another on his return. His illness was now diagnosed as Bright's disease, a serious infection of the kidneys. To escape the hot, summertime bowl of Florence, they moved to the Villa Torricella at San Domineo in the hills above Florence and later in the summer they spent several weeks in Siena. Pyle was comparatively well in that hill town above the enervating heat of the plain, and its beauty excited his interest.

But upon their return to Florence he suffered another attack. He lay in a coma much of the time and when that lifted, speech was difficult and his mind was clouded. He died a few days later on the ninth of November 1911.

XIV

FOUR TEACHING DISCIPLES

It was natural that some of Pyle's students should feel an evangelistic impulse to pass his message on to a new generation. Quite a number did just that, but they did it mostly in a peripheral, intermittent way. There were four young men, however, who allied themselves with art institutions and made an important commitment to years of teaching; their classes influenced hundreds of students. Three of them, Walter H. Everett, George Harding and Thornton Oakley, held classes in Philadelphia; one, Harvey Dunn, taught in New York and Leonia, New Jersey.

Philadelphia had attracted an enclave of Pyle students. Quite a number had been native Philadelphians and others had found it a comfortable place to work. The city boasted a fair number of publishers and was within two hours' ride of New York. It had acquired the reputation of having a quiet but appreciative atmosphere — a good place to get work done. The large art student population had been attracted by three important art schools and one or two smaller ones.

Walter Everett was the first of the Pyle students to undertake the instruction of a large class of students in an accredited art school at what was then the Pennsylvania Museum School of Industrial Art. He had studied at the school, bicycling up in the early morning hours from his home in southern New Jersey, riding across the Delaware River ferry and pedaling to Broad and Pine Streets. Later, Everett had entered Pyle's classes at Drexel and had attended some of the Wilmington composition classes. He knew exactly what to expect at the Museum School of Industrial Art, his old alma mater. It had an exceptionally strong faculty. It had been founded in the centennial year of 1876 upon a revolutionary concept for that time — that of building upon a firm base of the arts of design, of teaching students to solve problems in a wide variety of materials and uses, and of grappling with the endless challenges that the industrial revolution could offer to the art of functional design. It looked boldly at the mightiest force of the times, industrialism, in contrast to the regulation fine arts schools, which, except for a few exceptional teachers, paid only lip service to creation and contented themselves with imparting the skills of objective delineation. The Museum School had felt the demand of students for illustrative education, had tried to satisfy it with several routine academic instructors, but none had possessed the ring of authority. Everett had passed through these amateurish hands and, discouraged, he had enrolled with Pyle and had come upon what he needed. So he came into the breach at a needed time, found a group of students (most with more than average ability) eagerly awaiting him and was able to mold many of them into worthy professionals.

Everett was cocky and confident, short but broad and deep-chested, with knotted arms like a wrestler. He had a strongly modeled, dark-skinned, rather handsome and pugnacious face that seemed to threaten bad temper. All this left one unprepared for the eventual discovery that behind this manner was a vein of poetry. Although he possessed all the outward signs of a brusque man of incessant action, he was in his heart a dreamer — a daydreamer, incorrigibly lazy.

Everett was confident of his power to impart his considerable knowledge but he first had to prove it to himself, and he did. There was soon no question about his powers as a teacher. He needed an audience to which he could talk out his dreams and he had found it. His concern about his students was genuine and many of them became his loyal friends. He craved admiration and flattery and that came naturally from most. To the few that did not admire or could not flatter he turned cold.

His teaching routine was founded upon Pyle's with its crux in a weekly session of lecture and criticism of work prepared out of class. He adhered to this basic routine, but conformity to a set schedule bothered him. He was an improviser and his planned schedule often had to adjust itself to the notion of the moment. He was a brilliant demonstrator when the mood was upon him, and his students clustered about eagerly when he picked up charcoal or palette and brush in what was always a breathtaking exhibition of virtuosity. These were the electric intervals that fired the students to emulation and fortified their admiration and confidence. Following the contradictions of his own nature he encouraged them to dream and ponder, to allow their pencil and brush to lead them into graphic adventures. As soon as the first shadow of an impending picture crossed the mind, he urged them to take pencil in hand and lightly, sensitively, move it around the paper, not striving for sharply delineated forms, but tentatively seeking, believing in the intelligence of the fingers, following the behest of the pencil. These musing, half-dreamlike arabesques opened up a new pictorial world to many. It was often possible to glimpse tantalizing possibilities in these linear abstractions and, when clarified and supported by more objective drawing, new compositional conclusions came into being. For some this approach was nonsense, for others it was a fascinating and fruitful exploration into the subconscious.

Everett's own work partook of this sensitive quality. All his best pictures, even those of banal subject matter, had some flavor of an imagined world. His people were believable but not ordinary. Most pictures had their secret place; a tantalizing area where nothing was explicit, but where the eye was coaxed to muse and speculate. He preferred tonal subtleties, close values, edges that were lost and found again.

In spite of the special flavor of his work, he was a sought-after illustrator; in fact, quite a number of editors summoned their utmost patience and tact to get pictures from him. Yet he was difficult, for he hated deadlines. Things were put off until the last moment or beyond it. He loved the long indolent hours of dreaming about the pictures he would paint and when the day of delivery arrived he would go fishing to avoid the insistent telephone calls. Editors, wise in his ways, planned to spend the last twenty-four or forty-eight hours before deadline in his studio while he painted furiously and surely. Miss Dinsmore, art editor of *The Country Gentleman*, got excellent results by bringing her lunch and sewing bag and placidly knitting through the long hours. For once galvanized into action, he was amazingly rapid and certain — a true temperamental virtuoso.

There could have been a steady outpouring of pictures from his studio had he chosen to accept all the commissions pressed upon him and had he not been the victim of his innate indolence. But he was a provocative and exciting teacher to all except the excessively orderly minded and he awakened latent resources in many. His unexpectedness charmed them. For instance, he would dismiss a class suddenly and take them all for a carefree day in the country. He liked to gather a group of those who were closest to him and spend moonlight hours tramping country roads and fields, finding a hilltop from which to watch the sun come up. He left some imprint upon all of his students.

His years at the Pennsylvania Museum School of Industrial Art produced visible and successful results. His classes increased; new students came from distant points. But obvious success only annoyed him. The increasing numbers threatened his relaxation — the art editors, more importuning than ever, hemmed in his horizon. In a claustrophobic moment he resigned from the faculty. But he must have missed his contact with young talent, for a few years later he took over the classes that had been ably conducted by a former pupil of his, Maurice Bower, at the Spring Garden Institute and continued them for several years during the post World War I era.

The Pennsylvania Museum School, now with a considerable enrollment in its Department of Illustration and a reputation as the only possible successor to the Pyle school, was hard put to find a replacement. It inquired among the not inconsiderable number of former Pyle students in the city and finally picked young Thornton Oakley. The school opened a new, large studio-classroom on the third floor over the auditorium below, where the class could be remote from the usual school traffic, and constructed a new tidy office for the new department head. The junior and senior students, mostly resentful of a change, awaited the new regime.

The new instructor was eager but an inexperienced teacher. When he strode into the new studio for his first class, the students were assembled on rows of hard chairs, high stools and in the wide window embrasures — the senior and junior class veterans of Everett's criticisms with some basis for comparisons, the sophomores facing the unknown. Both instructor and audience were expectant and apprehensive. Oakley was large, tall, high-colored, with extraordinary beetling brows and quite unaware that his friendly frown was alarming.

He had rehearsed his lines, but at first the words seemed as though they had come from a textbook. Still, he was naturally fluent and as he warmed to his subject he forgot the script. He had faith fortified by the qualities of both the pedant and the evangelist. His earnestness came through nevertheless, and his doctrine, strange and bewildering upon first hearing, soon struck sparks of excitement into hopeful minds. Some seniors, admirers of their former teacher Everett, and in the cynical stage of their school years, were automatically critical; the juniors were impressed and struggled to sort out their impressions; the sophomores were completely won over.

Somehow, love seemed to be entangled in all the new philosophy. Oakley at the height of his enthusiasm said such things as, "Immerse yourselves . . . love your pictures. Love is the beginning of all masterpieces." To students who were just discovering that picture making was maddeningly arduous and frustrating and who had begun to have severe doubts concerning their innate gifts, these were words of emancipation. The news that art could be conquered by love, seemed radiantly promising to those who had little else to offer.

The opening lecture was succeeded by others, which preceded a criticism of the pictures prepared in out-of-class hours as homework. The pictures were piled on a table beside the instructor's easel and Oakley only elected to speak of the ones that aroused his interest. The students gradually sensed that he preferred those that were bold, sweeping and full of contrast — he had little time for the tonal subleties practiced by the Everett-reared older students. This shift in point of view created a schism in the student body — the pro-Everetts were resentful, although some tried to adjust to the new values; the newcomers were solidly pro-Oakley. The disadvantage of this partisanship was tempered by dividing the large unwieldy class into two critical groups; the pros and antis had to discuss their differences in the lunch and locker rooms.

The first few criticism sessions passed without any particular upset as Oakley selected for comment only those pieces that appealed to him, but the day came when he elected to go through the entire pile. He came to an inept picture by one of the most popular girls in the school, a sweet-hearted, devoted, hard-working girl, completely without talent. The disparity between her ambitions and her abilities had won her the help and sympathy of her classmates. The muddled picture was a fair target and the instructor virtually cut it to ribbons. But the tirade went on and the class became first uneasy, then shocked and embarrassed. When Oakley stopped, he became aware of the girl's sobs and the strangled voice saying, "But I loved the picture so . . . I loved it . . . I loved — it!"

No one could doubt the truth of her words, and the theory that love conquers all in the arts collapsed on the spot. Love did not disappear as a key motif in succeeding sessions, but henceforth its mention was tempered with qualifications that hinted at the true complexities of picture making.

No Pyle student could have admired his mentor more intensely than Thornton Oakley. The younger man stopped scarcely short of idolatry. None could have felt more charged with a sense of mission. Even his dullest student was touched by that. But the passing on of the intangible aura, so much a part of Pyle's approach, escaped his best efforts; the spirit shriveled into the letter, the overtones, the elusive intuitive values were lost in the search for a clean, tight doctrine. The doctrine, unwittingly, began to emphasize the can'ts at the expense of the cans. It finally hardened into a kind of ten commandments, lettered and fastened high on the wall of the composition studio.

The rigidifying process was accompanied by increasing unease among the student body as the whole publication and illustrative climate was changing. In a decade or two the expansion in this area was incredibly rapid. The magazines that had blazed the way for illustration, such as *Century, Harper's* and *Scribner's,* were fading, pushed into the shadow by rampant newcomers, with larger page size, bulk and circulation. Many new illustrators who were more aware of changing tastes and more varied in pictorial response had entered the field. Some of the Pyle landmarks were being obliterated. By this time some of Oakley's own students were professionally active, and he felt a sense of failure as he saw them abandon the formula he expected them to follow and build, each a personal pictorial language.

Oakley taught for over twenty years and some hundreds of students passed through his hands. Acquiescent or rebellious, he left something of himself with every one. His vision was narrow but it was intense, untested by any doubts or self-questioning. He was a personality and had his share of magnetism, but he had none of Pyle's gift for friendly and fatherly concern and never came close to his students. However, he had a high sense of his calling, and his responsibilities as artist-illustrator, and an awareness of illustration's far-reaching powers of communication. His former students have continued to debate his contradictions, the value of his contributions and his unrealized potentials, and he has not been forgotten.

*

A half mile north on Broad Street from the Museum School was a rival enclave of budding illustrators — the venerable Pennsylvania Academy of the Fine Arts, the oldest art school in the land. It had a matchless record of famous former students and had reluctantly aroused itself to respond to the times and opened its atelierlike curriculum to illustrative training. It had reached out and chosen another young Pyle pupil, George Harding, to head the new classes. Harding and Oakley had been easel-to-easel colleagues under Pyle for a number of years, and they were friends — by happenstance, not temperament. Now they were competitors, their rivalry barely concealed beneath the cloak of good manners. The different approaches aroused mutual curiosity and stimulated the students, and since the administrative policing was lax, particularly at the Academy, it was possible, with a certain amount of collaboration, to slip into both men's lectures and enjoy the best of two possible worlds. In this way, a good many young students learned that two teachers trained by the same master might evolve entirely dissimilar interpretations.

Harding's interpretation of his training under Pyle was expressed in terms of his aggressive, hardheaded, no-nonsense temperament. He was lean, muscularly active and impatient. That he had grown into an accomplished picture maker in only a few years was a tribute to Pyle's uncanny ability to discover the responsive chords in a budding artist, for Harding was a questioner and a chip-on-the-shoulder skeptic. But Pyle had released the warmth and imagination concealed behind the outwardly aggressive manner.

Harding's active nature had led him to take on a number of roving, artist-reportorial commissions; from the Grand Banks to Borneo; later he was an artist captain with the first American Expeditionary Force in France. He was a man's artist, at home with movement and muscle. In addition, he possessed a captivating, personal color sense, which never found proper scope in illustration but came into its own in his easel paintings. With it went a native decorative talent which led him into the sustained mural painting of his middle and later years. He had great vitality — in his sixties he took a major's commission to paint the Second World War in the South Pacific sector. Through a long life he was incessantly productive, a constant exhibitor and teacher until his last illness.

He conducted his classes briskly and with decision. He never hesitated to crack the whip, but he was reasonable and sympathetic and adept at getting the students to expect a great deal of themselves. His energy and enthusiasm were communicated to them as well as some of his hard practical sense, his push, will to achieve, his readiness to fight for the next achievement, no matter how small. He was an artist under the shell, but he was continually on guard against sentimentality and emotionalism.

His fame spread and he became an institution at the old Academy like most of his teaching colleagues on its seldom changing faculty. As Pyle had, in early middle age, he saw the possibilities in mural decoration, and how it fitted his innate gifts of color and design. After a few experimental ventures he gave himself over to this activity entirely and so busied himself to the end of his working days. His teaching interests shifted with this change of direction. A new course in mural decoration was created for him and the illustration classes were taken over by Edward Shenton, a former student of his and Oakley's.

The classes of Harding and Oakley ran parallel to each other for almost a quarter-century. For a much shorter time Everett taught at the Spring Garden Institute, so it was at least theoretically possible for an enterprising student to expose himself to three versions of the Brandywine spirit in a single week. It would have even been possible for some to slip over to New York and attend a fourth Pyle-motivated class with Harvey Dunn. This might have been begging for bewilderment, but a thoughtful pupil could have worked out the common denominators.

*

The fact that by the end of World War I, four extremely popular courses in illustration should be thriving, in addition to many smaller ones which were springing up throughout the country with every year, was just another indication of America's insatiable demand for the printed picture.

Harvey Dunn became a teacher by popular demand and for over a decade, he taught what was probably the most crowded class in illustration.

Young, and even older artists, attracted by the sweep and virility of his paintings, sought him out in his Leonia, New Jersey, home and studio. They found the man as commanding as his work and Dunn soon discovered his powers as a teacher. With an artist associate, Charles Chapman, he founded his school. It was in a large old Civil War mansion, surrounded by trees and lawns on the edge of Leonia. The tuition was trifling, only fifteen dollars a month. Many of the men lived in the old house for five dollars a month and cooked for themselves in the kitchen. In the sense that it was more of a dedicated community than a school, it was very like Pyle's Wilmington group.

Dunn came nearest to Pyle's personal mesmerism and possibly even surpassed his master. His height and bulk struck the eye, his rugged, handsome face was volatile, he managed to be both commanding and humble. Grant Reynard, who studied with him and became a lifelong friend, has evoked his presence in these words:

> He was a whale of a man, a veritable pioneer hulk of a man with a head reminding you of a cross between an Indian chief and a Viking. He looked as though he could easily bite a spike in two with one crunch of his broad jaws. You couldn't dress him up in city clothes. But in loose country clothes or a smock he was a king of men . . . It was years before I came to know that he was as gentle as a lamb under that steel frame and as sensitive in emotion as the artist he was. To discover this was like finding lilacs in a boiler factory.

Born near an old buffalo trace on the Dakota frontier, son of a sod house homesteader, Dunn was molded by that country of long horizons. Later in life, after Pyle had shown him other vistas and he had painted pictures of many climes and times, he said, ". . . my search of other horizons has led me around to my first."

He went to the front as a captain of engineers and war artist in World War I. His war pictures, now in the collections of the Smithsonian Institution, are among the most compelling and convincing of the time — "the shock and loss and bitterness and blood of it."

With his students, he had Pyle's gift of instant transference, now on the firm earth beside them, speaking of homely and common things, then off into the blue, somehow finding words to describe the indescribable. He often used the phrase, "The mysterious people," sometimes puzzling his auditors until they discovered he meant the unending mystery of just ordinary people. He sought, as he once said, "to render service to the majesty of simple things." His office was to open minds and hearts rather than teach ways and means, but when a student was truly trapped in an impossible picture, he would take brush in hand and demonstrate the way out. But copying the shape of things, he constantly reiterated, was only a means to an end. As one of his students said, "I had discovered that art was not a reproduction of nature but the picture was a thing born of ideas and creative impulses. Nature was only the dictionary."

When the classes threatened to grow beyond workable size, he accepted the offer of the Grand Central School of Art to join its faculty. Here he was relieved of all problems of space, services and administration, and from this base he reached hundreds of students over the years. Many of these students passed quickly into professional life and found the struggling and confusion in their minds and work brought into sharp focus in remarkably short time. By general consensus Dunn was the greatest teacher of illustration in his era.

During the era after World War I, the twenties and early thirties, he and his former pupils left a mark on American illustration. Among his protégés were Dean Cornwell, Harold Von Schmidt, John Steuart Curry, Grant Reynard, Mario Cooper, Clark Fay, Arthur D. Fuller, Albin Henning, Saul Tepper and J. E. Allen. Most of them adopted, to some degree, the broad-stroked dash of his oil technique. It was a school of masculine vigor, singing color and ample design.

The classes of these four men produced a considerable portion of the illustrative talent of the postwar period. Quite a number of them became teachers in turn, and some of their students became teachers. Four, five and even six generations of teachers have descended from the original

Pyle classes and the same number of generations of artists. Most of that talent has been illustrative, but it would be misleading to conclude that there is an obvious Pyle trademark evident in all their work. Time, change of fashion, the impact of different personalities and the crossfertilization of many influences have worked a myriad of changes in the look of their pictures and the character of their teaching. But at the core of the tradition has been the same concern with human values, the delight in the exercise of the pictorial imagination, the feeling that design should follow the behest of content and the conviction that the illustrator has a power over and a responsibility to his audience.

XV

THE WEB OF INFLUENCE SPREADS

AT THE TIME of his death, the Pyle influence on American illustration was clearly visible and it was to continue to be so for at least another decade. More than threescore Pyle-trained artists were making their marks, and from their ranks would come teachers to set new waves of influence in motion. The important magazine and book publishers employed a particularly high proportion of Pyle followers in their publications and since it was the tendency of many of the students to adopt the master's "manner," largely or in part, the "Pyle look" was easy to identify.

But even as this group worked at their easels and drawing boards, transformations were taking place under their very fingers. Growth, maturity, the impingement of new horizons on their consciousness, all the insistant persuasions of onrushing life were working their will upon their pictures. The Pyle influence was deeply imbedded in each former pupil's nature but it was not to be measured in terms of a Pyle look — these artists were placing the mark of individuality on their work.

Not only were techniques and compositional devices changing, but also subject matter was increasing in diversity and each artist was gravitating toward a field specifically congenial to him. Pyle had had his own favorite subjects, but he had never tried to foist them on others. It was rather routine for him to point out new horizons but he also persuaded some students to discover the magic in the familiarities of their own experiences. Most did. The sea held magic for a number. Anton Otto Fischer

with his youthful sailor days behind him painted the sea in his pictures
through a productive lifetime. Clifford Ashley, brought up on the whaler
and clipper lore of New Bedford and Mattapoisett, gave a great deal of his
time to painting the sea and the New England shores it washed, and in
later life wrote two books about seafaring: *Yankee Whaler* and *The Ashley Book of Knots*. William Aylward was a lifelong student of America's
early maritime and waterways history. He wrote and illustrated many
articles. He was a distinguished watercolorist with a splendid sense of
color and a limpid, brilliant brush. Several series of his colorplates in
Harper's, on early life on the Erie Canal and the sea battles of our young
Navy, have become collector's items.

Others turned in different directions. Thornton Oakley, born in Pittsburgh where he grew up watching the belching steel mills, became a de-
lineator of the industrial scene, capitalizing on the protean, decorative
shapes of smoke and steam, while his mother campaigned against the
smoke nuisance. In later life when Oakley turned to making pictures for
the texts of his wife's travel books, he experimented with a pen technique
founded on Pyle's heavy-line style.

Many of the students had been touched by the inevitable fever of the
western frontiers — the romance of the Indian, trapper, cowboy and
homesteader. For some, like N. C. Wyeth, this yearning for the West
had been a passion of their early years and resulted in some striking pictures. By his thirties, Wyeth had worked out of his early enthusiasm and
was beginning the historical and legendary paintings for which he became
famous. For William Henry Koerner, the West was the subject of almost
all his life's work. He delineated it faithfully and competently, with less
conscious drama than most, but probably with more truth to the day-by-
day monotony and matter-of-factness of reality. Philip Goodwin was
not a western specialist, but since he was an excellent portrayer of animal
life and the outdoor hunt, inevitably some of his scenes were laid west of
the Mississippi. Of all of them, it was Harvey Dunn who painted the
deep-down West, the stark poetry of the Dakotas. His childhood in a

prairie sod cabin had impressed upon him the wonder and terror of those endless open miles. This wonder filled him to bursting and picture making was his release. It pulled out of him his deepest memories and longings.

Edward Wilson, with his great facility, was equipped to deal with a wide variety of subject matter, and for years his adaptability made him a much sought-after artist in the advertising field. When he published his book, *Iron Men and Wooden Ships*, with its bold, rollicking pictures in flat-color woodcut technique, he attracted wide attention in the book world. From that time he devoted more attention to book illustration and his steady contributions to the classics of the Limited Editions Club have assured him a place as one of our finest romantic book illustrators.

Frank Schoonover, whose early work closely followed the Pyle pattern, made two trips through the north country of Canada and one to the bayous of Louisiana. These new experiences not only gave him fresh material but loosened and broadened his brushstroke and introduced more impressionistic color into his paintings. One of the most prolific of illustrators, a steady stream of pictures poured from his studio for years, and his productivity showed no abatement when he abandoned illustration for easel painting. He held classes, too, in his studio and taught many amateur painters. The younger and more gifted students he urged into accredited art schools for day-by-day training.

A number followed closely in the footsteps of Pyle throughout their lives. Three of them made important contributions to historical documentation. All three were avid students of our past and became as authoritative in their knowledge as many professional historians. Two, Stanley Arthurs and Clyde DeLand, expressed themselves almost entirely in paint, although Arthurs wrote some descriptive articles. Both were competent draftsmen. DeLand moved steadily and faithfully along the road of journeyman competence, while Arthurs, although uneven, had a restrained sense of drama and mood, and at his best his pictures had a quiet impressiveness. Many of his pictures, with accompanying text, were gathered together in a handsome volume, *The American Historical Scene*, and it is a summing up of a dedicated and useful life. The third artist, John Walcott Adams, with New England history in his bloodstream, formed his technique upon Pyle's fine-line, open-hatchwork pen style. His research was just as authoritative as that of Arthurs and De-Land but his pen imparted an ingratiating bustle and sparkle to his drawings. Whenever possible he depicted crowds of figures, characterful, natural and engaging. He presented the lessons of history as vignettes of ordinary life without trumped-up theatricality or self-conscious posing.

The women artists, with a few exceptions, give the impression that they formed a consistent school somewhat different from the men. A study of a large group of their work reveals, readily enough, that the paintings had been done by individuals, but the characteristics they had in common leap to the eye more readily than their differences. Their almost unfailing sense of the decorative, a shared technique and their natural inclination toward feminine, homely, reposeful subjects are there in almost every picture. Almost all had the gift of graceful draftsmanship with no inclination toward anatomical braggadocio. Almost all of them played small variations on the same basic technique. These women artists saw shapes largely in terms of line, and a linear arabesque formed the skeleton of their designs. Into this framework they introduced some reticent modeling (all this in charcoal). With a firm spray of fixatif, such a technique sufficed for monochromatic reproduction. For color reproduction, washes of transparent watercolor were brushed over the drawing and often some color and a few highlights were added in gouache.

Their imaginations were not notably engaged by our early history, our West, or the themes of mythology and legend. Some of them, having passed their childhood days in a late-Victorian climate, celebrated that time in their pictures, but mainly they portrayed the early years of our century. A collection of their pictures spread before us is a lesson in nostalgic charm. They make accessible the world of temperate emotions, grace and manners, the ample contours of feminine fabrics, the unharassed life. It is a record that unwittingly has become historical. We need it to complete our own perspective of that time.

Just the sound of their names calls up the kind of persons they were and from whence they had come — Elizabeth Shippen Green, Ethel Pennewill Brown, Ethel Franklin Betts Bains and her sister Anna Whelen Betts, Eleanor Crownfield, Frances Rogers, Olive Rush, Violet Oakley, Jessie Wilcox Smith, Sarah Stillwell Weber, Bertha Day, Wuanita Smith, Charlotte Harding, Margaretta Hinchman and others.

Their common interests, enhanced by similar backgrounds, are evinced in the close, often lifelong, friendships they formed with each other. Three friends of the Drexel Institute days, Elizabeth Shippen Green, Violet Oakley and Jessie Wilcox Smith shared the same studio in their early days, and then built their homes and studios nearby when prosperity came to them. Elizabeth Shippen Green became known for her early work in the *Ladies' Home Journal, The Saturday Evening Post* and a number of illustrated books. Later she had a contract for exclusive illustration with Harper. Her work was highly regarded and rightly so — it was work of distinction. She had also studied with Thomas Eakins and his probity shone through her drawing. Her work was strong but gracious, winning in what it revealed of human characteristics and always dominated by the need to weave a notable design.

Jessie Wilcox Smith's pictures bore many superficial similarities to those of her friends — she used the same basic technique, the considerable reliance upon the defining line, the tendency toward simple, flattened tones and colors, the general use of simple and conventional lighting. Her whole reputation was built upon her depiction of children and her treatment of this subject matter almost always expressed an affinity for a previous Victorian age. Her children were remote from sweat, dirt and savagery — dream younglings living in a world of improbable decorum.

Violet Oakley's early gifts were obvious and exceptional, and she was working hard at odds and ends of illustration while still attending classes. Her work matured rapidly, for she had natural deftness with a number of mediums and her draftsmanship was distinguished. Her early illustration was much of a piece with that of her colleagues but early on she set her sights on high goals. She developed a concern with philosophies and religions and searched for humanity's common denominators. Her pictures, conspicuously decorative, moved more and more away from the topical toward the universal. She yearned for size and large statements. Mural design was the obvious answer. A series of smaller commissions prepared her for the years which she would devote to the major project of her life — the extended series of decorations for the Pennsylvania State Capitol at Harrisburg. Throughout a long prolific lifetime her concern with messages remote from the whim and caprices of fashion saved her from much of the changing trends that created problems for her illustrator friends.

Charlotte Harding was the fourth of the young Philadelphia women to come from the early Drexel classes. She, too, had the decorative bent and indulged it with more freedom and daring than most. She searched out many an unhackneyed rhythm in her pictures — strange shapes and patterns delighted her and she worked out new ways of seeing the humdrum world. Unfortunately her strong sense of originality was handicapped by poor health.

The younger members of this large group generally followed the same pattern. It may be assumed that this predilection toward the decorative was innate, and that it received encouragement from Pyle, despite his deprecation of this particular gift in his later years. But it is highly likely that the pattern emerged partly because of mutual influence. The pressure of a teacher's style upon his pupils is obvious to all; what is seldom taken into account is the influence of pupil upon pupil, particularly the older upon the younger. Even experienced teachers may be surprised by the emergence of a class style that will sometimes fade, sometimes persist into maturity. Throughout the group there were echoes of this — variations on a basic tendency as in the magazine covers of Sarah Stillwell Weber, the fairylike compositions of Anna Whelen Betts and Ethel

Franklin Betts Bains, and the stylish pictures of everyday life by Frances Rogers. With the coming of the flapper age many of these able artists found themselves out of tune with the times. They were very susceptible to a change of climate. They looked at the caricature revelations of John Held, Jr., and saw the shapes of a new age.

There was a natural dispersal of the Pyle-trained artists in the years immediately after his death as they worked to find their niches in the world of painting, teaching and illustration. Since illustration was the goal of most, it was necessary for them to be in touch with New York, the publication hub of the country, so many moved there. But Philadelphia and Wilmington were within reasonable commuting distance, and so, the greater number of Pyle's former pupils set up their studios in or near one of the three eastern seaboard cities.

The Wilmington enclave was a closely knit circle. All the artists knew each other, had worked together and shared a common admiration and sense of indebtedness. Over the years the group accomplished many things and as attrition set in, it acquired new adherents. At the center was Mrs. Pyle and her grown children. There was a large group of close friends and admirers, professional and businessmen, and collectors of Pyle's work. There was Gertrude Brincklé, the devoted secretary and close family friend, and the two loyal former students, Stanley Arthurs and Frank Schoonover, whom Pyle had depended upon for so many things. Arthurs, preparing to paint a large decoration for the Delaware Capitol at Dover, needed a larger studio and rented that of his teacher. There he worked for the remaining years of his life, keeping the place almost unchanged and showing it willingly to interested visitors. Schoonover, consulted by Samuel Bancroft for his project of building a row of artist's studios on a high lot on Rodney Street, moved into the large double studio at the far corner of the building and there held his classes, painted his illustrations and landscapes and drew the cartoons for his stained glass windows. In nearby studios were Herbert Moore, Percy Ivory, Charles McClellan, Charles De Feo, Gayle Hoskins, Howard E.

Smith and others, and just over the state line, in nearby Chadds Ford, was N. C. Wyeth and his growing family.

The unity and energy of this Wilmington group produced a series of major accomplishments. The result of several meetings held shortly after Pyle's death was the formation of the Delaware Art and Library Association. Immediately the new Association made plans for a large retrospective show of Pyle's work. It was held in the ballroom of the Hotel Du Pont and opened on March 13, 1912. It was crowded daily beyond expectations. The evening paper headlines read:

GREAT CROWD VIEWS PICTURES

About 10,000 Saw the Howard Pyle Art
Collection During Yesterday

MANY COULDN'T GET IN

Contributions for the purchase of a permanent collection of Pyle's work came in so rapidly that by November of the same year the Association had become the owner of forty-seven paintings and thirty pen drawings. These, together with examples of the work of many former students, were shown in another large exhibition at the Hotel Du Pont in November of 1912. Realizing Wilmington's need for a museum and proper exhibition facilities, the Association changed its name and incorporated as the Wilmington Society of the Fine Arts. Lacking a home it confined itself, at first, to annual exhibitions of the work of Pyle and his former pupils. Later it extended its shows to include Delaware artists and later still to out-of-state members and invited guest artists.

In 1923 the large new Wilmington Institute Free Library, fronting on Rodney Square, was completed and the Association acquired the space of three rooms on the second floor for its home. Now it could expand its activities with a continuing series of varied exhibitions. The Pyle collection had grown by gifts. The society had met a need in the area and it grew steadily. In 1931, the estate of Samuel Bancroft, Jr., offered the society a plot of land on Kentmore Parkway with a provision to endow a gallery wing in a proposed museum building to house the Bancroft Collection of Pre-Raphaelite paintings and memorabilia. On June 5, 1938, the Delaware Art Center was opened. Besides the Bancroft Pre-Raphaelite wing and a large central gallery for transient exhibitions, there was a Howard Pyle wing housing the now very large Pyle Collection. At last it had found a permanent home. It had become by far the most important and complete collection of its kind — a mecca for Pyle enthusiasts. The only other considerable assemblage available to the public is the Thornton Oakley Collection in the Central Free Library on Logan Square in Philadelphia. There are still many Howard Pyle pictures in private collections in the Wilmington and Brandywine area; the largest, and second only to the Art Center Collection, is that of Howard Brokaw, a grandson of Howard Pyle.

Under the directorship of Miss Constance Moore, a friend since childhood of the Pyle family, the Art Center grew and expanded its activities. The Wilmington Academy of Art, working in its basement classrooms, grew to fill the large modern educational wing which now houses it. The Center devoted more and more time to educational activities for the public and private school children. When Miss Moore retired in November of 1957, she had the deep satisfaction of knowing she had nursed the Center with its museum and school through its beginning years and had seen it reach a robust maturity. She was succeeded by Mr. Bruce St. John who has guided its steady progress and has planned for its future enlargement. The Center has been the rallying point for the arts in the lower reach of the valley and with its junior sister organization, the West Chester Art Association, not only have the valley artists been supported and the past preserved but there has been a steady succession of outside exhibitions of all media and trends.

Between 1921 and 1925 four important books on Howard Pyle and his work appeared. Willard S. Morse, a longtime friend of Pyle and collector of his work, and Gertrude Brincklé, under the sponsorship of the Wil-

mington Society of the Fine Arts, undertook the arduous task of compiling a bibliography of all Pyle's works, writings, paintings, murals and
illustrations. It was completed and published in 1921; *Howard Pyle, A
Record of his illustrations and writings*, an invaluable book of reference.
Four years later, young Charles D. Abbott expanded an earlier essay and
thesis into a full-length biography. *Howard Pyle — A Chronicle* is notable for the many letters quoted in the text. It was written with the help
and approval of Mrs. Pyle, and Abbott was able to consult many of the
family, friends and associates who are no longer alive.

Two other books, anthologies of Pyle's work, appeared at about the
same time. In 1921 Harpers published *Howard Pyle's Book of Pirates*, a
compilation by Merle Johnson of Pyle's pirate stories and pictures. It was
copiously illustrated, of course, the pictures being reproduced from the
old plates. It was an immediate success in every way and led to the second
compilation in 1923 of *Howard Pyle's Book of the American Spirit* in
which most of Pyle's pictures of Early American history were reproduced. These two books constitute a gallery of two of the most important sectors of Pyle's work. They are the most convenient and concentrated way of studying the Pyle picture making, but they are collector's
items and difficult to come by.

In a few years the Pyle students found their way to many parts of the
country in pursuit of their interests, but besides Wilmington, the other
important concentrations were in Philadelphia and New York. Philadelphia and Wilmington were close enough for the two groups to keep in
close touch. The artists of both cities exhibited in each other's shows, the
Wilmington illustrators often came up to see the book publishers and Curtis Publishing Company's editors and the Philadelphia artists staged a
memorial show of Pyle's work and held a symposium of speakers in his
memory in 1923. Most of the Philadelphians clustered in the older, rook-
ery buildings of the central city — Wuanita Smith and Richard Blossom
Farley facing Washington Square, Walter Everett and Clyde DeLand in
the old Baker building, George Harding and Thornton Oakley in the

more tidy Fuller building before they moved to the suburbs, and Margaretta Hinchman in her ample studio in the trim old brick house on Walnut Street. Three old friends built houses close by on the slope above the narrow, wooded Cresheim valley. Violet Oakley reigned in her high, impressive studio filled for so many years with the huge canvases for her Pennsylvania Capitol murals. It is now the Violet Oakley Memorial Foundation, a repository for her abundant work. A stone's throw down the road was Jessie Wilcox Smith's house and studio and Elizabeth Shippen Green (Elliot) and her husband Huger Elliot, some years later, built partway down the slope. In nearby Germantown were Katherine Richardson Wireman, Sarah Stillwell Weber, Ethel Franklin Betts Bains and Anna Whelen Betts. Out beyond Philadelphia, in Chester County, Henry Soulen built his studio beside his plastered stone farmhouse.

The New York group never enjoyed the same cohesion as the Philadelphians or Wilmingtonians. Many alighted there briefly, only a few made it their home. Harvey Dunn remained across the river in Leonia, New Jersey, with the long summers spent in his beloved Dakotas. Douglas Duer, Harry Townsend, Remington Schuyler, Thornton Skidmore, Edward Wilson, Balfour Ker and Ernest Peixotto were among the large group that had studios in or near to New York for varying periods of time. William Aylward, a suburban resident, taught for a number of years at the Newark School of Art.

So the web spread. It was a visible force in the magazine and book fields, less significant in the rapidly expanding area of advertising. By the second quarter of the century it was noticeably altering its look in natural response to the changing times. New trends, new techniques and viewpoints came flooding in, modifying and being modified. The many graduates of the large classes of Dunn, Everett, Oakley and Harding were becoming a noticeable influence in illustration by the 1930's. Artists like William Emerton Heitland, Dean Cornwell, Saul Tepper, Rudolph Pott, Edward Shenton, Grant Reynard, Henry Pitz, Katherine Milhous, Marguerite deAngeli, Maurice Bower, Harold Von Schmidt, Harry Morse

Myers, Steven R. Kidd, Frank Street, Ralph Pallen Coleman, Mario Cooper and others were forging reputations. Color was more widely used, magazine pages were becoming larger and, probably galvanized by the adventurous layout experiments of the growing advertising field, the whole concept of magazine and book design was beginning to experience rejuvenation.

As the second quarter of the century moved on, the first generation of *Pyle* teachers retired, one by one, and a second took their places. Harvey Dunn was succeeded by his student Dean Cornwell, who in his turn influenced some hundreds of young illustrators and painters. At the Pennsylvania Academy of the Fine Arts, Edward Shenton took over the illustration classes from his teacher George Harding and some years later taught the same subject at the Moore College of Art. At the Philadelphia College of Art, Thornton Oakley gave way to his former pupil, Henry C. Pitz.

During these years, through the midcentury and into its third quarter, the enrollment in most art schools increased considerably and courses in illustration proliferated. Illustration was a popular subject because it was one of the few art disciplines that seemed to offer a rewarding livelihood. In addition it held the promise of reaching a large audience and to many it seemed a somewhat romantic profession. Finally, when more and more art training stressed the nonrepresentational, it offered scope for those whose talents inclined toward figurative delineation. During the past decade, in the face of a decreasing demand for pictorial illustration in the magazine and advertising fields, the illustration courses have become a training ground for television designers and directors, motion-picture animators, industrial illustrators and an increasing number of children's book illustrators.

All this seems a far cry from the illustration of Pyle's day. And yet the more recent revolutions have been no more drastic than those of his own time, which encompassed the transition from the wood engraving to the photomechanical processes and the simultaneous rapid development of color reproduction. Modern illustration has been an art of change. Although there has been a remarkable chain of artists and teachers descending from Pyle, who have influenced many others by their pictures, teaching and in some cases writings, it must be clear that this has not been a routine transmission of formal doctrine. There was no doctrine to begin with, only a communication of the excitement of pictorial creation. Pyle's original enthusiasm opened wide the door to several vistas; the penetration into man's character, the observation of and delight in the endless repertory of attitudes his body takes, the wonder in and study of nature's forms and moods, the involvement with the nation's early history, the imagination-stirring knowledge of the myths and legends of the race. These were the things central to Pyle's own interests and the majority of his students were captured by the glimpses they caught of these vistas. Inevitably many discovered vistas of their own and their mature work often departed markedly from the Pyle look.

At the present time, there are no Pyle students teaching and only a few who were the students of Pyle's students. But there is a considerable group of a third and fourth generation of the Pyle line in many of America's art schools and some private classes. Some of the familiar names are Albert Gold, Mario Cooper, Joseph Krush, Beth Krush, John Geiszel, Isa Barnett, Grant Reynard, Steven R. Kidd, Howard Woerner, William Erwin, John Forster and Andrew Theis. Although the obvious Pyle look has almost disappeared from American illustration, its influence is there in less readily recognizable ways and the tide of favor is now turning toward it again.

XVI

NEWELL CONVERS WYETH

THE SEEDS that Pyle planted were potent — few were completely wasted, many had their modest blooming, and some bore extraordinary fruit. When he first interviewed the strong young New Englander Newell Convers Wyeth before the crackling fireplace logs in his studio, his immediate instincts told him that here was superior metal. As the boy answered his questions, he grew more certain. He liked what he saw and what he heard.

Young Wyeth came away from that interview walking on air. He had found Pyle to be all that he had expected and more. He was accepted as a student on trial. He kept repeating Pyle's cautionary words over and over to himself, "My work showed promise and was practical; he emphasized that hard work, constantly applied and the living of a simple life were the two things that would bring about my making." Once back to earth he found a studio to share with a fellow student, Philip Hoyt, for a dollar a week. He next found a room for two dollars and board for four: he thought a budget of thirty dollars a month might be stretched to cover everything but clothes and materials.

He fell into his new life gratefully and easily. His new classmates stimulated him, for their high talents were obvious. Here was a new level of attainment to reach for. There was a bracing atmosphere of dedication and work, and he liked the sense of competition. The students were friendly and helpful too. Two of them, Clifford Ashley and Henry Peck, were his own friends. They had been his classmates at the Eric Pape

School of Art in Boston, had preceded him into the Pyle group and it was their glowing accounts that had spurred him into making the journey to Wilmington for the interview. He liked the town and particularly the country that lay behind it. His new friends showed him the roads and paths that crisscrossed the valley and by tramping them he discovered Chadds Ford and its rounded hills with the old stone houses. The valley contained so many small, intimate monuments of earlier days that he could scarcely be oblivious of a comforting feeling of continuity. He sensed, from the first day, a kinship with the region and a stimulus from the legend that had formed around it. The valley had worked a spell. There was promise there — material for a creative mind. The sights and sounds, the echoes of its early history at every turn of the road, its clan of eager artists, were part of the air of expectancy that opened a door into an empire of the imagination — all this expressed what has come to be recognized as "The Brandywine Tradition." Here Wyeth planned to send down his roots. Over the course of his daily walks with assorted friends along the valley road up to Chadds Ford, he soon set the school record for covering the distance — one and a quarter hours.

Pyle soon pieced together the background of this eager, gifted boy who had walked in for his interview on his twentieth birthday. On his father's side he came from an old Massachusetts family that had included many Harvard men, and reached back to the early settlers' days. His mother was a daughter of John Denys Zirngiebel, a Swiss horticulturist who had studied with Louis Agassiz. There had been artists in the Zirngiebel family in Switzerland and young Wyeth felt that he had inherited his early passion for drawing from them; it was his mother rather than his father who had encouraged his talent.

The Wyeth acres in Needham ran down to the banks of the winding Charles River, and there were meadows, fields and woodlands around the house for a child to explore. There were three brothers for playmates. Young Newell drew them and the family, the water, trees and all the things around him. As he grew a little older, he discovered the polo field at nearby Karlstein, and presently he earned a local reputation for his drawings of horses. As he moved through his middle and later teens he attended first the Mechanic Arts High School, then the Massachusetts Normal Art School and finally the Eric Pape School of Art.

That schooling provided a solid foundation for his work with Pyle. He could draw well, not only from the posed model but also from his imagination and retentive visual memory, and his figures had bounce and motion. Crayons, ink, brushes and pigments were already old friends. He was ready for the enlarging experience of Wilmington and the Pyle group. In this apprentice time he grew like corn in the night.

He fell naturally into the pattern of long hours of concentrated work, drawing and painting from the model, constructing imagined heads in a wide range of types and expressions and putting his best into the compositions to be submitted at the weekly criticism meetings. His first composition was a New England haying scene, a familiar theme since childhood, and it aroused Pyle's interest and that of the class. He found that the outdoor days of his childhood were an unexpected treasury of memories that he could pillage for countless subjects. Then too, he was beginning to sense the possibilities in Pyle's passion for the Early American background.

Like almost every American boy of his time, his head was filled with a kaleidoscope of cowboys, Indians, trappers and homesteaders, prairie schooners, trading posts, galloping horses and long-horned cattle. He had had no direct experience of the West, but its images had been planted in his mind by Remington, Catlin, Shirlaw, Zogbaum and other picture makers of the West, by magazine stories, dime novels and photographs. Blessed with volatile imagination, he felt himself bursting with inexhaustible ideas for pictures. In a letter to his parents he describes one of his subjects:

> My composition today was two boy Indians, naked, cautiously climbing up over a rock which looked over a deep black hole of water at the sharp turn of a winding brook. Everything is dark save two bright

glimmers of evening sky which are shown through the dark mysterious woods which form the background. One of the Indians has a fish spear uplifted, ready to dart into the transparent water upon any trout that happens to be lurking there, the other boy is told by a gesture to hold back.

It was undoubtedly this sort of picture that he took with him when he returned to Needham for the Christmas holidays. As he was aggressive and had a native sharp eye for opportunity, he wanted to experience some contact with the mysterious world of publishing, which would have such a command over his future. He stopped over in New York and carried his portfolio around to a number of publishers. He came from the art editors' offices exhilarated and much more secure about his illustrative ability. They had treated him as a serious professional, and he had a manuscript in his pocket from a magazine prophetically named *Success*. He had a great deal to tell the family in Needham.

Shortly after his return to Wilmington a color sketch of a broncobuster he had submitted to the Curtis Publishing Company in Philadelphia was approved and he settled down to make a finished painting of his first important commission. A few months later a Wyeth *Saturday Evening Post* cover was on newstands across the country and he was doing his best to dissemble his pride in the face of the congratulations of his fellows.

Pyle was both happy and apprehensive for his new student. He probably feared that Wyeth might become overconfident and smug — perhaps the boy was rushing ahead into professionalism before all the foundations were secure. So he prescribed a cessation from all professional effort for a while and suggested that Wyeth concentrate on disciplined drawing from cast and model.

This monotonous grind curbed the youngster's jubilation and posed a test for his impulsive nature, but he had a strong will; he gritted his teeth and slaved away. This was the response that Pyle wanted to see. In a few months he told the boy that his period of trial was over, he was a full-fledged member of the H.P.S.A. (Howard Pyle School of Art) and eligible to wear its gold and red button in his lapel. He released him from the ban on professional work and the young enthusiast could go back to painting the images that had been teasing his brain.

Not all Wyeth's hours were spent at the easel. His explosive muscles and exuberant nature had to express themselves in other ways and he was not the only energetic one in that highly charged company. Games and horseplay, the long walks over the hills, the swimming and skating with the Brandywine so close at hand, sleighrides, hayrides, pranks, parties and practical jokes were all healthy escapes from the hours at the easel.

All these experiences were the stuff of growing up. It was a period of rubbing up against both people and ideas, taking part in arguments, colliding with other doctrines, hearing new names and seeing new pictures, coming alight with new enthusiasms. He got to know the picture collections in Philadelphia at the Academy and Memorial Hall, and he came upon the impressionist landscapes of the New Hope group which later influenced his outdoor color schemes. His progress was rapid and he was winning his colleagues' respect. In the meantime commissions were beginning to come in and he was able to send some money back home and save a little.

These were happy days that he remembered always — there were the daylight hours of concentrated painting and drawing, the relaxation as the skylight overhead darkened, the expectation of Pyle's hand on the knob and the talk, spurred by the mood of the moment. These conversations at dusk left a deposit in the mind that could be mulled over as Wyeth walked to his boardinghouse through the winter streets.

Like hundreds of other young artists he couldn't get cowboys and Indians out of his head, but he found himself making pictures of a West he had never seen. Pyle's insistence on firsthand, immersed knowledge had sunk in and Wyeth discovered he couldn't be happy about such picture making until he had seen the land with his own eyes. His savings were meager but he thought he could manage the trip to the West. He left for a Colorado ranch. He was an excellent horseman and was able to take part in a roundup and the hundred and one chores of cattle-raising. The days in the saddle, squinting at new horizons, soaking up the life of the cowhand, filled his retentive pictorial memory with a crowd of images.

Most of his small store of money was stolen, but dismaying as this was, in the end it seemed an advantage. He was forced to take employment, and so when he moved south to a Navaho reservation in New Mexico he paid his way by becoming a mail-rider. This made him feel as though he were a participant in the life of the West not merely a spectator; he felt his future pictures would ring more true.

His visit to the West was one of his most fruitful experiences. He came back, his head crammed with impressions, his portfolio filled with drawings. In a relatively short time he had absorbed a great store of animated impressions upon which he drew for years. The immediate result was an article for *Scribner's Magazine* on western sheepherding accompanied by some excellent pictures. The article attracted a good deal of attention and a series of western pictures followed as the art editors became aware of this young ebullient talent. These pictures were virile, but they were subtle too. Most were painted from the warm earth-color range of the palette; the rainbow hues of the impressionists were still in the future for Wyeth. He was now able to project a mood, to use the fugitive effects of outdoor light to create electrifying patterns of tone. Pyle had opened his eyes to the mystery of shadows, and his own observations had taught him the dramatic effect of stray shafts of sunlight.

Although he was still to work with Pyle until he was told he was a graduate, he now had a rising reputation in the publishing world. He was no longer an apprentice, but a well-rounded, practicing illustrator. With a steadily increasing income, he now felt that his father should be reimbursed for the expense of his education. He wrote to him that he hoped to accomplish this during the following year and in passing he confessed a certain extravagance: "Costumes and material. I have a chest of military costumes that is invaluable to me and is the envy of H.P. himself."

Pyle not only envied the costume collection but possibly certain of Wyeth's characteristics as an artist as well. They had many things in common, yet their natures were divergent. With Wyeth, thought and action were usually instantaneous and simultaneous. Pyle's emotions worked through layers of Quaker reticence, although a sudden explosion of temper was not impossible. He was the older, of course, by almost thirty years and the grooves of creation were well worn. Wyeth was impetuous and young, impatient with preparation, inclined to the headlong attack. Pyle's was a steadying and helpful influence.

Both possessed the two-pronged ability to scrutinize with a sharp, perceptive eye the shape, weight and texture of the concrete objects in our daily lives, and to give scope to that sweep of fancy that invests these things with significance and glory. The fusion of the scrupulous eye and imagination was their common gift. Wyeth needed a little more time to master this. As Pyle moved into his later years the evidence of his writings and pictures indicates that the scrupulous eye was assuming the ascendancy over the imagination. Wyeth, in his last years, was still searching for a more perfect fusion of the two elements. It is certain that he was working for effects just out of reach up to the point of his death.

Wyeth's life was a continuing search. His bounding optimism had its reverse side — he had his moments of despair. From the first days in Wilmington he sent a steady stream of letters home to his parents and brothers, and most of them have been saved. The letters make up an intimate chronicle of his daily life and work, and he seems to hold nothing back. The reader sees him as he rides on the crest of a wave or drops into the trough. He flays his weaknesses and cheerfully boasts of his triumphs. There is no sparing of himself, sincerity rings through. He is sharply critical of his own work and motives and constantly challenging himself to do better.

In one of his letters to his mother he mentions casually an event that was to bring about a major change in his life. He speaks of plans for a sleighing party and for going to church: "I met a Miss Bockius the other day and she being a Unitarian asked me to go. I accepted with pleasure."

This casual meeting turned out to be the prelude to love, complete and final. For about a year Wyeth's letters were strangely silent on the subject of Miss Bockius, but the young pair had decided to wait until N.C.'s work had moved ahead another step and the bread-and-butter problem was solved. Apparently the solution came shortly after a year, for on the evening of April 16, 1906, Carolyn Bockius and Newell Convers Wyeth were married in the First Unitarian Church of Wilmington.

For a short time they remained in town but they had set their heart on the country, and when they found a suitable house to rent they moved out into the Brandywine hills at Chadds Ford. N.C. now had open land at his doorsill and he was happy. He could spend exhausting long hours in the studio and still feel the need to tramp the hills. And he needed the feel, smell and look of the woods and fields. It was second nature to him to scan the outdoors with a pictorial eye, sniff the wind and anticipate change on his very skin. This closeness to nature crept into his pictures. His letters almost always contain a mention of weather and the outdoors. On a wintry, seven-below-zero day he wrote, "I walked to Sugar Loaf in the evening and came nearer to freezing certain protruding features of my face than ever before. When I got back my face felt like a mask I could take off and hang in a closet."

Wyeth was never an armchair painter. He was on his feet all the time and moving. He favored large canvases and broad brushes. He needed to back off from his canvas, squint and evaluate, advance and place a deft stroke. Those outside the studio could hear the steady, heavy pacing back and forth. He covered miles in a day. Usually his brush strokes were swung from the shoulder, occasionally for a small, crisp detail he used the steadiness of a mahlstick. He needed room to maneuver and his pictures reflected it.

Many of his illustrations were painted in two or three days, sometimes in one. A small, quick pencil sketch or two usually sufficed to crystalize the important factors of a problem. Then his emotions rose to a peak of creation and his painter's hand worked with resourcefulness and authority. Like all ranking artists he had a brain in his fingers. His drive and facility were the admiration and envy of his colleagues. One of them, Thornton Oakley, said, "I am in despair over my own work when I see how easily and fluently Convers works on his pictures."

Instinctively the imagination that ignited his pictorial conceptions, communicated itself to his entire frame, all his senses. The sense of pulse and motion that is so apparent in most of his pictures was a natural transfer of the impulsive movements of his own strong body. He *felt* his pictures in every fiber, a feeling that reached down his long arms, through the knowing fingers and on to the canvas. He was becoming a master manipulator of light and shadow. His years of keen observation of nature's world had amassed a great repertoire of effects, upon which he could draw at will. He liked to revel in the unending dialogue between the secrecy of mysterious darks and the jeweled shimmer of sudden lights. These patterns, with their first impact upon the receptive eye, arouse great expectations. The mind is awakened to the possibility of revelations — the movement of figures, the clash of emotions, the exposition of character, of textures, shapes and rhythm — all the factors of a narrative picture.

He was attracting a large audience hungry for his inspirations. The publishers were aware of that hungry audience and they sought him out. He was in the happy position of being offered more work than he could undertake; he could refuse the less appealing commissions. He was a colorist and fortunately for him the era was ripe for color illustration. Four-color process reproduction was now an accustomed and widely used method. The advertisers had seized upon it and the magazine editors had to use it more and more lavishly on the editorial pages in order to keep pace with the advertising pages. The use of color was spreading rapidly in book illustration too. The illustrator was caught in an era of quick change and of keen competition as well. American illustration was different from what it had been in Pyle's early days. The sheer quantity of pictorial wealth that was displayed in America's publications was several times what it had been a generation before. The variety and versatility of its expression were beyond anything that had been seen. All types of rich talents were being attracted by its opportunities, its audiences were varied, united only in their demand for pictorial food, their tastes ran through a wider and wider gamut. The American magazine astonished the rest of the world; it was widely copied. Not only through sheer weight of pictorial material but also in variety and high quality of attainment, American illustration had become the most notable in the world.

It was the best of fields for an ambitious, gifted young figurative painter. Wyeth liked the goad of competition from talented rivals, the satisfaction of communicating with a wide-flung audience, the stimulation of tackling new and enticing problems. Part of the adventure of the illustrator was the constant encounter with the unexpected, the manuscript that forced him to delve for new information and search for a fresh range of expression. It was anything but a routine life. No matter what his background had been, a few years' active participation in the field endowed him with a liberal education. He became an expert at quick assimilation and a resourceful researcher. The successful illustrator has been defined as, "An artist who knows something about everything and everything about some one thing."

Almost all ranking illustrators are specialists in this broad or narrow sense. In their early days they may well find it desirable to accept the next job offered without quibble. The range of subject matter and interpretation can be breathtaking but such an exercise in flexibility can be a salutary apprenticeship and a test of one's resources. When an artist has achieved a certain reputation and can exercise the privilege of picking and choosing, most tend toward the subjects and outlets that cater to their gifts. Wyeth, stimulated by his western visit, plunged into a long series of pictures with that background but gradually as he worked and probed at his material, he became conscious of the gaps in his knowledge. Later he turned away from the western scene toward the subject matter of history, legend and outdoor contemporary life. A newspaper interview of the early twenties quoted him as saying that he was abandoning the western subject because his firsthand knowledge of it had not been deep and constant enough.

*

In a few years N.C. and Carolyn were as much a part of Chadds Ford life as though they had lived there all their lives. N.C., with his open nature, quickly made friends. He was genuinely interested in all kinds of people, their peculiarities, their interests, the work of their hands. He knew the ways of farm life, so they had a great deal in common. The older inhabitants had become accustomed to the ways of artists who had been roaming their fields for some years; they had discovered that they were less peculiar than they had feared. Even those least aware of his stature as an artist could measure N.C. by his size and strength. After he had worked his way through a number of friendly wrestling bouts with the strong men of the neighborhood and thrown all the local champions, there was no question about his acceptance. They could now brag about *him*, about his ability to hold two filled milk cans at arm's length. Then they liked to show visitors the large signboard he had painted to hang over the village barbershop. It was painted in the vein of the old Colonial signs, a blue-coated, tricorn-hatted general with the lettering, "This is where Washington and Lafayette had a close shave." The sign was a village landmark for years.

His letters home to his parents and brothers constitute an almost daily chronicle of the Chadds Ford life. There was homely news of Carolyn putting up Mason jars of green beans from the garden, N.C. picking five barrels of apples, a vaudeville show of local talent at Gallagher's Hall for an admission of five cents and almost always a mention of the weather, a reflection of N.C.'s innate sensitivity to the rhythms of nature. Then there was the happy news of the firstborn, Henriette, in 1907. In letter after letter her baby ways are lovingly described: "May 29 — The Butcher was here this morning and he weighed Henriette — 19½ lbs." A few years later:

Dear Papa: Last evening Henriette was repeating some of her nursery rhymes for the entertainment of visitors (sedate visitors at that), when she astonished us all with her powers of deduction, as follows,

> *Goosey, goosey gander*
> *Where will I wander?*
> *Upstairs and downstairs*
> *In my ladies* (hesitation here) *water closet.*

I perceived in a moment that she could not remember the word *chamber*, so substituted what to her was the true meaning of the word as she knew it.

The other children enter the chronicle as they appear: Carolyn — 1909, Nathaniel — 1911, Ann — 1915, and Andrew — 1917. There are descriptions of the new house built on the wooded hillside which looked down across the meadow fields threaded by Harvey's Run to the hills rising from the roadside of the Baltimore Pike. The new home, with its sturdy brick walls, white trim and a wide veranda was made possible by the Scribner's fee for the illustrations for Stevenson's *Treasure Island*. Next came an ample studio built above the house on the brow of the hill. The large studio room with its high glass Palladian windows to the north and a small anteroom were soon filled with N.C.'s accumulation of props and mementos, costumes, chests, firearms and swords, a birchbark canoe, bookshelves, ship models, busts and bottles. Outside he planted an orchard and a few steps away was an outcropping of large boulders shaded by a tangle of trees which often suggested background elements for some of his adventure settings. The studio was a natural hilltop nest for him, remote, yet looking down upon his home and the hills and fields with which Wyeth had identified himself.

The children were growing up and at every stage of their growth they figured in their father's pictures. Ann recalls posing dutifully while listening impatiently to young Andy's carefree hi-yipping outside the studio windows. When the pose was finished there was the walk with Father down the road to Gallagher's store and the reward of a bag of chocolate mints. The children also furnished the models for "The Giant," a large decoration for the Westtown School in nearby Chester County. Anyone — family, friends, neighbors — might be pressed into service, for professional models were not available in Chadds Ford. Besides, N.C. usually painted without models, from his abundant pictorial memory and when he felt the need for model reference it was usually for a brief study only. He was a great improvisor and a few hints from a living presence were all he needed — he could change character and proportions at will. Mrs. Wyeth grasping a long rifle could be converted into an unshaven frontiersman with a few flicks of the brush.

The growing children also gave their father an additional excuse for indulging one of his irrepressible passions — for dressing up, playacting — he loved to change his personality under cover of a strange costume. Halloween, Christmas or any plausible event could be reason for a fun-filled, dramatic improvisation. Over the years, the children were treated to a long succession of Kriss Kringles — there was even one that climbed to the chimney on an icy roof and slipped with almost tragic results. Each year produced a new variation on the Kriss Kringle theme. Once N.C. suddenly appeared before his astonished children festooned with glowing strings of tiny electric light bulbs. His audience expected and demanded the unexpected. The love of the pageantry of Christmas seemed to stem from N.C.'s mother and her Swiss forebears. It has left an ingrained impression on succeeding generations of the family — their impulse to dress up can be ignited very easily.

*

With the publication of *Treasure Island* in 1911, Wyeth moved into his harvest years. The pictures attracted wide attention and they are certainly among his best. They marked the beginning of a long series of illustrated classics for Scribner's and other publishers. Almost every year a new book with a fresh set of glowing pictures was added to the list which included such classics as *Kidnapped, The Black Arrow, Robin*

Hood, The Last of the Mohicans, Westward Ho!, The Mysterious Island, Robinson Crusoe, The Deerslayer, The White Company, The Oregon Trail. The format of the books followed a standardized pattern. Wyeth was not a book designer and always left the details of design to the editors and production men. The result was a squarish-paged book, usually about seven inches by nine and a quarter, with the colorplates tipped in by hand at intervals. It generally had a four-color paper jacket, with the same picture pasted on the linen binding, a two-color endpaper panel and sometimes chapter headings in line. This format proved so popular that not only was it adopted by Scribner's for their entire series, it was also imitated by other publishers. The early twentieth century was not an era of inventive and resourceful book design — an awakening to good design had to wait until the late twenties or early thirties. N.C. was galvanized only by the large areas of canvas to be covered with flowing brushwork and bounding shapes. He was fortunate to have come into his ripe years at a time when color reproduction had become perfected and relatively inexpensive. The long series of book illustrations gave him scope to exercise his color gifts and they show gradual experimentation and enlargement of his color vocabulary. His palette, beginning largely in the earth-color range, added much of Pyle's medieval richness and splendor; then, attracted more and more by our American landscape impressionists, his color range was often heightened and ventured into the rainbow spectrum. Blue shadows crept into many of the outdoor subjects and there were some experiments with pointillist pastel hues. This last was abandoned when it became apparent that the engravers found it almost impossible to preserve the subtle balance of the hues.

His fertile color vocabulary was intimately allied to his need to express the range of nature's moods. Even in his concentrated hours before the easel he seemed to be conscious of nature's vagaries beyond the Palladian window and he searched his manuscripts to find the settings for the repertoire of outdoor effects stored in his memory. Fog, rain, beating sun, slush and snow, the chronicle of the seasons, the story of leaf, bud and blossom, the groping anchor of great tree roots, the sense of the silent, fierce competition of the underground rootlets, the level light of the fading sun — these were some of the things he understood and craved to communicate.

In these enveloping settings his figures moved and lived, lavish in bone and muscle. It is easy to detect his love of the endless wonders of the moving body. But not all was movement; his pictures sometimes concerned themselves with the relaxed, the brooding, the grave and contemplative. It was largely a man's world he conjured up; women are there but they are unresponsive and passive — the viewer is seldom drawn to them.

In addition to the steady stream of book illustrations, there were often magazine manuscripts to be interpreted. Most of the important magazines, such as *Collier's, Harper's, Scribner's, McClure's, The Saturday Evening Post, American, Ladies' Home Journal, Country Gentleman* and *Metropolitan* wanted him on their pages. These commissions were more varied in subject matter and they often gave him the opportunity to deal with contemporary material. Then, from time to time, he consented to do some paintings for advertising, usually unwillingly and with repentant afterthoughts. Nothing in his makeup enabled him to understand the sharp, merchandising thinking of an advertising agency. Like many others, he was sometimes lured by the glittering fees they offered which were several times greater than those prevalent in the book and magazine fields. But there was always a price to pay. He was used to the friendly atmosphere of freedom allowed by the book and magazine editors and now he discovered a whole array of functionaries that had to be satisfied: advertising directors, copy heads, agency presidents, account executives, the client's advertising executives and finally, the last straw, the president of the client company and even perhaps, his wife and young daughter who had just entered art school. He growled every time he came across one of his advertising reproductions, for they seldom showed him at his best.

Even with the incessant press of work he found the time to roam the
hills and the Brandywine meadows with sketching traps and acquisitive
eyes, probing, rejoicing, remembering. But there were images other than
those of the Brandywine in his memory — those of the rocks and blue
water of the Maine coast near Port Clyde where the Wyeth family spent
the summer months. The valley and the Maine coast furnished almost all
the material not only for his illustrations but also for his easel paintings.
By the late twenties and the thirties his easel pictures were being widely
shown and greatly admired, but there were always the doctrinaire critics
who used the word "illustrator" as a denigrating label. He resented the
implied barrier between illustration and painting but his life was too filled
with projects to enter into controversy. Both the illustrator and painter,
he believed, were artists engaged in pictorial communication. The illustrator, he knew, could reach a large audience, but he was hampered by
size requirements and reproductive restrictions and limited in his choice
of subject material. Both, he believed, should be measured by the degree
of their talents, not by artificial compartments contrived by critics.

Down the long perspective of the arts he could see that the illustrative,
the narrative element had emerged strongly in the work of master after
master, from Giotto to Rubens, Grünewald to Blake, Dürer to Daumier,
Bruegel to Delacroix, from the cave paintings of Ajanta to Japanese
prints. If that element had sadly deteriorated into mindless anecdotage at
the hands of some Victorian painters, that was a failure of talent, not principle. For Wyeth, the artist practiced what came to his hand. The painting, the print, the illustration, the mural were not segregated expressions,
they were simply different mediums for his prodigious talents.

His painting hand had always craved size. He usually made his illustrations about as large as was feasible for reduction down to the small dimensions of the book or magazine page but still he sometimes felt cramped.
Some of his colleagues like George Harding and Stanley Arthurs were
working on mural decorations and the challenge of those large spaces excited him. He seized the opportunity to paint a long panel of an Indian

hunt for a hotel in Utica, New York. With this experience behind him
he moved on to larger projects. One of the most important and successful
was the commission to paint two large lunettes for the Missouri State Capitol. These were Civil War subjects and one, which proved most popular,
was a handsome battle piece of the fight at Wilson's Creek, painted in soft,
vibrant hues of blue, green and muted golden pinks.

As his reputation as a muralist spread and as new commissions came in,
even the impressive studio on the hill proved insufficient. He built a long
addition to it, separated from the old studio by great doors and accessible
by going down a flight of wide steps. It had the advantage of great height
and was equipped with ladders, scaffolds and a movable platform. Even
his craving for size was satisfied; climbing ladders and reaching from
scaffolds took care of his ambitious muscles. Two large commissions
came from Boston, one for a set of five upright panels on the theme of
maritime commerce for the First National Bank of that city and two decorations for the Federal Reserve Bank. A succession of orders followed:
five panels in the new Hubbard Memorial Building of the National Geo-
graphic Society in Washington, a large mural in the Federal Savings Bank
in New York City, panels in the Metropolitan Life Insurance Building,
New York, the Wilmington Savings Society and the First Mechanics National Bank of Trenton, New Jersey and a triptych for the Chapel of the
Holy Spirit in the National Cathedral in Washington.

These were prime years. His great strength and energy were undiminished. He usually rose at dawn and fortified himself with two or three
grapefruit halves, a huge pile of hot cakes and four or five eggs. Often his
daughter Ann was his only breakfast companion. Sluggish with sleep she
was sometimes interested in more modest fare. He would say in wonder-
ment, "My, you're a picky eater."

Up the hill to the studio in the morning light, he would face last night's
canvas in the merciless brightness of the new day or prepare to attack a
new one on the easel. Often he would put a Beethoven or Sibelius record
on the Victrola to get himself off to a good start. After a long day's work

at the easel, he would come down the darkening path to the house, stretching his arms saying, "I wish the day was just starting." Visitors and guests dropped in frequently at the studio and dinner table, drawn by his pictures and personality. There was constant good conversation. When N.C. went for the morning mail or to pick up something at Gallagher's store there was almost always a yarning session with the neighbors. He had listened to his Port Clyde neighbors too, and had built up a large repertoire of Down East, often Rabelaisian, stories which he loved to relate with an authentic Maine twang to any listening ear.

Meanwhile the children were giving strong premonitions of their futures. They had lived a large part of their young lives out-of-doors. They had been enfolded in the warm life of the home with a wise, affectionate and devoted mother and an irrepressible father. They knew the life of the studio, they had watched picture after picture come quickly into being and move out into the mysterious world of publication. They were used to people, to the talk of artists, writers and editors, to their farmer and working neighbors.

N.C. discovered that a small art school had spontaneously recruited itself from his family circle. Although young artists were constantly seeking him out and he gave liberally of his time to them, sometimes seeing that they were comfortably settled nearby for periods of time, he had no plans for organized classes such as Pyle's. But young Henriette and Carolyn showed unmistakable signs of talent as did Andrew, the youngest, at a later date. At an early age they were working in the studio and Wyeth would not permit their effort to be a hit-or-miss affair; it had to be concentrated work, the early beginning for a lifetime for dedication. Thus all three developed under their father's eye and eventually moved into maturity and professional life. Nathaniel, the oldest son, and Ann, the youngest daughter, had other talents. Nathaniel, as a growing boy and young man, spent much of his time in the basement workshop occupied with his precocious models of ships, locomotives and other mechanical things. This was not the now prevalent assemblage of small, mass-produced parts — he created an authentic structure of frame and details, carefully and accurately machined and finished. Nathaniel, the scientist-to-be, was an artist in his own field. Ann was the young musician of the family, preparing herself to become a composer.

Among the many young aspirants who came for N.C.'s help, three remained with him for long periods of work and moved into notable careers. Paul Horgan, with his dual talent for drawing and writing, finally concentrated his full powers on his writing and has become one of our important novelists and descriptive writers. Peter Hurd and John Mc-Coy became part of the family circle when they married Wyeth daughters and became painters of distinction.

The 1930's and early 1940's were years of abundance. Book and magazine illustrations, murals poured from the studio on the hill. Interspersed between mural and illustrative commissions were Wyeth's easel paintings. As he grew older these became more and more the vehicles of his most urgent conceptions. He resented increasingly the hampering restrictions of illustration, particularly those of advertising. His best and most private dreams could scarcely expect to find suitable outlet in illustration or even in mural decorations. Many of his canvases were loving portrayals of bits of the land and life that meant so much to him, but frequently he attempted a fusion of this concern with a tide of romantic fantasy which was such an essential ingredient of his nature.

His best canvases, such as "Island Funeral," convey this happy fusion. This painting was the result of attending the funeral of an old neighbor and friend on Teel's Island near Port Clyde, Maine. In the painting there was no attempt at a literal delineation of the actual occurrence. His composition was the result of brooding and contemplation, of trying to convey the significance that underlay the actual event. From the perspective of an imaginary viewpoint high above the island, the inevitable end of a life is framed in an immense landscape of water and rock-skeletoned land. It is seen as part of the cycle of nature.

In middle life, to know the man was to understand his pictures. He was volatile, active in body and mind, capable of a gamut of moods, self-critical but confident of his powers, also friendly, humorous, sharp and knowing. Physically he was still tall and powerful with a thick, solid torso, long rather slim arms and legs and a large head with mobile features. A crown of curly, touseled hair spread from a broad brow and there were bright, observant eyes behind spectacles. He was seldom withdrawn, his personality advanced to meet one, and his circle of friends widened through the years. Then, on the morning of October 19, 1945, as he was driving with a young grandson, his station wagon stalled at a grade crossing near his home, in the path of a freight train. The creative tide was suddenly, tragically stemmed.

But Wyeth's influence is still felt. The long series of children's classics found its way into homes across the land and fed the minds of tens of thousands of young people. The books have been worn with repeated rapt handling and saved from generation to generation. But there are new readers every year, for almost all the volumes are still in print. The Wyeth pictures have enriched our lives by making us see the strange, the improbable, the life that is larger than that of everyday.

XVII

A FAMILY OF ARTISTS

THE WYETH STUDIO on the hill at Chadds Ford not only saw the birth of a long stream of illustrations, paintings and mural decorations but also, completely unforeseen, its atmosphere nurtured five important artistic talents as well. Certainly N.C. must have had some premonitions of the futures of the youngsters who played and scribbled under his eyes. He is on record as having made a prophecy about Nathaniel, his oldest son, when the boy was about five years of age. After watching him draw small wheel shapes cleanly and painstakingly down in the corners of his paper he is reported to have said, "He's going to create, but it won't be in art." Time proved him right, for Nathaniel went on to become one of Du Pont's most imaginative and inventive scientists.

All the children drew, but in three the pictorial talent was conspicuous. Henriette, the oldest, was the first to mature as an artist. She was small and fine boned and her talent was elusive, imaginative and special. She could work hard — they all had that capacity — and she and her younger sister Carolyn accepted the drill of delineation and month after month of drawing in charcoal from white painted geometric solids, still life, plaster casts and living models. They all went to the Quaker School for their early schooling, but by the age of twelve they were being tutored at home. From that point on, the studio was their important classroom.

Henriette was precocious, and at sixteen her work showed independence and a flavor of its own. She felt the need to match her talent against the outside world, and the school of the Pennsylvania Academy of the

Fine Arts promised her an opportunity to encounter new attitudes and measure herself against values outside the family circle. At first her parents were dubious of the long and continuous effort it would require to get up to early classes in Philadelphia and back in the evening, but it was soon evident she was determined. She was up at six on dark winter mornings and down the road in time to catch the morning local train. Then she returned on the evening train after a hard day's work. Young Peter Hurd rode this same train to his first appointment with N.C. Wyeth and, upon asking the conductor the way to the studio, was introduced by him to a fellow passenger, Henriette. Peter describes his first reception by the daughter of his teacher-to-be and future wife as cool and detached. He set out to change her attitude with complete success.

Carolyn chose to stay in the studio and work under her father. She resembled him in looks and with her forthright and positive personality, she had little time for superficial graces — she pursued her own undeviating way. She says of her apprenticeship, "I stayed with charcoal for about six years. Andy was out of it in a year and a half because he was much faster and much more fluent than I." By the time young Andy had moved from scribbling to earnest study, Peter Hurd was one of the group. He boarded nearby and brought his work in for criticism. Soon he was one of the family. The fifth artist to join the circle was John McCoy, who, after study at Cornell, two summers at the American School in Fontainebleau, France and a short time at the Pennsylvania Academy of the Fine Arts came to N.C. for criticism and then to work beside Andy in the lower studio. While the young men drew or painted they could hear the footfalls of N.C. in the upper, older studio, as he advanced and retreated before his canvas. When the footfalls ceased, they put on a spurt of work, for they knew a visit might be impending. Downhill at the house, Ann would be at the piano or playing records, in the course of her preparation to be a musician and composer.

It was a closely knit and self-sufficient group, greatly inventive, full of pranks and resources — they stimulated and struck sparks from one another. The family were used to visitors of all kinds — there was a steady stream of them — some welcome, some not. When bores and time-wasters toiled up the hill, the word flew around and everyone scattered to cover. There were some who concluded that the Wyeths were never home.

Although temperamentally different from Pyle, N.C. had the same ability to light the creative spark in others. All who came close to him felt his power. Paul Horgan called him, "The greatest natural teacher I have known." Since Horgan became a distinguished writer rather than an art-ist, this bears out John McCoy's comment that N.C., "Really didn't talk about the mechanics of picture making. He opened our eyes and minds to life and made us want to express what we found." As with Pyle, the message, the education, was twofold and complementary: first, the en-largement of vision, the implanting of the thought of great possibilities in each pupil; second, the hard, steady, concentrated study of the pictorial language.

These were fruitful years on the hill for the younger talents. They could feel themselves growing. And their growth, although it centered around the inspiration and personality of N.C., drew strength from the place and its atmosphere, the surrounding countryside, the alternations of nature, the warm home, the enfolding presence of the mother dealing affectionately and understandingly with the hundred and one problems presented by volatile natures. Of course, they learned from each other.

They progressed toward their individual maturities. Henriette was soon exhibiting at the Pennsylvania Academy Annual and other national shows. An accomplished painter before the age of twenty, she found that a great deal was expected of her as the daughter of N.C. All the children experienced this pressure and they rose to it. Their parents had expected excellence as a matter of course, and it was natural that they should expect it of themselves. Nor did they feel obligated to follow any previous pat-tern — they would work out their own ways of expression. In many ways Henriette's work was in distinct contrast to her father's — sensitive

and feminine against his Baroque masculinity. Her approach was contemplative rather than agitated, tentative and exploratory rather than direct. Her early canvases were creations of fancy in which she exploited
her gift for pattern and color. She had a gift for portraiture too, and over
the years the list of her portrait paintings has been growing steadily.
Many of these have been commissions, but there are numerous renderings
of family and friends and of time-marked Mexican and Indian faces.
These last are often among her best. Almost all the subject matter of her
later pictures stems from the background of her second home after her
marriage to Peter Hurd and their move to his native New Mexico.

Peter had attended the New Mexico Military Institute and from there
he had received an appointment to West Point. Everything pointed to a
career in the Army except his love of drawing. He was athletic, an outdoor man, a fine rider with certain romantic notions about Army life, but
the compulsion to make pictures outweighed all else. He withdrew from
the Point and, not to disappoint his father too much, entered Haverford
College. But that was a short-lived interval; after his Chadds Ford interview he cast his lot with art. He spent about five years with N.C. Soon
he was finding more and more work as an illustrator and exhibiting increasingly widely. All in all, he spent some twelve years in the Brandywine where several of his and Henriette's children were born.

But he had a strong hankering to be back in the dry country, to be with
horses and live the ranch life. He made an exploratory trip to Roswell in
the mid-thirties and, circling around the country, found what he wanted
fifty miles away near San Patricio. He bought an adobe ranch house with
thirty acres in the foothill country. Over the years the ranch — and it is a
working ranch — has grown to a thousand acres and the house is part of a
compound. Both the Hurds are prolific picture makers but they do not
lead an immersed studio life. They exhibit throughout the country, their
paintings are in many important collections and many awards have come
their way.

Peter, grounded in the customary oil technique by Wyeth and the

Pennsylvania Academy of the Fine Arts, took up the ancient technique of egg tempera about 1935 and soon discovered it to be his natural medium. He interested his father-in-law in it and later he taught it to young Andrew. The dry and somewhat brittle medium of egg tempera seemed eminently suited to Peter's delineations of the Southwest. There are now a long line of pictures of the San Patricio country, a pictorial chronicle of the land, its moods and seasonal cycles, its light and shadow, its peace, its violence and its people. There is an equal abundance of portraits. Some of Hurd's finest work sprang from his experience as a combat artist for *Life* during the war. Pictorial reporting of the war scene was a natural outlet for his active nature. He adapted himself to the new conditions by putting aside his stroke-by-stroke tempera technique for rapid brushing in watercolor and any quick mixture of mediums. These war sketches are pulsing with life and immediacy and mark an extension of his powers.

After the war he went back to the ranch and his painting of the Southwest. An early painting, "Eastbound Mail Stage," done in the 1930's under the W.P.A. artists' project, was a favorite of President Johnson's and was hung in the White House office where he could see it every day. When Hurd was given the commission to paint an official portrait of the President, he gave it his best effort and was completely unprepared for the President's remark, "It's the ugliest thing I ever saw," a sentence repeated in every newspaper in the land. The clash of opinions that ensued was a nine days' wonder and is now a scrap of history.

*

The Hurds have spent the greater part of their creative years in pictorial celebration of the Southwest. They love their land and its life. Its compulsions are in their bones, Peter's by birthright and Henriette's by adoption. Both have national reputations but are more prideful of the esteem of their neighbors. Unconsciously they have opened the eyes of their neighbors to the grandeur of their country and made them feel they are participants in a drama of life. Their pictures have gone into many private and museum collections — there is a wing devoted to the work of Peter Hurd in the Roswell Museum.

The meaning of these pictures for the people of the Southwest has been well expressed by Paul Horgan, a lifelong friend:

". . . like people everywhere, the Southwesterners go through their days pretty much unaware that they are living and using the raw materials of art — they do not reflect as they raise a windmill, or drill an oil well, or cultivate an orchard, or water their cattle, that all life, any life, everywhere and anywhere, is worthy of record in works of art. It is only when someone not only lives their life with them, but also sees it with a fresh vision every day and puts down the vision itself as if it were entirely new, that they are struck by the meanings, the values and the beauties of their own commonplace dignity.

Every one of the Hurd pictures is a demonstration that the pictorial insight awakened by the Brandywine spirit and the Wyeth tradition is not provincial, not limited to set themes or any regional boundary. It can transfer itself. It can thrive in any place or condition that feeds the spirit and excites the hungry, picture-making eye.

Wyeth's other gifted student, John McCoy, brought his apprentice days to an end when he married Ann Wyeth. Ann, whose first symphony was played by the Philadelphia Orchestra before she was twenty, was not only immersed in her music but later began to paint in watercolor. John gradually shifted his technical interest from oil to watercolor and has become one of the country's ranking aquarellists. A quiet, ruminating man, his pictures reflect these qualities. He has considerable technical dexterity but this is not for display. At this time when brush wizardry and splash brilliance have been outstanding characteristics of the American watercolor school, McCoy's pictures await contemplation and receptive inspection. They make no concessions to instant visual shock; they make their way into the consciousness by accumulated study; their message is not dissipated in a few seconds. Living in Chadds Ford and spending the summer months near Spruce Head, Maine, McCoy draws his subjects almost entirely from these regions. He is particularly drawn to the dark spruce woodlands of Maine and the tumbled boulders and slanting rock ledges reflected in blackened pools of still water. The abstract patterns of rock shapes fascinate him and one's first glance at a McCoy picture often interprets an abstract message before its realistic content discloses itself.

McCoy's most typical papers are saturated with mood, a dark, brooding poetry that penetrates by reticence. He has the high esteem of fellow artists who have shown it in many ways. They have placed him on the selection and award juries of many national exhibitions and honored him with many medals and prizes. He has long been a member of the faculty of the Pennsylvania Academy of the Fine Arts and is Vice-President of the Wilmington Society of the Fine Arts. His has been the kind of reputation that requires time for growing.

Carolyn has been the most retiring of the family, painting quietly in her determined, individual way, living with and caring for her mother in the house and studio on the hill. Like her brother Andrew, she finds her subjects close at hand, often small, ignored things that the average eye would never pause to investigate. She sees things simply and strongly and paints them without added graces or concessions to the picturesque. She cherishes the precepts of her father but her canvases bear no outward resemblance to his. She has nothing of his spectacular flair but she has inherited his probity and has followed the honesty of her own eyes. She has exhibited only rarely — she is indifferent about it — and her work is not widely known.

Two generations of Wyeths, with a third generation beginning to move into the public eye, have been compared so many times with the Peale family, our only other multi-talented artist family, that there is probably little left to explore in that direction. Neither has a clear answer to the mystery of inherited talent, but the infinite fascination of that mystery has fed the Wyeth legend and they have grown accustomed to living in the center of a modern version.

The family has felt all the pressures, seductions and annoyances of increasing publicity, but it has not loosened their roots or swept them from their purposes. Their closely knit attachment, the protection of country living, their hardheaded common sense have dealt wisely with distractions and they are essentially untouched by them. The practice they had as children, scuttling to cover from unwelcome intrusions, has not been forgotten — they refuse to become the victims of publicity.

XVIII

ANDREW WYETH

THE YOUNGEST WYETH, in his scampering years, could not have dreamed that he was to become an important figure in the legend that had already grown up around his father and his father's teacher. He was well acquainted with legends at an early age but they were the sort that belonged in books. These were the glittering tales that tempted their readers to daydream and had stimulated artists like Howard Pyle and his father to make pictures that could not be forgotten.

King Arthur, Charlemagne and Robin Hood were in the pictures and texts he pored over, dreamed about and acted out with his older sisters and brother or a companion of his own age, the little Negro boy, Doo Doo. The outcropping of large boulders in a patch of woodland behind the studio provided a natural stage for small heroes who wished to act out giant parts. There were other larger-than-life figures in the books — Merlin, Jim Hawkins and Long John Silver, Deerslayer and Uncas, Alan Breck, Otto of the Silver Hand, Sir John Chandos and Robinson Crusoe. This radiant mixture of heroic figures inspires many imaginative youngsters, but more often than not the resultant glow is short-lived — the adult, lockstep world tramps it under.

Happy circumstances and an exceptional talent kept young Andy out of the lockstep world. The ample brick house on the hill overlooked a world saturated with nourishment for the imagination. Every step that the youngest Wyeth took was over an old battlefield. The countryside was crisscrossed with forgotten Indian trails and the newer roads of the white man. Andy's father knew the history of the early days and the tactics of the Brandywine battle by heart. The books on the living room shelves illustrated by his father, Pyle, Schoonover, Arthurs and others were filled with pictures of these events.

He had all the time in the world to roam this rural world. His formal education was a matter of a few weeks. Except for some tutoring at home he was master of his days. He was often alone, a solitary wanderer, but he came to know his land — field, fence, farmhouse and barn. The hours at home could be spent with his companies of lead soldiers and the castle and battlements that his brother had built for him. There was also a miniature theater and he could make things in the downstairs workshop where his brother Nat was putting together remarkably skillful model ships and mechanical constructions. The youngest of an inventive and imaginative family, Andrew was surrounded by an atmosphere of resourceful accomplishment; in addition, he had two older sisters to watch who were working steadily with charcoal and paint. Talent was expected of the son of such a father, increasingly so, as there were painters in the maternal (Bockius) side of the family as well.

When Andrew was twelve, Scribner's reprinted a number of Pyle's children's classics in a special edition, with new frontispieces and prefatory essays by some of Pyle's now famous students. N.C. Wyeth prepared his essay and pictorial frontispiece for *The Merry Adventures of Robin Hood*, and young Andy contributed pen-and-ink head and tailpieces for the essay. These small line drawings in the Pyle tradition were his first published drawings. At that time he thought of illustration as his destined field and later he did accept book and magazine commissions.

His father was his only art teacher. N.C. was quick to encourage any stirring of imagination but he believed also in a discipline that trained the eye and hand to analyze and depict with the immediacy of a natural function. The imagination was not to be harassed by a fumbling execution. Andrew drew day after day from casts and studied from Rimmer's *Art and Anatomy*. He drew from still life and from the posed model and learned to turn his back upon the model and draw from memory. He was rapidly sharpening a remarkable instrument of expression.

Part of the time he was in the open with his watercolors, free to paint what he liked. He was discovering the expressive possibilities of that medium and it was a release from the indoor disciplines. His sketches were dashed in with impatience, and they were full of his outdoor discoveries — wind, chance-caught lights, the glitter of sun on water, roof and earth, the haze of distance, the tangle of weed-grown foregrounds. He was discovering an innate expressionism and splashing it out in his own terms.

He had his first one-man show at the age of nineteen when several members of the Arts and Program Committee of the Philadelphia Art Alliance became excited at the young power in his work and invited him to exhibit in the Art Alliance galleries. A year later the Macbeth Galleries in New York put on a second show and he reached a larger audience. At twenty he seemed launched on a career as a brilliant watercolorist of the brush-dexterous American school. The possibilities beyond that were not yet visible to many.

In the summer of 1939 at the family summer home near Port Clyde, Maine, Roy Mason, a well-known painter and friend of N. C. Wyeth, brought a visitor to meet the great illustrator. He was Mr. Merle D. James. His summer home was in Cushing, on the shore of the St. George estuary, a short distance from Port Clyde across the water but many miles farther by road. Andrew happened to be home and met the visitor. The next day Andrew returned the call and met Mr. James' youngest daughter, Betsy. Shortly after, he had enlarged his sketching territory to include the far side of the St. George River. After a summer of extended sketching trips, N.C. remarked to his son, "Andy, you're not getting any work done. Why don't you marry the girl?"

Andrew Newell Wyeth and Betsy Merle James were married on May 15, 1940, and came to live in Chadds Ford in the converted white schoolhouse at the foot of the hill below the family home. This was home and studio until their recent restoration of the old miller's house, mill and granary beside the Brandywine a mile or more up the road. The schoolhouse is still the Wyeth studio and Jamie, Andrew's son, has his own studio a few steps away in the former living room.

In 1941 Andrew illustrated Henry Seidel Canby's *The Brandywine* in the *Rivers of America* series for Farrar and Rinehart. The book included a number of double-page tonal drawings and pen drawings at the beginning of each chapter. There were a few years when he said that it was a comfort to have a manuscript on his desk to be illustrated, for when grocery funds became low, he could turn to it and replenish the larder. He painted a much-admired cover for *The Saturday Evening Post* but when they offered him a contract for steady assignments and he was tempted, Betsy intervened and insisted that he give his time to painting.

He not only determined to give all his time to painting but also he began to experiment with a new medium that brought about an expansion of his powers. His brother-in-law, Peter Hurd, had experimented with the age-old technique of egg tempera and found it congenial to his talent. He taught the technique to N.C. and both became deeply interested. It seemed the answer to a problem that had been mounting in Andrew's mind. He feared the ease and responsiveness of watercolor (it is a medium of despair for the maladroit; it sparkles and beckons to the gifted). He needed the balance of a medium that required long, slower application, with all its necessities of planning, patience and the hoarding up of one's initial creative spark. It was the antithesis of the sketch technique and gave him encouragement to probe and reflect.

*

Then came that autumn day when N.C., driving back from the village with his small grandson, stopped to watch corn being shocked in a nearby field. Driving on up the tilted road, he passed through a familiar railroad crossing and was struck by a train. Grief and loss played their part in making Andrew grow up quickly as an artist. His father had had great hopes for him and the boy knew he would have to become more than a facile painter. In his own words he became possessed of an overpowering urge "to prove that what he started in me was not in vain."

A few years later, in the winter of 1950–51, he passed through another wrenching crisis. A critical operation brought him to the edge of death and his recovery was slow. He patiently regained his strength by slowly walking his fields, too weak to carry sketching equipment or to use it. Toward the end of this convalescence, when he first began to paint again, he had to support his painting arm in a sling supported from above. This brush with death left its mark — on his personality and thence to his pictures.

The loss of his father and his illness naturally have played their part in shaping Andrew Wyeth and his work. His pictures express him directly, and in a time of so much depersonalized and anonymous painting it is necessary to remind ourselves that here is an artist, painting not a theory, but his life. It is necessary to point out too, that he is not only the dedicated picture maker. He has an abundant sense of fun, he can clown and mimic, he has a store of jokes and enjoys a relaxed time with his friends. Like all the family he loves to dress up, to paint his face and work himself into another personality. Christmas and Halloween are welcome occasions for family capers, masquerades and impromptu pranks. Then he slips back into his storybook youth with great ease.

Wyeth lives on his meadow acres in a fine old Pennsylvania stone house furnished simply but with great distinction. He and Betsy have seen their two sons grow up in this atmosphere, the older, Nicholas, now an art scholar and dealer in New York and Jamie, the younger, a rising painter living at home. Behind the house is the old mill and granary, very much as it stood when Knyphausen's artillery fired over them from the hilltop across the stream. Andrew likes to quote historic eyewitness accounts of the British regulars forcing the crossing and pausing to powder their muddy leggings with flour before falling into formation to advance up the near hill.

Up and down the stream and up in the hills are the things and people he paints. He is loved and trusted by his neighbors and they are used to his figure in the fields, their barns and their kitchens. Usually they pay no more heed to him than they would to one of their own families. He is at ease with country people, white and black, and speaks their language. They know he belongs to their land.

The Wyeth present and past are entwined with this countryside, along with the past of the nation, and Andrew allows these things to speak through his pictures. The same voices speak in his Maine pictures but like the native speech, they are more tart and reticent. Practically all of his summer pictures seem to be of Maine, not simply because that is the time he knows that state best, but because not even summer green can disguise the bones of the land; the granite skeleton is never far beneath the skin and often breaks through. South in the Brandywine corner of Pennsylvania, the summers are lush and the land is screened in curtains of green. It is an opulent time and corpulent rhythms do not speak to Wyeth. He waits until the embroidery thins: he loves the spare months, the brown autumn-death of the vegetable year, the bony trees of winter, the sloshing freshets and mud of spring. When he paints the spring, he almost always catches its first, sneaking, deceitful green — the early pretense of diffidence while secretly bulging its underground muscles to crack open the year.

His pictures are both near and farsighted. He can peer down at a minute filagree of dry weeds, stones and moss, and paint it in loving detail, or cast his eyes over a mile of folded ridge and depict its anatomy so knowingly that one feels the ground under one's feet. The combination of delicate detail with broad and sweeping contours is one of his strengths — his pictures can be beautiful in the inch and in the mile.

Man, or some small monument of his — a road, a fence, a furrow — appears in almost all the pictures. Often there is a dialogue between man and his land — the pride, the wonder, and the pathos of the ancient relationship. Always one can sense the attachment of the two, even in those pictures which may be considered portraits. People, for Wyeth, are marked by their work and their environment; he cannot think of them as statistics, cases or abstractions. He seems to have an uncanny ability to see deep and true and is unswayed by any impulse to flatter, idealize or satirize. But a compassionate penetration emerges. He loves every mark that life has left on a face or hand and without exaggerating or diminishing it he allows it to tell its story. So his figures have a history; they possess all the dimensions. They exist solidly in a solid world. They seem to have a past and a future. His figures are not merely convenient space-filling shapes but willful and contradictory organisms with something to yearn for in their futures and something to ache for in their past. These figure paintings are all of people known and loved. They are a portrait collection of friends. It would not be entirely accurate to say that he has painted all his friends; many are missing. His immediate family is there — his wife, Betsy, and the two boys, Nicholas and Jamie. Many of his Chadds Ford and Cushing neighbors are there — the German farmer, Carl Kuerner, and the Negro farmer, Adam Johnson, crippled Christina Olson, Dr. Margaret Handy from the stone house on the hill above his studio, Tom Clark, the Delaware Moor, Willard Snowden, the studio caretaker, and Ralph Cline, from the Spruce Head sawmill.

The pictures of rooms are portraits too. The empty rooms, or those with a figure at window or doorway are lonely, aching documents of generations of living, of the comfort of four close walls, of the immensity of outdoors that is filtered through a patch of door or window. Light plays a thousand subtle patterns on floor, walls and ceiling. It searches out the scars of living, sometimes kindly, sometimes harshly. The Wyeth light is a northern light, reticent yet penetrating, reflecting itself from plane to plane into the remotest shadow pocket. The eye wanders through a gamut of subtle grays, warm and cool. No matter how sharply drawn or painstakingly rendered an object may be, there are still layers of air between it and the beholder.

Layers of air building space in depth is a consistent Wyeth weapon.

Felix Octavius Darley.

Defeat of General Braddock, Felix Octavius Darley. Watercolor and pen.
Collection of the Historical Society of Delaware. Photograph Frick Art Reference Library.

Washington Entering New York, Felix Octavius Darley. Pencil.
Collection of the Historical Society of Delaware. Photograph Frick Art Reference Library.

HOWARD PYLE.
Wilmington Society of the Fine Arts.

WRECK IN THE OFFING, Howard Pyle. Wood engraving from gouache.
This gouache, published in 1878, was Pyle's first work to appear entirely unretouched
by other hands until it was turned over to the wood engraver.
Harper's Weekly.

KING ARTHUR, Howard Pyle. Pen and ink.
Charles Scribner's Sons.

Endicott Cutting Out the English Cross, Howard Pyle. Gouache.
Harper's Weekly. *Collection of Howard Brokaw.*

PIRATES, Howard Pyle. Watercolor. Unpublished.
Collection of Howard Brokaw.

ON AND ON HE FLEW, Howard Pyle. Pen and ink.
Wilmington Society of the Fine Arts.

OTTO OF THE SILVER HAND, Howard Pyle. Pen and ink.
Charles Scribner's Sons.

HOWARD PYLE AND STUDENTS AT CHADDS FORD, SUMMER, 1903.
Standing, from left to right: Alan True, Howard Pyle, Arthur Becher, Harry
Townsend, Clifford Ashley, Francis Newton, George Harding, Philip Goodwin,
Ernest Cross, Walter Whitehead, Thornton Oakley, William Aylward,
Anna Whelen Betts, Gordon McCouch, Henry Peck.

N. C. WYETH.
Wilmington Society of the Fine Arts.

N. C. WYETH PAINTING MURAL.
Permission Mrs. N. C. Wyeth.

Magazine Cover, Maxfield Parrish.
Scribner's Magazine.

Mural Panel, Series on William Penn, Violet Oakley. Oil.
Decoration in the Pennsylvania State Capitol, Harrisburg.

AN HOUR SLIPPED BY, Jessie Wilcox Smith.
Charcoal touched with transparent and opaque watercolor.
Harper's Monthly Magazine.

EARTHQUAKE IN RABUT, George Harding. Oil.
Collection of the Pennsylvania Academy of the Fine Arts.

BIBLICAL ILLUSTRATION, Walter Everett. Oil.
Collection of Maurice Bower.

WATER FOLK, Sarah S. Stillwell. Charcoal.
Harper's Monthly Magazine.

THE HARBOR FRONT, Thornton Oakley. Charcoal.
Harper's Monthly Magazine.

HER LAST PORT, William Aylward. Watercolor.
Collier's.

OUTFITTING THE WHALER, Clifford Ashley. Oil.
The Wilmington Society of the Fine Arts.

HOPALONG CASSIDY, Frank E. Schoonover. Oil.
The Wilmington Society of the Fine Arts.

DEEPER AND DEEPER, Edward A. Wilson. Ink and monochrome watercolor.
The Limited Editions Club.

STAGE COACH DAYS, John Wolcott Adams. Pen and ink.
Collection of Henry C. Pitz.

THE GOOD SAMARITAN, Herbert Moore. Oil.

ILLUSTRATION, Anna Whelen Betts. Charcoal and watercolor.
The Wilmington Society of the Fine Arts.

SIEGE OF THE CASTLE, Andrew Wyeth. Pen and ink.
This pen drawing was executed by Andrew Wyeth at about the age of fifteen and is one of the many done during his early years. Its complexity, its wealth of detail are notable, and there is no mistaking the influence of the romantic, legendary world of Howard Pyle and N. C. Wyeth. The drawing is reproduced here for the first time, the only example of its kind to be published. *Collection of Mr. and Mrs. Andrew Wyeth.*

FUR HAT, Andrew Wyeth. Pen drawing touched with watercolor.
Collection of Mrs. Andrew Wyeth.

BURNING SHIP, Edward Shenton. Pen and ink.
Collection of Edward Shenton.

THE WYETH FAMILY.
From left to right: Betsy James Wyeth, Andrew Wyeth,
Carolyn Wyeth, John McCoy, Mrs. N. C. Wyeth, Anne Wyeth
McCoy, Caroline Pyle Wyeth, Nathaniel C. Wyeth.
Permission Mrs. N. C. Wyeth.

MUSHROOM PICKER, James Wyeth. Oil.
Collection of James Wyeth.

VINAL HAVEN, Philip Jamison. Oil.
The Wilmington Society of the Fine Arts.

LIGHT FROM THE WINDOW, George Weymouth. Oil.
Collection of George Weymouth.

The space relationships are almost always simple and dramatic, but fastidiously adjusted to each other. And within each major shape or space are a hundred subtle, intertwined tones and colors which do not menace the integrity of the major shape but afford an endless interest for visual exploration. For the viewer the first emphatic impact of a Wyeth picture and the following delight of inch-by-inch inspection is characteristic.

Wyeth's inner biography is painted into his pictures. The objective forms are the reflections he catches of himself. He is often described as a patient chronicler of his small world, but he is not a pictorial historian — he is a dreamer walking his world until the dream crystallizes. He walks it, expectant, waiting for a message. The collision of the dream with the objective world produces his pictures. This conjunction is chancy, never certain, never under control of the will, a creative gamble. His eyes are full of appetite; he sees many things that suggest themselves as pictures but he must wait to see if they will root. He waits for unmistakable demands.

The demand often comes in an electric moment — often a chance-caught shaft of light upon a hundred-times-familiar face or object. It is not the unfamiliar that he hunts, it is the moment of ignition upon the deeply accustomed. And although this moment has come upon him hundreds of times and seems trustworthy and true, it yet obeys its own laws beyond planning.

When the moment arrives, there is extraordinary dexterity ready in his fingers. It is a birthright gift, sharpened by years of study and practice. Wyeth has paid a price for it, of innumerable hours of calculating scrutiny and patient recording of what the eye has found.

An impressive reservoir of facility is ready to his hand. Never common in any age, exceedingly rare in a time that pretends scorn of it, that is too gutless to undergo the rigors of disciplined competence, that derides something it secretly aches to possess, this facility tends to become a controversial factor. Wyeth himself is suspicious of his own digital gift, as were his father and Pyle before him. He has a lurking fear, perhaps a hangover from the Puritan age, that the servant might become master. Wyeth's technical ability seems to invite over-evaluation or excessive depreciation. Thousands gape at it and see little or nothing else, but to brush it aside would be a slavish concession to the tide of the moment. Most of the critics speak that retarded language, a deprecation of skill, partly because they are bereft of insight into technical matters. It is impossible to imagine a Renaissance, Baroque or Romantic artist apologizing for his virtuosity — he would glory in it and so would all his audience. He would have deep joy in the exercising of his natural powers. It is impossible to imagine Wyeth's art without this gift.

When the moment of creation arrives, no matter how intense or overpowering, the ultimate fate of the picture rests in the fingers. The mind can work only through them. Wyeth can scarcely plunge into a tempera panel; tempera is not a plunging medium. It is not for the improvising temperament. It invites planning and stage-by-stage development, so its earliest versions lie outside the medium itself, usually in preparatory drawings and watercolor studies. As these studies accumulate, Wyeth broods over the material and watches the concept grow in his mind. The first pencil drawings are the jottings of a moment, a graphic shorthand that would mean little to most, but which are the first gropings in the transmission of an idea to a two-dimensional surface. They are succeeded by careful, accurate drawings of details which are relevant to the picture. There can be many of these, each a step in greater knowledge and understanding.

These informational drawings are paralleled by watercolor notes, which are often thumbnail jottings but sometimes ambitious full sheets. They are in a different category from the watercolors painted on location for their own sakes — they serve as breaks in the slowly achieved temperas or in the fallow periods between them. Their first function is information about a projected problem, but some of the happiest examples of the Wyeth brush are to be found among them. They are seldom exhibited and when they are, most audiences are likely to give them only a passing glance. Because they are unpretentious, their beauty too often goes unremarked.

When the masonite panel with its seven coats of sandpapered gesso, its smooth ivorylike surface, is ready to be attacked, it is a time of trepidation for the artist. Wyeth has no formula for the first stroking in of the images. He is not the cocky artist who lacks the imagination to be frightened by the possibilities of a blank panel. Every new picture is a step off into space, and he is not certain he can fly. It is not unusual for him to use the spur of impulse to lay in the picture's essential skeleton, then at the first warm hint of success, to flee — to return next morning to see if it tells the same story to a cooler mood. With creative luck the picture moves — toward the unknown.

Beside the easel are the tools and materials of the trade. Dry powdered pigments, distilled water, egg yolk, springy-haired red sable brushes and a metal-cupped palette. The pigments are finely ground earths and minerals — no gaudy colors but a great variety of rich, subtle hues. Some come from the standard dealer's list, some are specially imported from strange foreign lands or from the New Mexico country near the ranch of his brother-in-law, Peter Hurd. A row of these colors in their glass containers suggests a long range of muted harmonies. This is the Wyeth palette.

The tempera technique is founded upon patience and an accumulation of innumerable small brushstrokes. It is one of the most ancient of the artist's techniques and modern innovations have scarcely changed it. A little egg yolk and distilled water, rubbed together with pigment, picked up upon the brush and stroked onto the panel, are all the mechanics of it. The rest is skill and inspiration. It is a slow technique and this is the reason that only two, three or four temperas come from the Wyeth studio in a year. With all this time for gestation, ideally the picture should move from sketched outline through tone-by-tone and shape-by-shape development to its fated conclusion. Sometimes this happens. But often the growing picture dictates its own direction. Wyeth has painted a herd of cows and painted them out again; he has changed a barking dog into a sawed off, splintered tree trunk; he has painted a figure into a landscape or painted one out. Even the slow-moving tempera has to give way to change and modification.

The pictures evolve under the cold, flooding light from the large north window. Their muted color is intensified by the gray, cheerless walls of the squarish studio. The room is bare of everything except the essentials for work. On the floor, in an arc around the easel, are scattered the drawings that record the search for detail and intensive knowledge. Some sketches may lean against the walls or lie on a shelf or chair. They are there, not to be copied, but to fortify the mood. These drafts are means to an end and may be walked on, heedlessly. But for Betsy, many of them would be thrown away.

The temperas have been extensively documented. They are the pictures that are talked and written about — they bring the staggering prices, they are reproduced, they draw the crowds. But they are not the complete Wyeth. Those who have not studied the drawings and watercolors have only a partial knowledge of the artist. Those who catalog him as a greatly gifted plodder do not know his reach; he is more diverse in expression than the simplifiers would have it.

A fundamental Wyeth diversity asserts itself when a tempera and a watercolor are placed side by side. Even the uninitiated can sense the difference. The mediums are dissimilar, of course, but they are convenient vehicles for releasing shifts of temperament, each permitting the expression of a different set of qualities. The watercolors release the immediate, encourage the passing comment, are supremely fitted to the pictorial pounce. The tempera medium was chosen consciously as a brake on impetuosity. Wyeth complains that he is naturally a "messy painter." The patient stroke-by-stroke procedure of the temperas has made for orderliness, has forced him to husband the first creative glow and not expend it in a riotous hour or two. The two mediums have fed each other; they have tended to establish a balance of opportunities.

In the temperas, the will is sometimes dominant; the watercolors are usually full of desire. The average person, looking at the tempera panels, feels that *there* is security, senses a safe, step-by-step advance toward a foreseen goal. He feels reassured — he is unaware that the medium has its treacheries. But it is just as dangerous to paint a slow tempera inch-by-inch as to dash off a watercolor in an hour, for the laborious tempera constantly threatens to become tedious, overwrought, boring. On the other hand, the sense of gamble, the adventure of bringing something off, of producing a near miracle — this in a watercolor usually communicates itself to the many. So the watercolor is cataloged as a delightful, even indulgent record of scraps of time; the tempera induces reverence because it represents so many more work hours.

Wyeth is a great watercolorist, perhaps our greatest. His aquarelles have an aura of search — the artist is on the hunt; he has not yet worked out total answers. There is little precedent in America for the Wyeth temperas; for the watercolors there is much. Behind Andrew's watercolors is the great American school of watercolor painting — deservedly called great. The school is not just Homer, Sargent, Burchfield, Marin or Demuth; it is also a small army of able aquarellists, too numerous to be given individual mention. Their numbers began to swell when the first influx of European-trained Americans found their way back to their native land in the closing years of the last century. Some brought the brown pigmentation of Düsseldorf and Munich, some had picked up the delightful transparencies of the English School (and its predilection for form-enveloping outline). But the greatest number were missionaries of late French Impressionism and they had been awakened to a shimmering world of ricocheting light and color. Practicing their new vision on the brisker American scene, their technique picked up tempo, their brush language became emphatic and direct, and the American watercolor began to have a look of its own.

At first the watercolorists were largely a landscape school. The school turned its back on the pampered look of the European countryside and rejoiced in the bite and spicy atmosphere of North America. It celebrated its native land in a freshened technique. It developed some formulas but essentially it was an exploratory force. Its range of expression was great, from Childe Hassam to Arthur Davies, from Frank Benson to Maurice Prendergast. It included talents as diverse as William Glackens, Birger Sandzen, Preston Dickinson and Reginald Marsh. These watercolorists have multiplied over the years. They have soaked up many influences: the giant rhythms of the brief Mexican Renaissance, a great deal from the Orient, the brush calligraphy of Japan and China, compositional angles from the still- and motion-picture cameras, montage and collage, many illustrative procedures, the dry geometry of the Bauhaus and Mondrian, hints from cave paintings, Fayum heads, child art, folk art. All the multitudinous extensions of modernism are somewhere in the brew, for this is the great pictorial melting pot of America. There are artistic isolationists of all persuasions in it but basically it is a nationwide communion of testing, searching and discovering. Tradition and modernism are cross-fertilizing each other. Something new and our own is molding itself. There is not a country in the world that can match it in vitality and diversity.

Wyeth has gone his lone-wolf way, without involvement in the whims of the moment, but he is not unaware of what appears in American exhibitions. He has served on many watercolor juries and knows the big national shows as exhibitor and visitor. There he sees the work of fellow artists who are telling their versions of the American spirit and there he sees many of his imitators. He is exhibiting less and less frequently in America's open shows, but the watercolor exhibitions see more of his work than the oil shows, which curiously enough welcome the egg-tempera medium.

The constant dialogue between the two contrasting mediums has important consequences upon both. The temperas feed greatly upon the discoveries of the watercolors; they give Wyeth the reassurance that the headlong temptations of the aqueous medium will never run away with him. The watercolors come about during those intervals in the long incubation of the temperas when release into the open is a necessity and for when, after a panel is completed, the mind is empty, depleted and in need of replenishment. The watercolors are a rebound from discipline; they are open to surprise, they carry the bounce of release from long commitment. With less conscious responsibility weighing him, Wyeth often has his biggest say in them. They are the best of vehicles for the sudden insight that comes freely and without warning.

With all their spontaneity, they are clothed in solidity, and the technical answer lies in their combination of fluid washes and drybrush. There is nothing mysterious or new about drybrush; it is probably as old as the medium itself. The first artist who squeezed most of the water from his brush, loaded its damp hairs with pigment and stroked it on paper was practicing drybrush. For generations the American illustrator has used the method as an accustomed technical resource. In this way the artist is able to create textures that are a relief from the blandness of the usual transparent wash. Drybrush lends body and a feeling of solid modeling to the work.

The Wyeth watercolor palette is just as spare as that of the temperas. The earth colors dominate it. It has no need of one of modernism's spectacular gifts — the uninhibited rainbow palette freed from the tyranny of representational color. This consciously narrow spectrum yields countless harmonies and the color range with its inclination toward low tonality shows the link between materials and mood. Mood permeates the Wyeth pictures. Large audiences have felt it and responded. Many have given it labels, such as "that feeling of loneliness" or "the near presence of death." If there must be labels, these are not inaccurate or misleading. Those intimations are there in the pictures.

No one could miss the obvious story of the empty rooms, the houses and barns with their accumulated scars of human effort but without the humans themselves or the solitary figures in picture after picture. And the almost complete absence of dialogue between human and human, in a world devoid of communication between man and man, is inescapable. If "loneliness" is the name for it, and it seems unlikely that there is a better, it is the loneliness of every thinking human aware of a world that is dear and familiar yet unknowable and treacherous. The sense of the fated incompleteness of communication and the despairing limits of self-knowledge is there too.

The first glance at a Wyeth picture may well tell a story of pastoral quiet, of loved, worn monuments of man, of the comfort of a long-lived-in landscape. The tenth should dispel all feeling of coziness. The drifted snow is never cozy — or almost never. There are dark secrets in many corners. The nibbling of time is present in almost every picture. Time and dissolution give hints of their advance. Drama, consciously sought, is inherent in the Wyeth quest and inextricably entwined with mood. It is not the drama of violence or the theatrical ignition of passion, but the drama of inevitability, of the long endured, of facing the best and worst — drama, achieved by understatement, not the drama of a moment but of a lifetime.

Where are the Wyeth pictures that say, "Rejoice"? There is a small watercolor called "May Day," an unpretentious moment of poetry. Just a few white blossoms of the spring beauty reaching for the sun out of the dark.

*

The sheer bulk of comment on Wyeth presents a massive personal problem for him and for any who investigate it to achieve a better understanding of his work. On the whole he has fared extremely well with the critics and received much sympathy and abundant praise. At a time when critical opinion has set its face against realism in any form, he offers a prime target; yet, he has felt comparatively little laceration from the claws of even the vehement Left.

His experience with the critics almost duplicated Robert Frost's. When Frost's earlier poems first found response in a public that was notoriously indifferent to verse, most critics felt ready to pounce. They pic-

tured him as the Yankee farmer down from his hills, with his salty, la-
conic lines, a throwback to a bucolic, naïve age. But they did not
pounce, or only a few did, for there was a sense of high accomplishment
and original utterance that conveyed a hint of hesitation to their antago-
nistic minds. There was a longish period of great condescension and unease among them and among "the serious readers of modern poetry," before real discernment and awakened appraisal arrived with Randall Jarrell
and others.

Wyeth's work had the same unsettling effect upon those critics who by
the laws of the critical climate of their time should have been and were
innately hostile. But again some glimmer of high quality threw their routine convictions into confusion. They decided to accept him as good of
his kind and perhaps smother him with faint praise and offhand patron-
age. For years he has been tolerated as an example of the broad-
mindedness of the avant-garde critics. In this they had the comforting
feeling of leading from strength, there was no danger in tolerance. But
that is rapidly coming to an end. Seeping through the whole fabric of the
"mystique" of modernism are doubts and insistent questions. This means
panic for some, reappraisal for others. The obvious alternatives are re-
newed and fiercer attacks or a shifting of the sights to a new horizon.
The critical attacks on Wyeth are likely to become more cutting, since
their word for him is now "dangerous," meaning, dangerous to their tenets. The twist of the times has tried to make a crusader for realism, a fig-
urehead for a cause, of a man who hasn't the slightest interest in critical
warfare, who is concerned only with following his star.

The critical language of the age has been a chilly affair, increasingly
cerebral, increasingly circumscribed. It seems to make the bland assumption that it should speak only to an isolated segment of our consciousness
— a specialized aesthetic sense. These spokesmen seem unable to con-
ceive that art might speak to the whole man. The Wyeth *oeuvre* is a
denial of this assumption. He has involved himself with the human condition, not its momentary flickers but the eternal strands of it. It must be

described in a language that moves at blood temperatu ? and in which a pulse is felt. Here our present-day indoctrination in the dangers of sentimentality confronts us — a bit of overeagerness and we are on the queasy ground of the folksy and corny. Wyeth himself has probably best summed up the dilemma: "Most of what is said and written about me seems to be set to the tune of 'Turkey in the Straw.' "

His pictures do not move to that tune. They have no truck with the self-consciously quaint; he is not a midcentury A. B. Frost. He is moved by the things that have been part of his life since he first opened his eyes. The shapes, textures, smells and sounds that were the stuff of his growing years are the material of his pictures. Wyeth has never lost his sense of wonder. It is as simple as that. His life has passed through some wrenching experiences that have only deepened his attachments. Only a distorted intellectual climate could misunderstand the naturalness and rightness of this.

He does not range far but he can work in depth. It would not be much of an exaggeration to say that his subjects lie within leg distance of his Chadds Ford and Cushing studios. He has chosen to cultivate intensely his own garden.

Those who know his territory through his pictures and then explore the Brandywine hills and the sandy fields of Cushing are usually surprised and often disappointed. Picture and place are never identical. They are surprised to discover that Wyeth, the realist, is not a slave to fact. He makes of the facts he sees, as much or as little as will fortify his vision; he has no interest in compiling a pictorial catalog of details. On the contrary, his pictures are usually exercises in subtraction. Shape by shape, and detail by detail they are simplified. This search for simplification, which is an inherent characteristic of his mind, points to his affinity for the abstract — a quality seldom attributed to him. He has often spoken of himself as an abstractionist but this self-appraisal is usually passed off as an amiable whim or a private joke. It is only natural that the average admirer, his eye tutored by long years of realism, should fail to pierce through the skin of appearance to essential form. But the contemporary critic or artist, dealing daily in nonobjective shapes, also is seldom able to discover the essential abstractions if they are veiled by the merest hint of realism. To most, abstraction either exists *pure*, or not at all. The interpenetration of natural and abstract forms, which has been going on since the cavemen decorations through the rise and fall of many a culture and style, has been a natural and habitual interdependence. The so-called "composition sketches" and "idea doodles" of countless artists through the ages are a vast dictionary of intertwined abstract-realistic forms. They prove over and over again the abstract or near-abstract genesis of countless realistic pictures. Any Victorian book of pictorial composition will reveal that even that most factual and literary-anecdotal ages knew that a picture's barest skeleton was an assemblage of abstract forms.

Wyeth's simplifying eye performs a natural abstracting function. He sees through the accidentals and incidentals of nature's profusion and is aware of basic, elemental shapes and their relationships to each other. This is scarcely an exceptional gift. Many picture-loving persons have experienced it, often without being aware of it. Coming upon an unfamiliar picture suddenly, at a distance, there is a message of delight and excited interest. It is a message of shapes, tones, colors and their design. Only seconds later, upon approach and examination, it is possible to discover "what the picture is all about." Its first message is of the abstract essentials; the content awaits other messages. This duality is an ancient thing, but the modern abstractionist is content with the first message.

The first message is important but insufficient for the Wyeth idea of fulfillment, and it is the Wyeth idea of fulfillment that has generated the Wyeth legend. It has been the answer to a need; a deep-seated and insistent need of many people — many kinds of people. It is partly an awakened nostalgia for the older America and partly a search for traits of permanence and for reassurance that art is more than a mere kaleidoscope of shifting fads and follies.

The legend is a healthy one, and like all legends not to be measured by the yardstick of commonplace fact. It magnifies and paints with a radiant palette. It transforms its materials to fit yearnings and great expectations. It has found a hero in the person of a quiet, unassuming, hardworking artist. He has been caught in an unforeseen tide of adulation and has learned to live with it as benefactor and victim.

Fortunately Wyeth seems possessed of a natural armor against unwelcome invasion. He can vanish into the landscape like an Indian, he can say no to platform appearances, the radio and television, although no-saying is difficult for him. He has tacit protection from those around him, his friends and neighbors and especially his resourceful and understanding wife, Betsy.

The circumstances of his life have shaped Wyeth to become a special instrument, not only for the making of some of the most revealing pictorial documents of our time but also as an example of what we had well-nigh forgotten — that superior pictures are multifaceted, that they speak not merely to a special aesthetic sense but to the whole man. His work reminds us that the deeper soundings may be attained by passing through the door of appearance, and that even after centuries of picture making our eyes have only begun to explore the everlasting festival of the visible world.

XIX

THE FUTURE OF A TRADITION

THE PRESENT MOMENT has brought the Brandywine influence to a new peak that is largely due to the ascendancy of Andrew Wyeth and the bright promise of his young son James. The present and the future of the tradition would appear to be largely involved in these two talents, although the future may move in other directions. The "Wyeth dynasty" — now a familiar phrase — is a convenient label for outsiders while it remains an embarrassment to those who must bear it, with its connotations of the establishment. Nevertheless, there is so much competence in the Wyeth circle that the family's prominence is inescapable. The youngest generation has its share of inherited gifts and a few more years will undoubtedly disclose their true proportions.

Young James is a prodigy as were his father and grandfather. The appearance of dazzling talent in three successive generations has captured the imagination of the country and expressed itself in both accurate and inaccurate publicity. Early praise and widespread reporting can pose a threat to a young talent, but James has handled this problem with aplomb and mature evaluation. The Wyeth art education pattern has been repeated in this youngest generation — as Andrew was taught by his father, so Andrew has been the art teacher of James, although James had a year's preparatory training from his aunt, Carolyn Wyeth. It is natural that the work of James should be strongly marked by his inheritance and training, but his pictures are not docile restatements of theme and manner — they are becoming full-bodied and confident documents. James, in his early twenties, has great technical capacity at his fingertips — he is searching his familiar world for his own themes and his brush is working out his own style.

Besides Jamie Wyeth, Michael Hurd, the son of Henriette and Peter Hurd, is painting and majoring in art, and two granddaughters of N.C. have married painters. George Weymouth, who married Ann, daughter of Ann and John McCoy, and Peter Rodgers, married to Ann Carol, the daughter of Henriette and Peter Hurd, are artists of considerable ability in their own right. A McCoy son, John Denys McCoy, has channeled his pictorial talent into the field of the experimental motion picture and has directed a number of unusual films. Andrew Nathaniel Wyeth, the son of Caroline and Nathaniel Wyeth, is now working in this same field, and another son, Howard, is a musician.

Beyond the Wyeth circle the tradition shows its influence in a less concentrated way. Aside from the network that has spread into many areas of the illustration field, there are numerous painters and draftsmen resident in the valley who have been touched by it. Philip Jamison, educated in the illustration classes of the Philadelphia College of Art and influenced by the work of Andrew Wyeth, in his early post-college years, has built an individual and expert painterly expression upon this foundation. He has a mounting reputation, particularly in the watercolor field. Dorla Dean Slider is one of the most able among the considerable group that have adopted the Wyeth idiom. Paul Westcott is a veteran painter of importance, who is in no sense a follower but a sensitive artist whose natural inclination is to move in the same general direction as the tradition. Edward Shenton, in a lifetime of illustration, has drawn many pictures of his southeastern Pennsylvania countryside, particularly to accompany books written by his wife, Barbara Webster, which deal with the same background. Carol Pyle Jones, a descendant of one of the oldest valley families, the same that produced Howard Pyle, has made use of the tradition as a base upon which she erects what are often brilliant imaginative improvisations.

There are many other able painters such as the Studio Group of women artists who have purchased the old Pyle studio and make it their headquarters. With the active Delaware Art Center as a rallying point in the lower Brandywine and the West Chester Art Center in the middle valley, the artists enjoy the advantage of abundant exhibition and forum activities. These two institutions are part of a rich cultural environment that has been so much enhanced by the concern and generosity of the wide-flung Du Pont family. Their famous Longwood Gardens at Kennett Square, Winterthur, with its magnificent collections of American arts and design, and the Hagley Museum, nestling in its Brandywine ravine where many of the early mills were built, are not only monuments to the valley's pride in its beauties and achievements but also focal points for the pilgrimage of thousands.

It would be misleading to infer that the region's concentration of talent is bent only upon the exploitation of tradition. Probably every phase of the multitudinous facets of past and present art is represented in it. The valley's artists are a microcosm of the present state of the arts. There are many who rebel against and vehemently deny the influence of any Brandywine tradition; but, after all, rebellion is a response to influence.

The work of two of the Brandywine's most important painters refuses to be tucked neatly into the tradition. Horace Pippin and Edward Loper were both solitary painters who worked out individual pictorial languages with little or no schooling or contact with other artists. Pippin appears in many of the surveys of American art, always classified as a "primitive." That label is in itself an indication of a tradition, of an instinctive awareness of a folk-art idiom. Pippin's powers were much above those of the average "primitive" — his best pictures are rich evocations of a deeply brooding nature. They are far above the "quaint" level that so readily tickles sophisticated tastes. Loper's work is scarcely "primitive" but it partakes of a similar unpretentious poetry. His pictures are not widely known but he has an audience of loyal admirers.

Looking back to the vintage years of Felix Octavius Darley and the early efforts of Howard Pyle, one can sift through the mountain of books, magazines and other printed material to which they began to contribute. We can search out the thousands upon thousands of reproduced pictures that originated in the studios of the Brandywine School and in the imaginations of the artists who painted and studied there to discover one of the most important records of our social history.

Illustration is one of the most significant sources of historical and social material, and scholars, for the most part, have neglected it. It is true that of late, more pictorial material has been appearing in the scholar's books, so there is an increasing awareness that the picture can convey an illuminating message. But pictures have been used mostly to enliven the text and have not been accepted as legitimate primary historical documents. Too often, the scholar accepts without question the idea that only written documents or perhaps artifacts are valid evidence. Pictures have been outside the province of his discipline and, confronted with them, he suffers unease and insecurity.

The traditional scholar needs to be taught that illustration provides not only a revealing insight into the artists who produce it but into the minds of the public that absorbed it. The illustrator's picture is not always a delineation of how things actually looked or how they might have looked — *but how a mass audience expected things to look.* The visual image is an important index to the expectations and satisfactions of its audience. The illustrator is not the ivory-tower artist by nature; he must be of his world in order to report upon it. The mass of people accept him as a pictorial spokesman. Over the years the illustrator in American history has compiled a monumental record of the American public's yearnings and sentiments, fads and follies, appearances and accomplishments. And to the delineation of the simple facts, he has brought to bear the great gifts of his probing eye and interpreting mind.

The pedantic historian will seldom admit that indisputable facts are the lesser part of his material. If a recital of indisputable facts had been the only mission of the historians, there would have been no Gibbon, no Parkman, Burckhardt, Green, Michelet or Toynbee. The facts without interpretation are inert. At the heart of all great history is imaginative reconstruction.

The pictorial artist reconstructs in just such a way. His mind stores up all the authentic material he can find and then projects itself into that material. The artist acts out the characters of his pictures, trying to think their thoughts, imagining the feel of unaccustomed garments on his body, moving through rooms of another age, adapting himself to strange furniture. He tries to live the life of another milieu and because imaginative projection is his birthright, he may often make a better job of it than the footnote-haunted scholar.

The Brandywine tradition is only a part of the vaster American illustrative art, but its artists were particularly involved with the historical, and it produced an impressive array of creators concerned with their country's past. For years their pictures touched a nation's imagination and furnished it with images of its great and lesser days. Just as three of the region's early evolved artifacts — the log house, the frontier rifle and the Conestoga wagon — became widely used symbols in the American mythology, so the Brandywine illustrators developed many images of our historical archetypes. The buckskinned frontiersman, the ax-wielding settler, the ragged Revolutionary soldier, the pioneer wife and mother, the plantation aristocrat and a score of others are some of the types they have impressed on the American consciousness. The long picture gallery of their art has left its imprint in the nation's memories and its contents are still in use, now ready to be reviewed and reevaluated.

Since the tradition has been largely an art of illustration, it has moved into the present under a cloud of critical scorn or neglect. In the jargon of today's art critics, no more withering phrase can be uttered against a picture than, "It is illustrative." The same dismissive phrase points up one of the modern critic's most noticable blind spots. Such a mind finds itself unable to accept one of the most natural and ancient attributes of the picture — the narrative element. That mind can examine Michelangelo, Blake, Dürer, Veronese, Hokusai, Delacroix, Degas, the cave artists of Lascaux, the Greek vase painters, the medieval missal-illuminators, the Byzantine mosaic designers (let the list grow and grow), and remain impervious to the themes that ignited the creative impulses of these arts.

If the Brandywine tradition has refused to sacrifice the element of narration and that of figurative form to the trend of the moment, time may prove that it has nourished these elements against the day of renewal. The future may discover that it has need of these discarded gifts. On the other hand, any tradition runs the risks of repetition and stagnation. Its triumphs could lead to manner and method — a way of seeing and doing, accessible to any mediocre talents. A practiced method discourages the fresh eye and the investigating mind that keeps a tradition healthy.

A tradition, such as that of the Brandywine, which has refreshed itself for more than a century, may not face the problem of self-renewal in the immediate future. But its wariness about some of the opportunities offered by modernism could prove a limiting factor. It is possible to theorize that modernism's amazing dictionary of strange, new abstract forms, its fresh and daring color combinations, never experienced by the old masters, and its freedom of design and technique, are all elements that could be absorbed into the tradition with vitalizing effect. With so much to give, the tradition should demonstrate an equal capacity to take. Cross-fertilization of tradition and modernism may be the design of our future.

BIBLIOGRAPHY

INDEX

BIBLIOGRAPHY

Books

Abbot, Charles D., *Howard Pyle — A Chronicle*. New York and London, Harper and Brothers, 1925.

Arthurs, Stanley, *The American Historical Scene*. Philadelphia, University of Pennsylvania Press, 1935.

Bland, David, *A History of Book Illustration*. Cleveland and New York, The World Publishing Company, 1958.

Canaday, John, "Andrew Wyeth and Our Time," *The Embattled Critic*. New York, The Noonday Press, 1962.

Canby, Henry Seidel, *The Age of Confidence*. New York, Farrar and Rinehart, 1934.

———, *The Brandywine*. New York, Farrar and Rinehart, 1941.

Cantwell, Robert, *Alexander Wilson — Naturalist and Pioneer*. Philadelphia and New York, J. B. Lippincott Company, 1961.

Clark, V. S., *History of Manufactures in the United States, 1607–1860*. Washington, 1916.

Crane, Walter, *The Decorative Illustration of Books*. London, G. Bell & Sons, Ltd., 1896.

Ellis, Richard Williamson, *Book Illustration — A Survey of its History & Development shown by the work of Various Artists together with Critical Comments*. Kingsport, Tennessee, Kingsport Press, 1952.

Exman, Eugene, *The House of Harper*. New York, Evanston and London, Harper and Row, 1967.

Furthey, J. Smith, and Cope, Gilbert, *History of Chester County, Pennsylvania*. Privately printed, Philadelphia, 1881.

Holme, Charles, (ed.), *Modern Pen Drawings: European and American*. London, The Studio, 1901.

Horgan, Paul, *Peter Hurd — A Portrait Sketch from Life*. Fort Worth, Amon Carter Museum, 1964.

Kent, Norman, (ed.), *The Book of Edward A. Wilson*. New York, The Heritage Press, 1948.

Larkin, Oliver W., *Art and Life in America*. New York, Rinehart and Company, 1949.

Lehmann-Haupt, Hellmut, Wroth, Lawrence C., and Silver, Rollo G., *The Book in America*. New York, Bowker, 1951.

Lossing, Benson J., *Pictorial Field-Book of the Revolution*. New York, 1851–1852.

MacElree, Wilmer W., *Down the Eastern and up the Black Brandywine*. West Chester, Privately printed, no date.

Mahony, Bertha E., Latimer, Louise Payton, and Folinsbee, Beulah, *Illustrators of Children's Books, 1744–1945*. Boston, The Horn Book, 1946.

Miller, Bertha Mahony, Viguers, Ruth Hill, and Dalphin, Marcia, *Illustrators of Children's Books, 1946–1956*. Boston, The Horn Book, 1958.

Morse, Willard S., and Brincklé, Gertrude, *Howard Pyle — A Record of His Illustrations and Writings*. Wilmington, Wilmington Society of the Fine Arts, 1921.

Nesbitt, Elizabeth, *Howard Pyle*. New York, Henry Z. Walck, Inc., 1966.

Papers of the Historical Society of Pennsylvania, Relative to the Battle of the Brandywine. Philadelphia, Bulletin of the Historical Society, Vol. 1, No. 8, 1846.

Pennell, Joseph, *Modern Illustration*. London, George Bell & Sons, Ltd., 1895.

———, *Pen Drawing and Pen Draughtsmen*. London, Macmillan and Company, 1889. New York, The Macmillan Company, 1920, rev. ed.

Pitz, Henry C., *Illustrating Children's Books*. New York, Watson-Guptill Publications, Inc., 1963.

———, *A Treasury of American Book Illustration*. New York, Watson-Guptill and American Studio Books, 1947.

Read, Walt, *The Illustrator in America*. New York, The Reinhold Publishing Corporation, 1965.

Richardson, E. P., *Painting in America*. New York, Thomas Y. Crowell Co., 1965.

Thompson, William Fletcher, *The Image of War*. New York and London, Thomas Yoseloff, 1960.

Trevelyan, George Otto, *The American Revolution*. New York, 1939.

Wallace, Paul A. W., *Indians in Pennsylvania*. Harrisburg, Pennsylvania Historical and Museum Commission, 1964.

Watson, Ernest W., *Forty Illustrators and how they work*. New York, Watson-Guptill Publications, Inc., 1946.

ARTICLES, CATALOGS, PAMPHLETS, ETC.

Bolton, Theodore, "The Book Illustrations of Felix Octavius Darley." Worcester, Mass., *Proceedings* of the American Antiquarian Society, 1952.

"The Brandywine Story, 1777–1852." The Brandywine Battlefield Park Commission, September 11, 1952.

Carmine, Delesio, "Paintings by John W. McCoy." Rockland, Maine, William Farnsworth Art Museum, August 1955.

"Celebrating the 100th Anniversary of the Birth of Howard Pyle." Wilmington Society of the Fine Arts, March 5, 1953.

Coffin, William A., "American Illustration of Today." New York, *Scribner's Magazine*, March 1892.

Drexel Institute of Art, Science and Industry, Records (1894–1900).

Garrett, Charles Hall, "Howard Pyle — The Reader." New York, May 1903.

Haas, Irvin, "A Bibliography of the Work of Edward A. Wilson." *Prints*, February 1938.

Hawthorne, Hildegarde, "Howard Pyle — Maker of Pictures and Stories." New York, *St. Nicholas*, May 1915.

Hawthorne, Julian, "Howard Pyle, Illustrator." New York, *Pearson's Magazine*, September 1907.

Horgan, Paul, "Andrew Wyeth — Impressions for a Portrait," Exhibition Catalogue. Tucson, University of Arizona, 1963.

Howell, Edgar M., "The Look of the Last Frontier" (Pictures of Harvey Dunn). *American Heritage*, June 1961, p. 41.

Ingersoll, Robert, "N. C. Wyeth — Painter and Father of Painters Today." Philadelphia, July 4, 1965, p. 2.

Kent, Norman, "Edward A. Wilson: A Graphic Romancer." New York, *American Artist*, May 1944, p. 16.

Koerner, W. H. D., "Howard Pyle." Wilmington, *New Amstel Magazine*, November 1911, p. 477.

Lunt, Dudley, "The Howard Pyle School of Art." *Delaware History*, Historic Society of Delaware, March 1953, p. 151.

Martin, Pete, "N. C. Wyeth." Philadelphia, *The Sunday Bulletin Magazine*, October 10, 1965, p. 4.

Meryman, Richard, "Andrew Wyeth — An Interview." New York, *Life*, p. 93.

Mongan, Agnes, "Andrew Wyeth — Drybrush and Pencil Drawings." Cambridge, Mass., Loan Exhibition Organized by the Fogg Museum, 1963.

Moore, Constance, "The Wilmington Society of the Fine Arts 1912–1962." Published by the Society, 1962.

Oakley, Thornton, "Howard Pyle — His Art and Personality, An Address." Free Library of Philadelphia, November 8, 1951.

————, "Remarks on Illustration and Pennsylvania's Contributors to its Golden Age." *The Pennsylvania Magazine of History & Biography*, Historical Society of Pennsylvania, January 1947, p. 3.

Philadelphia College of Art, Records.

Pitz, Henry C., "American Illustration: Then and Now." New York, *American Artist*, June 1962, p. 51.

————, "Andrew Wyeth." New York, *American Artist*, November 1958, p. 26.

————, "The Book Illustrations of Edward Shenton." New York, *American Artist,* March 1961, p. 22.

————, "Book Illustration since 1937." New York, *American Artist,* 1967, p. 64.

————, "The Brandywine Tradition." New York, *American Artist,* December 1966, p. 29.

————, "Frank E. Schoonover: An Exemplar of the Pyle Tradition." New York, *American Artist,* November 1964, p. 64.

————, "George Harding." New York, *American Artist,* December 1957, p. 29.

————, "Howard Pyle: American Illustrator." New York, *American Artist,* December 1951, p. 44.

————, "Millions of Pictures" [two parts]. New York, *American Artist,* November 1961, p. 35, December 1961, p. 52.

————, "N. C. Wyeth." New York, *American Heritage,* October 1965, p. 34.

————, "N. C. Wyeth and the Brandywine Tradition." Harrisburg, Pennsylvania, William Penn Memorial Museum, 1965.

"Report of the Private View of the Exhibition of Works by Howard Pyle." Philadelphia Art Alliance, 1923.

Rhoads, Eugenia Eckford, "A Master Returns to His Studio." *Delaware Today,* December 1964, p. 16.

Richardson, E. P., "Andrew Wyeth." Boston, *The Atlantic Monthly,* June 1964, p. 62.

Schoonover, Frank E., "Howard Pyle." Washington, D.C., *Art and Progress,* October 1915, p. 431.

Trimble, Jessie, "The Founder of an American School of Art." New York, *The Outlook,* February 23, 1907, p. 453.

Vandercook, John W., "Howard Pyle." New York, *The Mentor,* June 1927.

Watson, Ernest W., "Giant on a Hilltop." New York, *American Artist,* January 1945, p. 16.

Weitenkampf, Frank, "Illustrated by Darley." New York, International Studio, March 1925, p. 445.

Wyeth, N. C., "Howard Pyle as I Knew Him." New York, *The Mentor,* June 1927.

Young, Mahonri Sharp, "Catalogue of Pictures by Howard Pyle." Wilmington, Wilmington Society of the Fine Arts, 1926.

————, "Peter Hurd and Henriette Wyeth Catalogue of Paintings." Columbus, Ohio, Columbus Gallery of Fine Arts, January 1967.

————, "Q and A with Andrew Wyeth." Philadelphia, *The Sunday Bulletin Magazine,* January 21, 1962, p. 10.

————, "Wyeth and Manet in Philadelphia." New York, *Apollo,* November 1966, p. 403.

INDEX